James Beard's

MENUS

for Entertaining

Revised Edition

MARLOWE & COMPANY
NEW YORK

First Marlowe & Company edition, 1997
Published by
Marlowe & Company
632 Broadway, Seventh Floor
New York, NY 10012

http://www.marlowepub.com

Manufactured in the United States of America

Library of Congress Cataloging-in-Publication Data
Beard, James, 1903–
    James Beard's menus for entertaining / James Beard. — Rev. ed.
        p.   cm.
    Includes index.
    ISBN 1-56924-765-X (cloth)
    1. Entertaining.   2. Menus.   I. Title.
TX731.B373   1996
642'.4—dc20   96-32203
                                                          CIP

CONTENTS

EDITOR'S NOTE

Menus for Entertaining, first published in 1965, proved to be one of James Beard's most popular cookbooks and showed off his flair for putting together innovative meals for a wide range of occasions. He once wrote that "planning a menu is much like planning a theatrical production. The first course is a prologue that holds a promise of what is to follow, and the entree must top the first course in interest and be the high point of the meal." Beard's earlier career as an actor no doubt kindled this perception of food as theatre. His own dinner parties and cocktail buffets were legendary.

Menus for Entertaining was lightly revised for a new paperback edition in 1986. The current revision has been more comprehensive, clarifying cooking instructions, updating recipes, adding a few where called for, deleting others, and bowing to political correctness with the abolition of the term "ladies' luncheons." Beard's introduction, inadvertently dropped from the 1986 edition, is restored here. The most significant feature of this revision is the inclusion of ten more elegant Beard menus. These date mainly from the last years of his life, and though twenty years separated them from his original collection of menus, his commitment to well-presented, good, honest food was undiminished.

John Ferrone
(1996)

INTRODUCTION

Entertaining is my main pleasure, my forte; and beyond that it is essential to my livelihood. I do it frequently with little help and often with none at all. It is not unusual for me to arrive home at 5:30 after a full day's work, with eight guests due for cocktails and dinner two hours later.

Whether you are entertaining at breakfast, luncheon, cocktails or dinner, you must plan carefully and make sure that most elementary chores are done in advance. Shop for food and liquor as far ahead as possible; check your linens or place mats, your silver and dishes a day or so before; get out any cooking equipment and serving dishes you will need. If you are lucky enough to have several hours before guests arrive, clean vegetables, set the table and arrange the centerpiece. If it is difficult, for one reason or another, to set the table in advance, try a serving method I often use. Simply put place mats and napkins on the dining table, and at the last minute put out plates and silver on a work area in the kitchen. Then invite your guests to come to the kitchen and dish up for themselves. Into a dirty kitchen, you say? You can keep it clear as you work if you stack all used utensils in the dishwasher or, as does one hostess I know, hide them in the cupboard under the sink. If you cook in handsome, decorative pots and pans, the food can be served right from the stove. One of the most popular restaurants near Wall Street in New York serves in just this manner. Patrons are ushered into the restaurant kitchen, where they select their meals from the array of delectable dishes on the stove. The men love it.

Choose menus that call for no more than one or two complicated jobs to be done at the last minute. Other dishes on the menu should be simple to prepare, or they should be the sort that can be made a day or so in advance. Most cooks, when they think of dishes in the latter category, automatically come up with beef bourguignon or coq au vin. I've become thoroughly tired of both dishes. There are fine terrines, cocottes, and other so-called casserole dishes available. But these must be cooked carefully and seasoned with discretion to achieve any kind of distinction. In the long run, such dishes take far more time and attention than a fine roast, a quick sauté, or a grill that is done at the last minute.

I find that American hostesses try to serve too many dishes at dinner. There is no need, for example, to have four or five complicated hors d'oeuvre with drinks. Such lavishness takes the edge off appetites. One or two items, not too rich, are enough—perhaps just olives, or radishes with sweet butter. The first course can sometimes be served in the living room with a chilled white wine in place of cocktails.

A first course isn't absolutely necessary, but if you have planned a grilled main course, it can prove a help. Most grilled meats cook quickly, and you should start them as guests sit down to their fish or soup, or whatever you have chosen. If there is a short wait between courses, no one will mind, particularly if you serve a pleasant wine that the guests can sip as they talk.

If you worry about timing and keeping foods hot, invest in an electric hot tray. With one of these you can hold a roast and vegetables for quite a few minutes at the right temperature. Also, there are many tasty dishes that can be prepared at the table in an electric skillet or chafing dish.

A sensible way to save yourself headaches in planning your menu is to take advantage of fine prepared foods available. If you live in a city of any size, investigate caterers and specialty shops that can supply you with first courses, such as pâtés, aspics, fish mousses and vol-au-vents with cream fillings, or desserts such as torten, pastries, and frozen sweets.

Entertaining is expensive, make no mistake, and this book is not dedicated to economy in the kitchen, although many menus presented here are relatively inexpensive to produce. It is dedicated to hosts and hostesses who want to provide the best for their guests, to achieve the finest in pleasures of the table effortlessly, graciously, and with flair. To entertain successfully one must create with the imagination of a playwright, plan with the skill of a director, and perform with the instincts of an actor. And, as any showman will tell you, there is no greater reward than pleasing your audience.

James A. Beard
New York
(1965)

BREAKFASTS

EARLY BREAKFAST

Entertaining at early breakfast usually means overnight guests—unless you happen to be catching a friend on the wing, between planes; or you happen to be one of those extraordinarily busy people who must do business or entertain from the crack of dawn on through the day. Actually, a business breakfast makes a nice change from the usual, hurried luncheon.

At no time are people's eating habits more fixed and less creative than in the early morning. Gauge your guests' appetites carefully: If you are faced with a "continental breakfast" appetite, at least find the best rolls and bread available and an interesting marmalade or preserve. If you think your guests might be afraid to stray too far from the bacon-and-eggs routine, try variations on these standards to give the meal a lift; offer a soufflé, or quiche, or a good omelet.

Here is a trio of menus for the early hours that are somewhat off-beat.

Three Light Breakfasts

I

Melon with Prosciutto
Crisply Toasted French Bread
Butter   Marmalade

Melon with Prosciutto

Use any available ripe melon. Peel and cut into rather thin strips—3 or 4 to a portion. Arrange on a plate with 2 or 3 slices of prosciutto over the melon, and serve with a wedge of lime or lemon. Have the pepper grinder handy.

NOTE: Westphalian or Smithfield ham may be used instead of prosciutto.

II

Hot Fruit Compote—Heavy Cream
Freshly Baked Brioche
Butter

Hot Fruit Compote

Prepare a simple syrup, combining 1 part sugar, 2 parts water, and vanilla to taste. Boil 5 minutes. Add mixed fresh (or dried) fruits: apricots, prunes, figs, peaches or pears. Bring to a boil, lower heat, and simmer until tender. Serve with heavy cream.

Freshly Baked Brioche

See p. 344.

III

Sautéed Mushrooms on Toast
Bacon Strips
Fresh Coffee Cake   Butter

Sautéed Mushrooms on Toast

6 tablespoons butter
1 1/2 pounds mushrooms
  (small caps)
1 teaspoon salt
1/2 teaspoon freshly ground
  black pepper

Dash Worcestershire
Buttered toast, as needed
Chopped chives and parsley
Bacon

Melt butter in a heavy skillet, add the mushrooms, and sauté over medium heat. Stir, and shake the pan from time to time. Cook until mushrooms are lightly browned and still firm. Do not overcook. Add seasonings.

Serve on buttered toast with chopped herbs and crisp bacon.

Coffee Cake

You may use a coffee cake from a good bakery, if you wish, but if you prefer to do your own, try this quick version.

1 1/2 cups less 2 tablespoons
  flour
2 teaspoons double-acting
  baking powder
1/2 teaspoon salt
1/2 teaspoon mace

1/2 cup sugar
1 egg, well beaten
1/2 cup milk
3 tablespoons melted butter
Butter and sugar for topping

Sift dry ingredients together. Combine with egg, milk and melted butter. Beat until smooth. Pour into a buttered 8- by 8-inch pan. Dot with butter that has been rolled in sugar, and sprinkle additional sugar over the top. Dust with mace or cinnamon. Bake at 400° for 25 minutes or until brown and puffy. Serve hot.

Four Hearty Breakfasts

—————————

I

Strawberries
Trout Sauté Meunière   Hash Browns
Thin Crisp Toast   Lemon Marmalade

—————————

Strawberries

Choose ripe berries. There is only one sure way of getting sweet ones: sample one in the market. Wash the berries lightly, and drain. (One great food authority once said strawberries should never be washed with water—only wine!) Serve with the hulls on, with a mound of powdered sugar in each plate. Also pass heavy cream or sour cream for dipping.

Trout Sauté Meunière

For 4 trout, melt 4 tablespoons butter and 2 tablespoons oil in heavy skillet. Dust trout well with flour. Sauté gently, turning several times until fish is cooked through but not overcooked, allowing 10 minutes per inch of thickness. Flesh should be moist but easily flaked with a fork or toothpick. Sprinkle with chopped parsley, and season with salt and pepper. Serve with lemon.

Serves 4.

Hash Browns

See p. 356.

II

Sliced Ripe Tomatoes
Broiled Flank Steak
Crisp Protein Toast   Butter

Sliced Ripe Tomatoes

Scald tomatoes, or sear over a gas flame, to loosen skin. Peel, and slice thin. Sprinkle with salt and freshly ground pepper.

Broiled Flank Steak

You will need a steak of top quality for this. Rub steak well with salt, ground black pepper and Tabasco. Broil steak $1^1/_2$ to 2 inches from the broiling unit (allowing for shrinkage and thickening) 3 to 4 minutes on each side for rare. Carve into thin slices, holding the knife at an angle of 45° or less. The diagonal slicing is essential for tenderness.

A flank steak of medium size will serve 3 to 4 people.

III

Grapefruit Sections
Sautéed Squab Chickens
Fried Cornmeal Mush
Butter   Honey   Apple Butter

Grapefruit Sections

Peel grapefruit so that white skin is completely removed. With a sharp knife, a small pointed one preferably, slice and remove each section. Dress with sugar. Add a little champagne or sherry if you wish.

Sautéed Squab Chickens

These generally weigh about 1 pound and are sold split. You decide whether you wish to serve a whole one or a half per person.

For 4 small chickens, heat 4 tablespoons butter and 1 tablespoon of oil in each of 2 large skillets. When the butter and oil are hot and bubbly, arrange the chickens, skin side down, in the pans, and brown nicely. Sprinkle with salt and freshly ground pepper, turn and continue cooking over medium heat for 12 to 15 minutes. Turn again, and test for tenderness. They should take 18 to 20 minutes. Remove to hot platter. Rinse the pan with ¼ cup cognac or Madeira, and add 2 tablespoons chopped parsley. Pour over chicken halves.

Serves 4 to 8.

Fried Cornmeal Mush

Follow directions on cornmeal package for making cornmeal mush, noting quantity required for the number of guests you are serving. Pour into a loaf tin and cool. Slice in ½-inch slices, and brown well on both sides in butter. Serve hot with honey and apple butter.

IV

Sherried Grapefruit
Steamed Smoked Black Cod or Sablefish
Rye Toast
Butter Steamed Potatoes
Cherry Tomatoes

Sherried Grapefruit

Peel grapefruit, and carefully slice into sections with a sharp knife, freeing the fruit from the tough membrane that separates each section. Arrange in individual serving dishes. Sugar to taste, and add 2 tablespoons medium or sweet sherry to each dish. Chill.

Steamed Smoked Black Cod or Sablefish

This comes in plastic bags that may be heated in water. If purchased loose, wrap in foil and heat in a 375° oven. Serve with chopped parsley, melted butter, and lemon.

Butter Steamed Potatoes

Choose small new potatoes of uniform size. Steam them in about $1/2$ inch butter in a heavy saucepan with a tight-fitting cover. Shake the pan several times during the cooking. Do not let potatoes overcook. Salt well with coarse salt and add freshly ground black pepper.

Cherry Tomatoes

Wash tomatoes but leave the hulls on. Allow some moisture to remain on the skins. Place in a bowl and sprinkle with salt (preferably coarse), or pass the salt separately, and pepper.

LATE BREAKFAST

Late breakfast (or "brunch," to use a word I dislike) can be served any time between 11 and 1. It is not the hour that makes it breakfast but, presumably, the fact that it is the first meal of the day. In content the menu for a late breakfast is hardly distinguishable from a light luncheon, and there are few types of food that cannot be considered breakfast fare. In the menus that follow, you will find such items as fettucine Alfredo and grilled porterhouse steaks.

Of course, one thing clearly distinguishes late from early breakfast: alcoholic drinks. Bloody Marys are good for such an occasion, and so also are various wine drinks. Champagne is perfection.

Breakfast can be as informal as you wish, but it can also be a rather sumptuous affair. I do a Christmas breakfast every year, to which I invite a dozen or so close friends. It is every bit as festive as a Christmas Eve supper.

A Mint Julep Breakfast for 12

Serve perfectly made mint juleps before breakfast.

Cold Smithfield Ham
Rye or French Bread
Eggs and Mushrooms in Tarragon Cream
Raspberry Preserve
Toasted Muffins
Pound Cake

Cold Smithfield Ham

Smithfield hams may be bought in many parts of the country already cooked. It will save you a great deal of preparation if you are able to find one or have time to order one through your butcher. Slice the ham very thin, and serve with thin rye or thin French bread and butter.

Eggs and Mushrooms in Tarragon Cream

14 hard-cooked eggs
2 pounds mushrooms
10 tablespoons butter
5 tablespoons flour
1 1/2 cups chicken or mushroom
    broth

1 1/2 cups cream
3 egg yolks
1 to 2 teaspoons dried tarragon
    or 1 1/2 tablespoons finely
    chopped fresh tarragon

Slice the eggs. Sauté the mushrooms lightly in 6 tablespoons butter, and keep warm while you make a cream sauce: Heat 4 tablespoons butter in a saucepan, and add the flour. Cook over low heat for a minute, then add broth, stirring continuously, and the cream. Cook until sauce is slightly thickened, then add lightly beaten eggs yolks, first beating a bit of the sauce into the eggs. Do not allow the sauce to boil after eggs have been added. Add the tarragon and salt and pepper, if necessary (the broth may provide seasoning enough).

Place the eggs and mushrooms in the sauce, and serve in a chafing dish or tureen, garnished with chopped parsley.

Have quantities of buttered toast muffins on hand and a good raspberry preserve. With coffee serve thinly sliced Pound Cake (*see* p. 349).

Champagne Breakfast for 8

Serve well-chilled champagne before and throughout the meal.

Tiny Croustades
Superb Chicken Hash
Link Sausage
Asparagus
Toasted Brioche
Damson Preserves

Tiny Croustades

1 loaf unsliced bread
Olive oil
Melted butter
6 hard-boiled eggs, finely
 chopped
Freshly ground pepper
2 tablespoons chopped parsley
4 anchovy fillets, chopped
12 to 16 anchovy fillets rolled
 with capers

Cut bread ½ inch thick. Remove crusts, and cut each slice in halves or thirds. With a sharp paring knife and a spoon, hollow out the center of each piece, leaving a base and a frame of bread. Brush with olive oil and butter, and toast both sides to a delicate brown.

Combine eggs, a grind of pepper, parsley, chopped anchovies and 2 tablespoons melted butter. Spread into the small croustades. Dot with butter, and add a rolled anchovy to each. Heat for 3 to 4 minutes in a hot oven. Serve hot.

Superb Chicken Hash

1 large onion, finely chopped	Tabasco
2 green peppers, diced	1 1/2 teaspoons tarragon
5 tablespoons butter	1/2 cup chopped parsley
2 tablespoons oil	1/2 cup blanched almonds or
4 cups or more cold chicken or	1/2 cup broken walnut meats
turkey cut in wide dice	8 eggs, slightly beaten
Salt and pepper	3/4 cup grated Parmesan cheese

Sauté the onion and green pepper in the butter and oil until just wilted. Add the chicken and mix well. Add seasonings and almonds and toss. Press the chicken down well in the skillet. Cover for just 2 or 3 minutes. When the chicken is thoroughly heated through pour in the beaten eggs, mixed with the grated cheese, and cook over low heat until set. If practicable, run the skillet under the broiler for just 2 or 3 minutes to brown the egg and cheese.

NOTE: If you are using turkey that has been stuffed, a little of the cold stuffing mixed with the turkey adds a pleasant flavor.

Link Sausage

Small pork sausage links are best for this occasion. Broil according to instructions for Broiled Sausages (see p. 16).

Asparagus

Wash and trim 4 pounds of asparagus. Lay flat in a skillet, and cover with water. Add salt and bring to a boil. Cook quickly until tender but still crisp. Serve with melted butter.

NOTE: If asparagus is out of season, serve a platter of radishes, celery and scallions instead.

Brioche

See p. 344.

A White Wine Breakfast for 6

Serve chilled Muscadet or Riesling.

Tiny Peppers Stuffed with Sausage
Table-Scrambled Eggs
Croissants   Raspberry Preserves

Tiny Peppers Stuffed with Sausage

*2 pounds ground pork, ³/₄ lean,
   ¹/₄ fat
2 garlic cloves, finely chopped
1 teaspoon thyme
¹/₂ teaspoon ground cardamon*

*¹/₄ teaspoon ground cumin
1¹/₂ teaspoons salt
¹/₂ teaspoon Tabasco
12 small green peppers or the
   lower halves of 12 large ones*

Blend meat and seasonings well. Fry a small piece and taste. Correct the seasoning.

Parboil peppers 8 minutes in salted water. Drain. Fill with the sausage mixture. Arrange in a shallow, oiled baking pan. Bake at 350° for 25 to 30 minutes or till sausage is cooked and delicately browned.

Table-Scrambled Eggs

Use either a chafing dish or an electric skillet.

*14 eggs
4 tablespoons water
1 teaspoon salt*

*2 or 3 dashes Tabasco
6 tablespoons or more of butter*

Beat eggs lightly, together with water and seasonings. Melt butter over low heat, and add eggs. Increase heat slightly, and scrape along bottom of pan with a wooden or rubber spatula until eggs form large curds. Do not overcook. Add more butter if you wish.

Croissants

You may buy croissants if you have a good French bakery in the neighborhood, or make your own (*see* p. 344–45).

A Vodka or Zubrowka Breakfast for 12

The vodka or zubrowka should be served icy cold. (Zubrowka is vodka with a piece of sweet grass in it, which perfumes it delicately.)

Smoked and Cured Fish
Sliced Tomatoes and Onions
Pumpernickel Sandwiches
Cucumber Sandwiches
Danish Pastry
Rolls and Butter
Marmalades
Cheese

Smoked and Cured Fish

1 pound best smoked salmon, thinly sliced
1 pound smoked sturgeon, thinly sliced
2 pounds smoked eel, skinned and cut from bones in thin fillets

2 or 3 whole smoked whitefish
12 pieces herring in sour cream
12 pieces herring in white-wine sauce

Arrange smoked fish on a platter, together with lemon wedges and capers. Each type of herring should be on a separate platter, with chopped parsley for a garnish.

Arrange a plate of sliced tomatoes and thinly sliced onions, a plate of thin pumpernickel and butter sandwiches, and a plate of cucumber sandwiches on white bread. Also provide crisp rolls and butter, and have a cruet of oil on hand for the fish.

Follow with Danish pastry and more rolls, with butter, cheese, and marmalades.

The vodka or zubrowka should be served throughout the fish course. Afterwards serve coffee and iced tea.

A Sherry Breakfast for 8

Offer a well-chilled fino sherry, a chilled medium sherry, and, if you wish, a cream sherry. With the sherry you might serve salted almonds and tiny green olives.

Broiled Sausages
Potato Galette
Broiled Kidneys
Watercress
Toasted Homemade Bread
Strawberry Preserves

Broiled Sausages

Choose 2½ pounds small pork sausages. Blanch in boiling water 5 minutes. Drain, and place under broiler, 4 to 5 inches from heat, and broil, turning once, till the sausages are golden brown and glazed. Remove to hot plate.

Potato Galette

See p. 356.

Broiled Kidneys

Remove most of the fat from 8 veal kidneys, and cut in half lengthwise. Remove the cord. Brush with butter or sausage fat (from the broiling pan), and broil quickly, turning once, for 5 to 6 minutes or to your taste. Salt and pepper.

Serve with a garnish of watercress.

Toasted Homemade Bread

See the recipe for Homemade Bread, p. 341. If you haven't the time or ambition to make your own, you can purchase frozen loaves of "homemade" bread ready to bake.

Slice bread fairly thick, toast well, butter, and keep hot.

A White Wine and Cassis Breakfast for 6

As an apéritif, serve chilled dry white wine with a touch of crème de cassis stirred in it.

Sliced Oranges, Mexican
Codfish Provençale
Croissants   Strawberry Jam

Sliced Oranges, Mexican

Peel 6 or 7 oranges carefully, or slice off peel with a knife, so that no white skin remains. Slice thin, and arrange on a serving plate. Dust with 6 tablespoons confectioners' sugar, and sprinkle with cinnamon. Serve at once.

Codfish Provençale

The sauce on this fish dish is a favorite in the South of France. It is called *rayte* and is often used as a dip for crisp bread sticks or raw vegetables.

1½ pounds salt codfish	1 bay leaf
1 cup olive oil	Touch of fennel
¼ cup butter	Pint of red wine
3 cloves garlic, peeled and chopped	1 can tomato paste
3 medium onions, peeled and chopped	½ cup pine nuts
	¼ cup capers
1 large can solid-pack tomatoes	1 cup black olives
1 teaspoon rosemary	Salt and pepper

First, put the salt cod to soak in cold water. It should soak at least 8 hours. Meanwhile, prepare the sauce. Sauté onion and garlic in the olive oil and butter. When they are just limp, add the can of tomatoes, the rosemary, bay leaf, fennel, red wine, and tomato paste. Blend thoroughly. Cook gently until slightly thickened. Add the nuts, capers, olives, and salt and pepper to taste, and continue cooking gently for about 30 minutes.

When the fish has soaked, drain it, and cut into square serving-size pieces. Roll in flour and sauté in olive oil until nicely browned. Pour the sauce over the fish and serve.

Croissants

See p. 344–45.

A Bloody Mary Breakfast for 12

Use either vodka or aquavit for the Bloody Marys.

Charcuterie
Radishes and Cherry Tomatoes
French and Rye Breads
Eggs with Ratatouille
Melbaed English Muffins   Marmalade

Charcuterie

Place a selection of salami, summer sausage, liverwurst, and mortadella on a large cutting board, with sharp knives for slicing. Place French and rye breads on a bread board. Provide plenty of butter, and bowls of cherry tomatoes and radishes.

Eggs with Ratatouille

12 small casseroles of ratatouille   12 eggs
(see p. 63)   *1¹/₂ cups grated Gruyère cheese*

The ratatouille may be made the day before and reheated in individual casserole dishes. Top each dish with a poached egg, and cover with shredded Gruyère. Return to oven just long enough to melt cheese.

Serve with Melbaed English muffins (*see* p. 270).

Sunday-Noon Breakfast for 6

Some of the California champagnes, such as Korbel, Almaden and Beaulieu, are delicious for summer drinking. Serve a briskly chilled champagne with a drop of crème de cassis before breakfast-at-noon. It livens up the appetite. Continue through the meal with plain champagne, well iced.

Melon with Port
Charcoal-Broiled Ham Steaks
Zucchini Frittata
Tomato Salad
Warm Brioche with
Preserves and Cream Cheese

Melon with Port

Cantaloupe, honeydew or Cranshaw are all perfect for this dish. Be sure the melons are ripe and sweet. Cut them in halves or slices (depending on size) and make two or three gashes in the flesh of each piece with a spoon. Add 2 ounces of port to each serving, and let melon stand a half hour to mellow.

Charcoal-Broiled Ham Steaks

Have your steaks cut about 1 to 1½ inches thick, and allow about 6 to 8 ounces per person. Slash the fat on the sides of the ham slices and broil slowly over medium coals, turning two or three times. The steaks will take about 12 to 15 minutes. If you like a glaze on ham steak, brush with a mixture of mustard and honey, and bring up the heat during the last few minutes. To serve, cut the ham into 2-inch strips.

Zucchini Frittata

6 to 8 small zucchini
3 tablespoons olive oil
2 tablespoons butter
8 eggs
1 teaspoon salt

$^1/_2$ teaspoon freshly ground
  black pepper
$^1/_2$ cup grated Parmesan
  cheese

Wash but do not peel the zucchini. Cut into $^1/_4$-inch slices and cook slowly in oil and butter until just tender. Beat the eggs with the salt and pepper and pour gently over the zucchini. Cook until just set. Sprinkle the cheese on top and run under the broiler to brown lightly. Let the frittata stand for a minute or two, and then cut in wedges and serve.

Tomato Salad

Scald or singe the tomatoes quickly, and peel them. Cut into thin slices, and arrange on a serving plate. Salt and pepper to taste, and dribble a little oil over them. Add lemon juice or red-wine vinegar to taste, and garnish with chopped fresh basil, chopped chives, and chopped parsley.

Warm Brioche with Preserves and Cream Cheese

Many French bakeries make a specialty of fine brioche, and good frozen ones are now available. Or, you may make your own (see p. 13).

Offer a choice of several preserves. Try black currant, ginger marmalade, pure apricot, damson plum, and raspberry; also, quince honey and pear butter. Serve with cream cheese.

An Elegantly Simple Breakfast for 6

Prunes in Madeira
Sautéed Calf's Liver   Bacon
Boiled New Potatoes
Toasted Rolls   Marmalade

Prunes in Madeira

These may be prepared in quantity and used when needed.

3 pounds choice prunes, pitted   *Madeira (or port or Marsala)*
* or unpitted*   * to cover*

Place the prunes in a large jar. Cover with the wine. Seal jar, and let prunes stand for 1 week before using. These will last indefinitely and will enhance many meals.

Sautéed Calf's Liver

12 thin slices of calf's liver   *Salt and pepper*
Flour   *¹/₄ cup finely chopped shallots*
5 tablespoons butter   *¹/₄ cup finely chopped parsley*
4 tablespoons oil

Flour the liver slightly, and sauté very quickly on both sides in the oil and 4 tablespoons of the butter. Salt and pepper to taste, and remove to a hot platter. Add shallots and parsley to the sautéing pan with the remaining spoon of butter, and cook for 1 minute. Pour over the liver. Serve with sautéed or broiled bacon slices.

Boiled New Potatoes

See p. 354.

A Piquant-Flavored Breakfast for 4

Rhubarb Compote
Kedgeree with Curry Sauce
Toast   Marmalade

Rhubarb Compote

Wash 1 to 2 pounds rhubarb. Cut in 3- to 4-inch lengths, and place in a casserole or baking dish. Add 1½ cups brown sugar. Cover, and bake at 350° for 25 minutes or until rhubarb is tender.

Serve hot or cold.

Kedgeree with Curry Sauce

May be made with fresh cooked, canned, or smoked salmon, although often made with other fish, such as cod, haddock, or finnan haddie.

1 pound salmon	*1½ cups Sauce Béchamel*
4 hard-cooked eggs	*(see p. 331)*
1 or 2 tablespoons curry	*2 cups cooked rice*
powder	*¼ cup chopped parsley*

Flake the salmon, and slice the eggs. Mix curry powder with the sauce béchamel. Place alternate layers of rice, fish, eggs, parsley and béchamel in the top of a double boiler or in a mold. Place over hot water and heat thoroughly. Unmold on hot platter.

You may wish to serve additional curried béchamel.

An Italian Breakfast for 4

Pasta for breakfast?—why not? Fettucine Alfredo is rich with dairy products and gentle enough to begin the day. With it serve a good Italian white wine—perhaps a Soave or Verdicchio. And offer a bowl of crisp celery and some grissini (Italian bread sticks) to munch on.

Figs and Prosciutto
Fettucine Alfredo
Celery   Grissini
Espresso

Figs and Prosciutto

Buy either the white- or purple-skinned figs, making sure they are fully ripe but still firm. Allow 2 or 3 per person. Serve on a plate with a slice of prosciutto for each fig. Pass the pepper grinder.

Fettucine Alfredo

1 pound fettucine
6 tablespoons butter
$1/2$ cup grated Parmesan cheese
$1/2$ cup grated Switzerland Swiss
or Gruyère cheese
$1/2$ cup heavy cream
Freshly ground black pepper

Cook fettucine to your favorite state of doneness. Drain. Melt butter over low heat or in chafing dish. Add the fettucine, and toss well. Then add the cheese, and toss gently until it is melted and blended. Last, add the cream and a generous sprinkling of pepper. When the cream is blended with the butter and cheese, remove pan from heat, and serve immediately.

A Pennsylvania Dutch Breakfast for 6

Dishes of the Pennsylvania Dutch region dominate this menu—scrapple, available in most sections of the country now; velvety apple butter, to be eaten with buttermilk biscuits; and shoofly pie, really a coffee cake in a crust and perhaps the best-known recipe from this part of the world. Eggs, pickled in beet juice and red wine vinegar, in the local manner, give a pretty color as well as the characteristic sour tidbit for the meal.

Red Beet Eggs
Scrapple
Fried (Sautéed) Ham
Buttermilk Biscuits and Apple Butter
Shoofly Pie

Red Beet Eggs

1 pound small firm fresh beets,
   peeled and trimmed
3 cups water
1 cup sugar

$^1/_2$ cup red wine vinegar
6 hard-cooked eggs, peeled
   and cooled

Bring the water to a boil in an enameled or stainless steel saucepan. Add the beets, cover the pan, and simmer over low heat for 30 to 40 minutes or until the beets can be easily pierced with a thin knife blade.

Transfer the beets to a bowl, using a slotted spoon. Add the sugar and vinegar to the liquid in the pan, bring to a boil, and stir until the sugar dissolves. Return the beets to the pan, and cook over low heat another 5 minutes.

Drain the beets in a sieve set over a deep bowl, and set them aside. Add the eggs to the beet liquid, and turn them to coat evenly. Add the beets to the bowl. Cool to room temperature, then cover with foil or plastic wrap and refrigerate for about 12 hours.

To serve, remove the eggs from the liquid and pat them dry with paper towels. Cut them in half lengthwise and arrange on a platter. Slice the beets 1/4 inch thick, and put them in a serving bowl with the beet liquid. Serve the eggs and beets separately.

Scrapple

Slice scrapple about 3/8 of an inch thick, lightly flour on both sides, and sauté in bacon fat or butter till brown and crisp.

Fried (Sautéed) Ham

Slice either ready-to-eat or country ham 1/2 inch thick. Trim off the dark edges but leave some of the fat. Sauté very slowly in a little ham fat and butter in a heavy skillet, turning several times, until ham is lightly browned and the fat is crisp. For a ready-to-eat ham allow about 10 minutes; for a country ham, about 12 to 15 minutes. If you are using a highly salted aged ham, first parboil it in water for five minutes. Drain it, pat it dry, and sauté 8 to 10 minutes in butter.

Buttermilk Biscuits

See p. 346.

Shoofly Pie

Makes one 9-inch pie

> 1 cup unsifted all-purpose flour
> 1/2 cup light brown sugar
> 1 1/4 cup vegetable shortening
> 1 teaspoon baking soda
> 1 cup boiling water
>
> 2/3 cup light corn syrup
> 1/3 cup dark molasses
> 9 inch unbaked, short crust
>   pastry shell

Prepare the crumb topping by combining the flour, sugar, and shortening in a bowl and cutting them in together with a fork or pastry blender to form a coarse, mealy texture.

In a deep bowl, dissolve the soda in the boiling water, and stir in the corn syrup and molasses. Allow to cool, then pour into the unbaked pie shell. Sprinkle the crumb mixture evenly over the top.

Bake on the middle rack of a 375° oven for 10 minutes, then reduce the temperature to 350° and continue baking 30 to 35 minutes or until the filling is just firmed when the pan is gently shaken. Do not overbake. Cool before serving.

Special Omelets for Breakfast

Serve Bloody Marys made with aquavit. You'll find that aquavit gives more flavor and will prime the palate for the unusual omelet to follow.

Red-Caviar and Sour-Cream Omelets
Crisp Hot Rolls   Butter
Cream Cheese   Strawberry Preserves

Red-Caviar and Sour-Cream Omelets

Prepare omelets in your usual fashion. Fill each omelet with about 2 tablespoons of chilled caviar, and serve with a dollop of sour cream on top.

LUNCHEONS

INFORMAL LUNCHEONS

Serving luncheon at home is a pleasing, effortless way to entertain. Guests are offered an apéritif or two, sit down to a two- or three-course luncheon, and linger a bit over coffee before leaving for their afternoon round of duties.

One busy woman of my acquaintance entertains six or so at luncheon in her handsome kitchen. These are friendly, informal occasions and a stimulating change from the ordinary cocktail or dinner event. One can do this sort of thing in an hour or two and be well rewarded. A simple menu such as sausage and an interesting omelet, cheese and fruit, or perhaps a fine chicken hash, is all that is necessary.

Although one thinks of luncheon fare in terms of light food, there are many hearty dinner dishes that are better consumed at midday. Cassoulet is one of these; feijoada is another. Both require long digestive periods. If eaten in the evening, these are apt to disturb one's sleep.

No cocktail hors d'oeuvre are necessary for a luncheon; menus should be appetizing but brief. In warm weather a cold plate, preceded or followed by a hot course, will suffice. Offer young, light wines that will not act as a sedative. Keep in mind the guest who has to return to the office or studio.

A Marseillaise Luncheon for 6

It would be nice to start this luncheon with iced vodka and perhaps a few shrimp to dip in a little of the aïoli. With the bourride drink a Pouilly-Fumé, and after lunch, coffee and cognac.

Bourride
French Bread
Peaches with Raspberry Puree

Bourride

2 pounds fish (bass, haddock, or flounder)
1 medium onion, finely chopped
Bouquet garni (thyme, bay leaf, fennel, peel of half an orange)
Salt and pepper
Boiling water
12 slices bread
Garlic
2 cups aïoli

Prepare the fish—fillets will do. Cut into small serving-size pieces. Place in the bottom of a saucepan, cover with the onion, add bouquet garni, and salt and pepper to taste. Add boiling water to a little more than cover, and poach 5 to 10 minutes.

While the fish is cooking, toast the bread and rub well with garlic. Place in a large tureen or deep platter. Prepare the aïoli.

When the fish is cooked, remove it and keep warm. Strain the bouillon and combine 3 cups of it, little by little, with 1 cup of the aïoli. Mix well without letting it curdle. Put it in a saucepan over very low heat, or over hot water, and stir with a wooden spoon until the sauce just coats the spoon. *It must not boil.* Pour this sauce over the pieces of toast, and serve the fish separately with additional aïoli.

FOR THE AÏOLI:

6 cloves garlic
3 egg yolks
Salt

1 to 2 cups olive oil or peanut oil
Lemon juice

Chop the garlic very fine or put it through a garlic press. Add the egg yolks, and beat in the electric mixer or blender.

Gradually add the oil until thickened to the consistency of a mayonnaise, then add lemon juice and salt to taste. The garlic flavor should be dominant.

Have plenty of crusty, hot French bread to accompany the Bourride.

Peaches with Raspberry Puree

8 to 10 ripe peaches
2 cups water
1 cup sugar

Dash vanilla
2 packages frozen raspberries
Candied violets

Drop peaches into boiling water for 3 minutes. Remove, and peel as quickly as possible. Have ready a boiling syrup—the water and sugar cooked together for 5 minutes—and transfer the peaches to this immediately after peeling. Cook till just tender, then cool in syrup. Arrange in a serving dish.

Whirl raspberries in a blender and strain or put through a food mill. Spoon over peaches, and chill. Serve with whipped cream, if you wish, and garnish with candied violets.

A Good, Hearty Luncheon for 4

The only hard work here is in the preparation of the brioche. Serve Alsatian wine.

Sausage en Brioche
Hot Potato Salad
Toasted French Rolls
Orange Marmalade Soufflé

Sausage en Brioche

1 or 2 coteghino or kielbasy
   sausages
Basic Brioche dough (see
   p. 344)

2 eggs
3 tablespoons heavy cream

Poach the sausage for 20 to 25 minutes in boiling water. Peel off the skin, and cool.

Prepare the brioche dough and allow to rise. Punch down, and roll out 1/3 inch thick. Cut piece, or pieces, large enough to cover sausage. Place sausage in center of dough, and make a neat package, tucking in the ends and then bringing the sides together to overlap. Place seam side down on a buttered baking sheet, and let dough rise for 10 minutes. Beat the eggs and cream together. Brush the surface of the dough with this mixture. Bake at 375° till brioche is done and lightly browned—about 35 minutes.

Slice, and serve with a variety of mustards.

Hot Potato Salad

2¹/₂ pounds small new potatoes,
  scraped
6 tablespoons oil
3 tablespoons wine vinegar

Salt and pepper
¹/₃ cup finely chopped onion
2 tablespoons chopped parsley

Boil potatoes in salted water till just tender. Cut in halves or quarters, depending on size, and toss with oil, vinegar, salt, freshly ground pepper, onion and parsley. Return to heat for a moment. Serve at once.

Orange Marmalade Soufflé

6 egg whites
1 cup orange marmalade

Whipped cream, if desired

Beat egg whites till stiff but not dry. Fold into orange marmalade, and pour into the buttered top of a 2-quart double boiler. Cover, place over hot water, and steam 45 to 50 minutes.

Unmold. Serve with whipped cream, if you wish.

A Light, Simple Luncheon for 6

Scallops Sauté, Provençale
Potatoes Anglaise
Apple Charlotte

Scallops Sauté, Provençale

2 pounds bay scallops
Flour
¹/₄ cup oil

Salt and pepper
3 to 4 cloves garlic, finely chopped
¹/₃ cup chopped parsley

Flour the scallops lightly just before cooking. Heat the oil in a skillet, preferably non-stick. (You may have to use 2 skillets for this amount.) When the oil is quite hot add the scallops. Cook for just a minute or so until the scallops lose their translucent look. Add the garlic and parsley, and toss with the scallops. Cook for a moment longer. Serve at once.

Potatoes Anglaise

These are simply plain boiled potatoes. Be sure to cook them so they are just tender and not soggy, about 20 to 25 minutes.

Apple Charlotte

About 18 slices white bread
Butter
6 tart apples, peeled, and
*   sautéed in butter*

1 teaspoon vanilla
1/4 cup sugar
Whipped cream, flavored with
*   sherry*

Trim the crusts from the bread. Sauté in butter until crisp and brown on both sides.

Place the apples in a heavy skillet with butter and vanilla. Cover and steam over medium heat till soft but not mushy. Sugar to taste.

Line a mold—a charlotte mold or bread tin—with overlapping pieces of bread on bottom and sides. Fill with apple mixture and top with bread.

Bake at 375° for 25 minutes or until golden brown. Unmold and serve with sherry-flavored whipped cream.

An Easy, Informal Luncheon for 6

Oeufs en Cocotte
Beef Salad Parisienne
Rolls
Tarte aux Abricots

Oeufs en Cocotte

12 eggs   *6 tablespoons cream*
Salt and pepper

You will need 6 small individual soufflé dishes or "cocottes" for this. Butter the dishes well, and into each break 2 eggs. Salt and pepper to taste. Bake at 350° for 10 to 12 minutes, or until eggs are just set. Add a spoonful of heavy cream to each cocotte, and bake for another minute or so. Serve at once.

Beef Salad Parisienne

2 to 3 pounds cold pressed   *1 green pepper*
boiled beef or beef à la   *Salad greens*
mode   *Vinaigrette Sauce (see p. 338–39)*
6 boiled potatoes   *Tarragon*
1/2 pound cooked green beans   *Chopped parsley*
1 cucumber   *6 hard-cooked eggs*
4 to 5 tomatoes   *Cornichons (small sour pickles)*
2 stalks celery   *1 onion, sliced*

Cut the beef into slices and then into smaller pieces. Combine with sliced potatoes, green beans, sliced cucumber, tomatoes (peeled and cut into sixths), finely sliced celery, and sliced green pepper. Dress with a good vinaigrette, heavily flavored with tarragon and chopped parsley. Garnish with sliced hard-cooked eggs, cornichons, and onion rings.

Tarte aux Abricots

Rich Pastry (see p. 347)   Apricot Glaze (see below)
Pastry cream   Whipped cream (optional)
Apricot halves

Make Rich Pastry, chill, and place in a flan ring. Line pastry with foil, and fill ring with dried beans (to prevent pastry from puffing up). Bake at 425° for 18 to 20 minutes. Remove foil and beans, and allow to cool. Spread with a thin layer of pastry cream. Then fill with fresh apricots poached in a simple syrup and cooled. Top with an Apricot Glaze. Serve with whipped cream, if desired.

For the Apricot Glaze: Melt 1 pound of apricot jam in a heavy saucepan over high heat. When it is melted and bubbling, remove from fire and force through a fine sieve. Keep warm till ready to use. Also use as a glaze for tarts or cookies.

VARIATION: Add 2 tablespoons cognac, bourbon or rum to the jam when it comes to a boil, and let it cook down for 2 minutes before straining.

A Modest but Delicious Luncheon for 6

Risotto al Frutti di Mare
Beet and Egg Salad with
Onion Dressing
Chocolate Génoise Roll

Risotto al Frutti di Mare

4 tablespoons butter   lobster or mussels
1 small onion, finely chopped   12 to 14 small clams
2 cups rice   Dash of sherry or port
1 cup white wine   Grated Parmesan cheese
3 cups broth (chicken or fish)   Chopped parsley
1 pound shrimp   Salt and pepper
1 pound crabmeat, scallops,

Melt the butter in a heavy skillet, and sauté the onion till just tender. Add the rice, and toss with a fork; do not let the rice brown. Add the wine, and cook until it has almost evaporated. Then add the broth, cover, and cook over low heat for 20 minutes or until the liquid is absorbed. If rice is not yet tender (to your taste), add more broth, and continue cooking.

For the *frutti di mare*: You may combine any type of seafood for this dish. If you are using the combination suggested above, prepare each variety of shellfish separately—boil the shrimp and crab (or buy ready-cooked), and steam the clams. Combine all three and heat over a low flame with a little butter and a dash of sherry or port. Fold into the risotto. Add grated Parmesan to taste and chopped parsley. Taste for seasoning.

Beet and Egg Salad with Onion Dressing

6 to 8 cooked beets, peeled and coarsely chopped	Mayonnaise
1 large onion, finely chopped	Tarragon
8 hard-boiled eggs, finely chopped	Greens
	Chopped parsley

Combine the beets, onion and ²/₃ of the egg. Bind with a tarragon-flavored Mayonnaise (preferably homemade, *see* p. 336), and arrange in a bowl bordered with greens. Decorate with chopped parsley and the remaining chopped egg.

Chocolate Génoise Roll

Basic Génoise recipe (see p. 360)	2 tablespoons cocoa
1¹/₂ cups heavy cream, whipped	2 tablespoons Grand Marnier
2 tablespoons sugar	6 ounces semisweet chocolate bits
	1 cup sour cream

Bake génoise in an 11- by 14-inch pan that has been buttered and lined with baking paper. When done, turn out on waxed paper. Allow to cool, and then spread with the whipped cream, flavored with sugar, cocoa, and Grand Marnier. Roll carefully by lifting the waxed paper at one end and allowing the génoise to fall gently inward. As you continue to lift the paper, the cake will roll forward. Finally, roll onto a board or plate.

Ice with Helen Evans Brown's Chocolate Frosting: Melt the chocolate over hot water, and combine with sour cream. Blend well, and spread over roll.

An Easy Luncheon or Sunday-Night Supper for 4

A light Swiss Neuchâtel would be pleasant with this meal.

Swiss Tarte à l'Oignon
Green Salad
Compote of Prunes

Swiss Tarte à l'Oignon

Cream Cheese Pastry or Rich	*Nutmeg*
Pastry (see p. 348)	*1 cup Gruyère or Emmenthal,*
3 tablespoons butter	*grated*
3 onions, thinly sliced	*5 egg yolks*
Salt and pepper	*1 cup cream*

Line a 9-inch tin with pastry. Place foil over the pastry, and fill with dried beans. Bake at 425° for 10 to 12 minutes. Remove beans (reserve for future use) and the foil.

Melt butter in a heavy saucepan over medium heat. Add onions and seasoning. Cover, and steam until onions are just tender. Remove to pastry shell, and mix gently with the grated cheese. Blend eggs and cream, and pour over the onion-cheese mixture. Bake at 375° for 25 to 35 minutes or till custard is just set.

NOTE: The pastry shell may be made in advance and frozen, either baked or unbaked.

Compote of Prunes

I keep a jar of prunes in my kitchen the year round, preserved in Marsala, port or sherry. Select about 2 to 3 pounds of dried prunes of good quality, place in a crock, and cover them with any of the three wines mentioned. They will be ready for eating in three weeks.

Serve in a compote with whipped cream, flavored with the same wine in which the prunes were steeped.

These prunes have many other uses—in soufflés, in hot compotes with other fruits, and as a flavoring for certain meats.

A Hearty Winter or Spring Lunch for 4

Beer is certainly the correct tipple for this luncheon.

Irish Stew
Homemade Rolls
Onion and Romaine Salad
Apples and Ripe Cheddar Cheese

Irish Stew

2 pounds lamb shoulder, cut in 1½-inch cubes
4 medium onions, thinly sliced
3 carrots, thinly sliced
6 medium potatoes, sliced
Salt and pepper
3 cups stock or water
Parsley

In a heavy casserole place alternate layers of meat, onions, carrots, and half the sliced potatoes. Season with salt and pepper and add enough stock or water to cover the mixture. Secure the lid and simmer over low heat 1½ hours. Add the rest of the potatoes and simmer another 45 minutes. Arrange stew on a hot serving platter; garnish with chopped parsley.

Homemade Rolls

See p. 342.

Onion and Romaine Salad

1 head romaine	Basic Vinaigrette Sauce (see
1 large Spanish, or sweet	p. 338)
Italian, onion	Chopped parsley

Wash and dry the romaine and place in refrigerator till ready to use. Slice the onion very thin, blend with vinaigrette sauce in salad bowl, and allow to stand for 1 hour. When ready to serve, add romaine and toss. Sprinkle with chopped parsley.

Apples and Ripe Cheddar Cheese

A Canadian, Vermont or Oregon cheddar is a delicious cheese in winter or spring. Be sure to get a nicely aged and flavorful one.

A Sunday Autumn Luncheon for 6

Serve chilled vodka with the blini and a cabernet sauvignon with the rest of the meal.

Blini with Sour Cream and Caviar
Butterflied Leg of Lamb
Barley and Almond Casserole
Tomatoes Provençale
Pear Tarte Tatin
Goat Cheese

Blini with Sour Cream and Caviar

1¹/₂ packages dry yeast	4 tablespoons unsalted
2¹/₂ cups lukewarm milk	butter, melted
1 teaspoon sugar	3 tablespoons sour cream
¹/₂ cup buckwheat flour	¹/₂ teaspoon salt
2 cups all-purpose flour	Golden caviar
4 eggs, separated	Additional sour cream and butter

In a large bowl sprinkle the yeast into the milk with the sugar, and stir. When dissolved combine with the flours and the egg yolks, lightly beaten. Stir slowly, then beat vigorously until the batter is smooth—by hand, in an electric mixer, or in a food processor. Put the batter in a clean bowl, cover with a dish towel, and let rise in a warm, draft-free place for 1½ to 2 hours, until doubled in bulk.

Punch down the batter, and stir in 2 tablespoons of melted butter and the sour cream. Beat the egg whites with the salt until stiff but not dry, and fold into the batter.

Brush a hot griddle or heavy skillet well with the remaining melted butter and drop the batter on by spoonfuls large enough to make pancakes 3 inches in diameter. When the bottom is lightly browned and bubbles have formed on the surface, flip over the blini and brown the other side. Keep warm in the oven, adding a little melted butter. Serve with more butter, sour cream, and the caviar. Makes 12 servings.

Butterflied Leg of Lamb

This is simply a boned leg of lamb that has been opened out and slightly flattened to make it fairly uniform in thickness. A 6- to 7-pound leg will yield about 5 pounds of trimmed meat.

4 to 5 garlic cloves, peeled	crushed
½ teaspoon salt	1 cup olive oil
1 teaspoon freshly ground	6- to 7-pound leg of lamb, trimmed,
black pepper	boned, and butterflied
1 teaspoon dried rosemary,	

Grind the garlic, salt, pepper and rosemary together, and then stir into the olive oil to make a smooth marinade; or blend the ingredients in a food processor.

Put the lamb in a shallow dish large enough to hold it, and pour the marinade over it, making sure all the meat is well covered. Allow it to marinate for 2 to 3 hours, or longer.

Preheat the broiler. Remove the lamb from the marinade, and lay it on the broiler rack with the cut side up. Broil 6 inches from the heat for approximately 15 to 18 minutes, depending on the thickness. Brush the surface with the marinade, turn the lamb with tongs, and broil fat side up for 16 minutes. Before the end of the cooking time remove the lamb from the broiler and insert a meat thermometer in the thickest part. It should register 135° for rare, 140° for medium rare.

Transfer the lamb to a hot platter or carving board, fat side down, and allow to stand for 5 minutes before carving. Carve slices cross-wise on the diagonal, from ¼ to ½ inch thick.

Barley and Almond Casserole

See p. 89.

Tomatoes Provençale

See p. 123.

Pear Tarte Tatin

SHORT CRUST PASTRY

2½ cups all-purpose flour
1 cup (2 sticks) unsalted butter,
  chilled and cut into small
  pieces

2 tablespoons sugar
3 egg yolks
Grated zest of 1 lemon

PEAR FILLING

¾ cup sugar, plus 3 or
  4 tablespoons
6 ripe but firm pears, cored,
  peeled, and cut into
  quarters or sixths

4 tablespoons unsalted
  butter, cut into tiny pieces
Juice of 1 lemon
2 teaspoons vanilla extract

Place the flour in a large bowl, make a well in it, and add the butter, sugar, egg yolks, and lemon zest. Knead until well mixed and the dough gathers easily to form a ball. Chill until firm.

To make the filling: Melt the sugar in a heavy iron or other 8- or 9-inch ovenproof skillet over medium heat until it turns a delicate brown. Remove the pan from the heat. Arrange the pears on the melted sugar, and mound up in the center. Sprinkle them with the 3 to 4 tablespoons of sugar, and dot with the butter. Sprinkle with the lemon juice and vanilla.

Preheat the oven to 350°. Carefully roll out the chilled pastry to a size that will fit inside the skillet. Lay it over the pears, and tuck down inside the skillet. Make 3 holes in the top with a skewer or sharp knife. Bake from 1 to 1½ hours, until the crust is brown and firm to the touch and the pears bubbling up a bit around the edges. Remove from the oven and let it stand 2 minutes, then run a sharp knife around the edge of the tart, and invert it onto a plate somewhat larger than the skillet. This must be done quickly and deftly so the pears don't fall off. Should they shift position, push them back into place with a spatula. Cut into wedges and serve warm or tepid with a domestic or imported goat cheese.

FOUR LIGHT LUNCHEONS

Luncheon for 4

This can be expanded easily to a luncheon for 6 or 8. Merely make two crab soufflés instead of one, and increase the number of oranges in the dessert. The mixture for the soufflé may be prepared ahead of time, the soufflé mold buttered, and the crabmeat placed in it. All that remains is for the egg whites to be beaten and the soufflé popped in the oven. By the time you have an apéritif it will be ready. For an apéritif there is nothing more refreshing than chilled white wine with a drop of cassis in it. Pass some good cocktail biscuits or salted Macadamia nuts with the drinks. If you wish to serve wine with lunch, continue with the same white wine used in the apéritifs; it might be a young Muscadet or a Pouilly-Fuissé.

Crab Soufflé
Melba Toast
Watercress and Raw Mushroom Salad
Grapefruit with Sherry

Crab Soufflé

1 small onion, finely chopped	black pepper
5 tablespoons butter	Dash Tabasco
3 tablespoons flour	1 teaspoon tarragon
3 tablespoons tomato paste	2 tablespoons cognac
1/2 cup cream	4 egg yolks
1 teaspoon salt	6 egg whites
1/2 teaspoon freshly ground	1 pound crabmeat

Sauté onion in butter until soft. Add flour and stir, then add tomato paste and cream and stir again until smooth. Add seasonings, including cognac, and cool slightly. Add egg yolks and beat well.

Beat egg whites until firm but not dry. Fold into mixture. Butter a 1½-quart soufflé dish. Place a layer of crabmeat on the bottom. Add ⅓ soufflé mixture, then another layer of crab and the remaining soufflé mixture. Bake at 375° for approximately 30 minutes. Serve with a hollandaise sauce if you wish.

Melba Toast

See p. 318–19.

Watercress and Raw Mushroom Salad

¼ pound freshest raw mushrooms	*Vinaigrette Sauce (see p. 338)*
	1 tablespoon chopped parsley
1½ bunches watercress	*2 tablespoons finely cut chives*

Slice the mushroom caps very thin and combine with trimmed watercress. Toss with vinaigrette sauce, and sprinkle with chopped parsley and chives.

Grapefruit with Sherry

6 grapefruit	*½ cup medium or cream sherry*
Sugar to taste	

Peel grapefruit carefully, removing all white film. Slice neatly into segments with a sharp knife. Arrange in serving dish or individual serving dishes. Sprinkle with sugar, if necessary, and chill. Just before serving add sherry to taste. Or pass chilled sherry and permit guests to serve themselves.

Luncheon for 8

A pleasant main dish with a most delicious soufflé for dessert makes entertaining as easy as you could want it. Drink chilled dry sherry before lunch while you pass the olives and filberts. If you plan to serve a wine with lunch, make it a Pouilly-Fuissé or a California Traminer.

Sherry   Spanish Olives
Toasted Filberts
Vol-au-Vents with Chicken and Sweetbreads, Suprême
Petits Pois with Mint   Endives with Beet Dressing
Apricot Soufflé

Vol-au-Vents with Chicken and Sweetbreads, Suprême

You may buy large vol-au-vents or small individual ones from a caterer or good pastry shop. If you use individual ones, bring them to the table hot and serve the chicken and sweetbreads from a separate bowl or tureen. The large vol-au-vents should be assembled beforehand. You may, of course, make your own vol-au-vents if you are willing to prepare a puff paste.

2 pounds chicken backs   *2 pairs sweetbreads*
1 pound chicken gizzards   *1 onion*
1 onion, stuck with cloves   *1 carrot*
1 tablespoon salt   *1 stalk celery*
Water   *1 cup white wine*
4 whole chicken breasts   *1 pound mushrooms*

FOR THE SAUCE:

6 tablespoons butter   *4 egg yolks*
6 tablespoons flour   *2 truffles*
2 cups chicken broth   *1 tablespoon lemon juice*
1/2 cup sherry or Madeira   *2 tablespoons chopped parsley*
1 1/2 cups heavy cream

Place the backs, gizzards, onion and salt in a deep pot, and cover with 2 quarts of water or more. Cook over low heat for 2½ to 3 hours, covered. Correct the seasoning and cool. Then chill, and remove excess fat.

Poach the breasts until just tender in 1 quart of the broth, adding salt if necessary. Do not overcook. Cool, and remove meat from bones. Return bones to broth, and reduce to 1 pint.

Allow the sweetbreads to stand in ice water for 1 hour, then trim. Dice the onion, and cut the carrot and celery in julienne strips. Place on the bottom of a large saucepan. Add the sweetbreads, the remaining quart of chicken broth and the white wine. Cover and poach for 20 to 25 minutes. Peel the sweetbreads, and return peelings to the broth. Reduce to 1 cup. Combine with the previously reduced broth. Strain and clarify.

Slice the mushrooms, and sauté quickly in 4 tablespoons butter. Remove the mushrooms and reserve the butter, adding 2 more tablespoons to the pan. Over low heat add the flour, and blend. Gradually stir in 2 cups of the reduced broth, and stir until thickened. Correct the seasoning, and add sherry. Then stir in the cream and egg yolks, and continue stirring till the sauce is perfectly smooth.

Cut the chicken and sweetbreads into bite-size pieces. Combine with the mushrooms and truffles. Heat with a little chicken broth, and combine with the sauce. Stir in the lemon juice. Keep hot over warm water. Correct the seasoning, and transfer to a warmed tureen; or ladle into vol-au-vent shells. Top with chopped parsley. If the vol-au-vents are 6 to 8 inches in diameter, serve cut in wedges.

Petits Pois with Mint

Use the frozen petits pois with butter sauce that come in a plastic bag. Follow directions on box. They are remarkably good. Add a little chopped fresh mint to the peas just before serving. You will need about 3 packages for 8 persons.

Endive with Beet Dressing

6 to 8 heads Belgian endive   Basic Vinaigrette Sauce (see
1 large cooked beet   p. 338)

Crisp the leaves of endive in cold water, and arrange them in a salad bowl. Grate the beet over them, and at the last minute add the dressing, and toss.

Apricot Soufflé

1½ pounds dried apricots
Sugar to taste
2 tablespoons cognac or
   ⅓ cup apricot liqueur
½ teaspoon salt

8 egg yolks
10 egg whites
1½ cups heavy cream, whipped
Sweet sherry or cognac

Soak the apricots in water overnight. Bring to a boil and cook for 5 minutes. Add sugar to taste and the cognac or apricot liqueur. Put through a food mill or a coarse sieve. You will need 2½ cups puree.

Combine the puree with the salt and egg yolks, and cook over low heat to thicken. Do not allow to boil. Cool slightly.

Fold in the whites, beaten stiff but not dry. Pour into 2 1½-quart soufflé dishes that have been buttered and sugared. Bake at 375° for 30 minutes or until brown and puffy. Serve with sweetened whipped cream flavored with a little sweet sherry or cognac.

Luncheon for 6

This meal is composed of a rather pleasant first course, a cold main course, and a light dessert. It is simple to prepare, and the main course can be done a day in advance. Precede the lunch with a good dry sherry, and drink a light white wine with lunch if you wish.

Canapé Provençale
Cold Red Snapper with Shrimp and Mustard Mayonnaise
Cucumber and Cherry Tomato Garnish
Nesselrode Pudding

Canapé Provençale

6 slices white bread
Butter
Garlic
10 eggs
½ teaspoon salt

¼ teaspoon Tabasco
3 tablespoons water
18 anchovy fillets
6 black olives
Chopped parsley

Cut the bread into rounds about 3 inches in diameter. Fry in garlic-flavored butter until crisp and brown. This may be kept warm in a napkin or foil for an hour or two. Just before serving, combine eggs with the salt, Tabasco and water, and scramble carefully. Do not overcook. Spoon the egg onto the fried toast, and garnish with anchovy fillets, black olives and chopped parsley.

Cold Red Snapper with Shrimp and Mustard Mayonnaise

1 or 2 red snappers—about 5 pounds in all	1 tablespoon salt
	Water to cover
2 pounds small shrimp	1 lemon, thinly sliced
1 onion	2 hard-boiled eggs, sliced
1 sprig parsley	Mustard Mayonnaise
1/2 cup wine vinegar	(see p. 337)

Trim the fish, which is handsomer if it has its head. Clean and devein the shrimp. Combine the onion, parsley, vinegar, and salt with enough water to cover the fish, and pour into a long fish boiler. Wrap the fish in cheesecloth, leaving ends long enough to use as handles. Bring the liquid to a boil and cook for five minutes. Taste for salt. Lower fish into liquid and reduce heat to simmer. Cook 10 minutes per inch of thickness. Fish should flake easily when tested with a fork. Remove from the bouillon and cool; then chill in refrigerator. Meanwhile cook shrimp in the same bouillon for 3 or 4 minutes. Remove, cool, and chill.

TO SERVE:

Remove skin from the snapper and arrange on a platter. Garnish with cooked shrimp, thinly sliced lemon and sliced hard-boiled eggs. Watercress is also a decorative touch with this. Serve with mustard mayonnaise.

Cucumber and Cherry Tomato Garnish

Thinly sliced cucumbers and cherry tomatoes may be used on the fish platter as an additional garnish or served separately as a salad. No dressing is needed. Just salt and pepper.

Nesselrode Pudding

1 pint light cream
4 egg yolks
1/2 cup sugar
1 can (8³/4 ounces) pureed
   chestnuts
1/4 cup Malaga or sherry

1/2 cup currants
1/4 cup seedless raisins
1/2 cup sugar
1/2 cup water
3/4 cup heavy cream

Heat light cream in a saucepan until a film shines on top. Beat egg yolks until light and thick, then gradually beat in 1/2 cup sugar. Add heated cream gradually and pour back into the saucepan. Cook over a very low heat, stirring constantly, until custard thickens slightly and coats a spoon. Remove from heat, stir in chestnut puree and Malaga or sherry. Freeze, preferably in the traditional way, in an ice cream freezer, since the fruits are added later and should be all through the pudding when it is presented.

Cook currants, raisins, sugar and water together over a moderate heat until the fruit plumps up and the syrup thickens. Beat heavy cream until it holds a soft shape. Stir the fruit and the whipped cream into the frozen custard. Pack mixture into a melon or charlotte mold and freeze until firm, either in a freezer or in a container of ice and salt (4 to 6 parts ice to 1 part rock salt). Unmold on a handsome, chilled platter, and garnish with marrons glacé and whipped cream.

NOTE: To prepare fresh chestnuts, make a slit in the skins of 20 plump chestnuts and boil for 5 minutes. Drain and remove shell and inner brown skin. Cook in a mixture of 1 1/2 cups water, 1/2 cup sugar and about an inch of vanilla bean. When tender, drain off most of the syrup and either blend chestnuts in a blender or work through a sieve to make a smooth puree.

A Low-Calorie Luncheon

This luncheon has simplicity yet a certain elegance. If you want to keep this truly low-calorie, you will eschew cocktails.

Consommé with Fresh Sorrel
Tiny Grilled Lamb Chops
Cherry Tomatoes in Dill
Toasted Protein Bread
Pineapple with Kirsch

Consommé with Fresh Sorrel

2 quarts consommé   ¹/₂ pound fresh sorrel
   (canned may be used)

Wash the sorrel well and cut it into thin strips. Heat the consommé to the boiling point. Serve in heated cups with a generous sprinkling of sorrel.

Tiny Grilled Lamb Chops

Ask your butcher well ahead of time to save you tiny rib chops and to French them. If they are 1-rib chops, serve 2 to a person; if they are double, have them cut full and serve 1 to a person. Provide some extras for those who have larger appetites.

Grill the chops quickly under a brisk heat, allowing about 5 to 8 minutes for 1-rib chops and 9 to 11 minutes for double. You can be the judge of how pink they should be. Salt and pepper the chops, and serve at once, with sprigs of watercress as a garnish.

Cherry Tomatoes in Dill

3 pints cherry tomatoes
1¹/₄ teaspoons salt

2 tablespoons butter
1 tablespoon chopped fresh dill

Remove stems from tomatoes and place in top of a double boiler over hot water. Barely heat through, then add salt, butter, and dill, and heat for an additional 4 minutes. Serve with a little chopped parsley.

Pineapple with Kirsch

Arrange thin slices of ripe fresh pineapple on a platter or on individual dishes, and at the last minute sprinkle generously with chilled kirsch or framboise. Or you may add the brandy at table in case some guests prefer their pineapple plain.

FORMAL LUNCHEONS

Formal luncheons are not as common in this country as they are abroad. However, some day it will occur to hosts and hostesses that this is an ideal way to entertain certain visiting personalities. Naturally, it is not a black-tie affair. Nor are the menu and table as elaborate as they would be for a formal dinner. Usually guests are bid for 12:30, with lunch served at 1 and the final course and coffee over by 2. The offering consists of apéritifs, three courses and one or two wines. You might start with cold or hot hors d'oeuvre and follow with a meat or fish dish and a vegetable or salad. Finish off with dessert and coffee—and brandies, if you wish. Although it is not customary to serve butter at a formal meal, you may want to serve it with the hors d'oeuvre and then throughout the meal.

Unless it is a very formal and important affair, choose lighter wines than you would offer for a dinner party. Beaujolais, Fleurie or Juliénas, and Muscadet or Pouilly-Fumé are a few perfect luncheon wines. And one should not forget the wines of California, especially if the guest of honor is a foreigner.

Keep flower arrangements and table settings simple. Place cards are optional, although I still like to present a written menu. Formal luncheons should be lively and amusing and without an air of duty or protocol.

A Formal Luncheon for 6

Serve a brût champagne with this if you wish.

Lobster and Zucchini Appetizer
Tournedos au Poivre Flambé
Grilled Tomatoes with Duxelles
French Bread   Gorgonzola Cheese
Fresh Pears

Lobster and Zucchini Appetizer

6 medium zucchini
Sauce à la Grecque (see p. 339)
Greens
3 or 4 lobsters—
about 1 1/2 pounds each
Thousand Island Dressing (see p. 338)

Poach the zucchini à la grecque. Remove from sauce and chill. They should be tender with just a touch of crispness in them. Arrange on 6 beds of greens, and decorate with slices of poached lobster tail and one lovely piece of lobster claw. Serve with Thousand Island Dressing.

Tournedos au Poivre Flambé

White peppercorns
6 tournedos, about 6 ounces
*   each*
Coarse salt
6 tablespoons butter
3 tablespoons oil
1/2 cup cognac
6 rounds fried toast
1 cup Basic Brown Sauce
*   (see p. 332)*

Roll or pound peppercorns till they are coarse. You may also whirl them in a blender. Press into the tournedos along with some coarse salt. Heat butter and oil in pan and sear the tournedos on both sides. Reduce heat and let them cook gently till they have achieved your desired state of rareness. They should never be served medium or well done.

Remove to a hot platter and pour off excess fat. Return the tournedos to the pan and flame with cognac. Place toast rounds on platter, and top with tournedos. Add brown sauce to pan and heat through quickly. Pour around the tournedos. Place a broiled tomato on each plate, and garnish with watercress. If it is to be a very impressive party you may top each tournedo with a slice of truffle. Serve very hot.

Grilled Tomatoes with Duxelles

6 tomatoes, red and ripe
Salt and pepper
6 tablespoons Duxelles
  (see p. 341)

Toasted buttered bread crumbs
Chopped parsley

Cut off the top $1/3$ of each tomato and discard. Sprinkle tomatoes with salt and a touch of pepper, and broil 5 inches from heat for about 6 minutes. Spread with duxelles, and return to broiler for 3 minutes or until brown. Keep hot till serving time. Dust with crumbs mixed with parsley just before serving.

Fresh Pears with Gorgonzola

Choose the ripest and best pears available. Serve with fruit knives and forks, and pass the cheese. It should be a fine ripe one.

Serve good French bread throughout the meal and again with the cheese, in case there are those who prefer it to the pears. And if you wish to serve a red wine with the cheese and fruit, it might be a fine old port. This would complement both.

A Formal Luncheon for 6

Crudités
Crêpes de Volaille
Quick Strawberry Sherbet

Crudités

Arrange a selection of cleaned and crisped raw vegetables on a platter—perhaps radishes, scallions and strips of cucumber. Pass the salt. Anchovies and good bread and butter go well here.

Crêpes de Volaille

2 fowl or roasting chickens
1 onion, stuck with cloves
1 bay leaf
Parsley

Salt and pepper
12 unsweetened crêpes (see p. 351)

FOR THE SAUCE:

5 tablespoons butter
5 tablespoons flour
1½ cups broth
1 teaspoon salt
Pinch nutmeg

Dash Tabasco
1 cup heavy cream
3 egg yolks, lightly beaten
¼ cup sherry or Madeira

Poach the chickens in seasoned water till just tender. Do not over-cook. Cool. Remove chickens, and reduce broth by one half over a brisk heat. Strain through a linen towel or napkin.

Prepare the crêpes. They may be done a day or several days in advance. Simply wrap in foil, and store in the refrigerator. They may even be frozen.

Cut the chicken into 1-inch pieces. Taste for seasoning. Prepare the sauce: Melt the butter in a saucepan, add the flour, and let cook for a minute. Then add heated broth slowly, and stir till sauce thickens.

Add seasonings and the heavy cream and then the egg yolks. (Do not allow the sauce to boil after this point.) Add sherry or Madeira.

Mix chicken with ²/₃ of the sauce, and heat through. Wrap chicken in the crêpes. Arrange in a baking dish or ovenproof serving dish. Pour remaining sauce over top, and glaze in a 450° oven for a few minutes.

Quick Strawberry Sherbet

2 packages frozen strawberries   Kirsch or Grand Marnier

Dice thawed berries, and place in a blender or food processor with about ¹/₄ to ¹/₃ cup kirsch or Grand Marnier. Blend, and then pour into ice trays, a serving dish, or individual serving dishes or sherbet glasses. Return to freezer to stiffen. Decorate with fresh strawberries, if you wish.

A Formal Luncheon for 4 to 6

Madrilene with Chives and Sour Cream
Poached Salmon, Beurre Blanc
New Peas
New Potatoes with Mint
Princess Charlotte Pudding

Madrilene with Chives and Sour Cream

Use canned madrilene. Pass a bowl of chopped chives and a bowl of sour cream, and let each guest help himself. Toasted crackers go well with this.

Poached Salmon, Beurre Blanc

3-pound piece filleted salmon

Court bouillon:

2 pounds fish bones and heads
2 bay leaves
1 onion, stuck with 2 cloves
1 or 2 stalks celery
1 $^1/_2$ tablespoons salt
   (approximately)

1 teaspoon peppercorns
$^1/_2$ teaspoon thyme
$^1/_2$ teaspoon tarragon
$^1/_2$ cup vinegar
1 pint white wine or dry
   vermouth

Beurre Blanc:

$^1/_4$ cup white wine
$^1/_4$ cup wine vinegar
1 tablespoon chopped shallots
   or onions

$^1/_4$ teaspoon salt
1 grind black pepper
3 sticks chilled butter, cut into
   24 pieces

Combine the ingredients for the court bouillon, except for the wine, and add enough water to cover fish bones and heads—about 4 quarts. Bring to a boil, and cook for 15 minutes. Taste for salt, and correct the seasoning. Add the wine, and continue cooking for 5 minutes.

Wrap the salmon in cheesecloth, leaving long ends to use as handles, and lower into the court bouillon. Poach at a feeble bubble 10 minutes per inch of thickness. Test fish with a fork or toothpick until it flakes easily. Be careful not to overcook. Remove salmon to a hot serving dish or gratin dish, and keep warm.

For the sauce:

Boil the wine, vinegar and onions together in a stainless steel or enamel saucepan until they are reduced to 2 tablespoons. Add salt and pepper. Remove the pan from the heat, and, with a wire whisk, beat in two pieces of butter. When this begins to cream, beat in another piece. Continue in this manner, holding pan over low heat or warm water, until all the butter is added. The resulting sauce will be creamy and light amber in color. Do not let it get too hot, or it will separate.

Serve with the fish.

New Peas

3 pounds new peas
2 to 3 cups water

Salt and pepper
6 tablespoons melted butter

Select the freshest, youngest peas you can buy, and store in the refrigerator until ready for shelling. Do not soak them in water after shelling. Bring 2 to 3 cups water to a boil—do not worry if this does not entirely cover peas—and add peas. Cook uncovered till just tender, about 10 to 15 minutes. Drain, season to taste with salt and pepper, and toss with the melted butter.

New Potatoes with Mint

Follow directions on p. 354 for cooking new potatoes. Allow 3 or 4 potatoes per person, depending on size of potatoes—the smaller, the better. When cooked, toss with butter and chopped fresh mint.

Princess Charlotte Pudding

6 egg yolks
6 tablespoons sugar
2 tablespoons cornstarch
2 cups milk
$1/2$ teaspoon vanilla
1 tablespoon unflavored gelatin

$1/4$ cup cold water
$1/4$ cup toasted filberts, chopped
2 cups heavy cream, whipped
Sugar to taste
Cognac

Combine egg yolks, sugar and cornstarch in the top of a double boiler. In a separate pan heat milk and add vanilla (kirsch or cognac may be substituted if you wish). Soak gelatin in cold water. Pour milk into egg mixture, and stir over hot water till mixture thickens. Add gelatin and stir until thoroughly dissolved. Add toasted filberts and the whipped cream, blended with the sugar and a touch of cognac. Pour into 12 individual molds. Chill.

Serve with raspberry sauce, sauce Melba or with crème de cassis. All these are available bottled.

SUMMER LUNCHEONS

When I think of an ideal summer luncheon, I think of a day like this:
I am sitting in a cool house in Provence with the hot sun beating
down outside. A few yards from the house there is a large tree with
thick foliage and deep shade beneath. Beyond is a field of bright
flowers, a range of hills and a brilliant sky. Soon guests will arrive for
lunch. It will be a cold one, prepared yesterday. I shopped for some
of the hors d'oeuvre at the local charcutier and robbed the garden of
crisp vegetables. We shall have drinks in the shade of the tree and
then move indoors. The table is set with gay placemats and Provençal
pottery of that indefinable golden shade. There is a centerpiece of zin-
nias, and carafes of white and rosé wine, well chilled.

There is salade de museau—made from the muzzle of the beef
long cooked. It is sliced paper-thin and tossed with a vinaigrette,
with chopped pickle, onion and parsley added. I bought a cervelat—
a cooked one that has a richly seasoned flavor and is utterly delicious. I made some peppers à la grecque, which are now cool and
reposing in their *ravier* with oil and vinegar and spice; also some tiny
onions, with the same beginning but to which I added a bit of
tomato puree, some saffron and finally some white raisins, cooking
the sauce till it made a glaze. There are fresh tomatoes and raw beets,
just pulled from the garden this morning; and fresh basil has been
chopped and mixed with the dressing for the tomatoes. There is a
chicken—a poulet de grain bought from the *épicier* rather than the
poultry dealer—because his are better. A sprig of fresh tarragon is in
the chicken's tummy, and butter and salt and pepper were used to
baste it first on one side and then on the other. The chicken is neither hot nor cold but that delicious in-between state where it has the
quality of crisp warmth. The one hot dish of the meal will be haricots verts gathered just in time to cook. They will be buttered well.

Cheese and lovely fresh peaches will follow and some black, black
coffee. This is summer lunching to me—color, good food, cooling wines.

A Summer Luncheon for 6

This is an ideal luncheon for beer.

Hot Ratatouille with Grated Cheese
Cold Roast Beef with Mustard Sauce
Pickles   Melba Toast or Rolls
Blueberries with Maple Cream

Hot Ratatouille with Grated Cheese

This great dish of Provence may be varied in so many ways. Here, we add mushrooms in quantity and cheese.

3 cloves garlic, finely chopped
2 onions, cut in thin slices
1/3 cup olive oil
1 green pepper, cut in thin rounds
2 medium eggplants, diced
6 very ripe tomatoes peeled, seeded, and diced, or

2 1/2 cups canned Italian plum tomatoes
1 teaspoon dry basil, or 1/4 cup fresh chopped basil
1 1/2 teaspoons salt
1 pound mushrooms, sliced
Grated Parmesan cheese

Sauté garlic and onions in oil till soft. Add the pepper and eggplant, and cook for 5 minutes over medium heat, tossing well and shaking pan. Add tomato and seasonings, and simmer 30 minutes, covered for half that time. Add mushrooms, correct seasoning, and continue cooking till mushrooms are just cooked through. Serve sprinkled with grated cheese.

Cold Roast Beef with Mustard Sauce

This should be cooked to rare perfection. Merely slice and arrange on a platter. Garnish with watercress and pickles of your choice.

FOR THE MUSTARD SAUCE: Combine 2 to 3 teaspoons dry mustard with 1 tablespoon oil and enough white wine to make a paste. Add a touch of salt and finely chopped tarragon.

You may serve the ratatouille and roast beef together if you wish.

Melba Toast

See p. 318–19.

Blueberries with Maple Cream

Sweeten blueberries with maple sugar or maple syrup. Serve with sour cream, and sprinkle with a dash of cinnamon.

A Summer Luncheon for 4

Serve a chilled Sancerre with this luncheon.

Crudités, Sauce Niçoise
Broiled Chicken, Rosemary Butter
Snow Peas with Mushrooms
Coeur à la Crème with Strawberries
Crisp Rolls

Crudités, Sauce Niçoise

The crudités should include green onions, radishes, celery, tiny artichokes, asparagus, turnips, carrots—all raw. Arrange on a platter, and chill.

FOR THE SAUCE NIÇOISE:

2 cloves garlic
12 anchovy fillets
18 capers

25 soft black olives
2 cups mayonnaise

Chop garlic, anchovy, capers, and olives very fine, and blend with the mayonnaise at least 3 hours before luncheon. Serve separately as a dip for the vegetables.

Broiled Chicken, Rosemary Butter

2 small broilers or 4 squab
   broilers
1/2 cup butter

Salt and pepper
1 teaspoon rosemary

Split the chickens if they are large; for squab chickens, merely remove the backbones, and flatten. Rub well with 1/2 the butter. Salt and pepper. Place skin side down on a broiler rack, and sprinkle bone side with a little rosemary. Combine remaining rosemary and butter.

FOR BROILERS: Broil for 13 minutes 3 inches from heat, turn, brush with rosemary butter, and broil skin side for another 12 to 13 minutes.

FOR SQUAB BROILERS: Follow instructions given above, broiling bone side 8 minutes, then turning for another 6 minutes.

Snow Peas with Mushrooms

1 pound snow peas
1 pound mushrooms
Butter

Salt and pepper
Chopped parsley

Trim snow peas, and cook in a small amount of boiling salted water till just heated through. Drain at once. Sauté mushrooms quickly in butter. Toss with the snow peas. Season to taste with salt and pepper, and garnish with chopped parsley.

Coeur à la Crème with Strawberries

See p. 178.

A Hot-Weather Luncheon for 6

Serve a Chassagne Montrachet.

Veal Scallopine with Lemon
Roesti Potatoes
Onion and Orange Salad
Apples Bonne Femme

Veal Scallopine with Lemon

1¹/₂ pounds veal scallopine
Flour
6 tablespoons butter
2 tablespoons olive oil
Grated rind of lemon

3 or 4 lemon slices
2 tablespoons lemon juice
White wine
Chopped parsley or tarragon

Dust the scallopine with flour, and sauté quickly on each side in the butter and oil. Add the lemon rind, slices, and juice, and simmer for 3 to 4 minutes. Add a dash of white wine (you may use vermouth). Remove to a hot platter, and sprinkle with chopped parsley or chopped fresh tarragon.

Roesti Potatoes

Parboil 6 medium potatoes. Peel and grate. Melt ¹/₄ pound butter in a skillet, add potatoes and cook well till they form a crust. Press into a cake with spatula, and turn and cook on other side. Salt and pepper to taste and add more butter if needed. When crisp and beautifully brown, slide out onto a hot plate.

NOTE: These may be made in small cakes and served individually.

Onion and Orange Salad

5 oranges
1 large Bermuda or Texas
   onion, or 2 red Italian onions
$^1/_2$ teaspoon crushed rosemary
6 tablespoons olive oil
2 tablespoons orange juice

$1^1/_2$ tablespoons vinegar
1 teaspoon salt
$^1/_2$ teaspoon freshly ground
   black pepper
1 large or 2 small heads
   romaine or curly chicory

Peel the oranges with a sharp knife so that the white film is entirely removed. Slice the oranges by cutting between each section, to loosen the fruit from its thin membrane. Slice onions very thin, and break into rings. Combine the orange and onion slices with the rosemary, and dress with the oil, orange juice, vinegar, salt, and pepper. Just before serving, add the greens. Toss well.

Apples Bonne Femme

For 6 persons choose 6 good-sized, firm apples. Core, then peel $^1/_3$ of the way down the apple. Place each apple on a round of toasted white bread, well-buttered and sprinkled with granulated sugar. Place 1 tablespoon sugar and as much butter as the core will hold into each apple. Top with another tablespoon sugar and a chunk of butter. Place these in a well-buttered baking dish and bake at 350°, basting every 15 minutes with the juices in the pan and additional butter and sugar, if necessary, until the apples are tender but not mushy.

Serve warm with heavy cream, which you may wish to season with a little grated nutmeg.

An Unusual Light Summer Luncheon for 6

Depending on the filling, woven eggs, a specialty of Thailand, may be served as a first course, a luncheon dish or a dessert. Here, it is just right for a light midday meal.

Woven Eggs
Tossed Green Salad
Raspberries in Red Wine

Woven Eggs

9 eggs
Peanut oil

FOR THE FILLING:

1 cup thinly sliced scallions (white portions)	*3 teaspoons lemon juice*
	3 tablespoons tomato ketchup
6 tablespoons peanut oil	*3 teaspoons finely chopped*
1 1/2 pounds lean pork, finely ground	*fresh coriander or*
	3/4 teaspoon ground
1 1/2 teaspoons anchovy paste	*coriander seeds*
1 1/2 teaspoons grated lemon peel	*3/4 cup finely ground peanuts*

Prepare the filling first. Sauté the scallions in the peanut oil till they are soft but not brown. Stir in the ground pork, and cook till brown, breaking up the meat with a fork. Blend in anchovy paste, lemon peel, lemon juice, ketchup, coriander, and peanuts. Continue cooking over low heat, stirring frequently, for 15 minutes longer. Correct the seasoning, adding salt if needed. Keep warm while you prepare the eggs.

Break eggs into a mixing bowl, and stir with a whisk until well blended. Do not beat. Strain through a fine sieve into another bowl.

Then divide eggs equally between bowls, since the cooking will be done in two batches. In a shallow skillet heat peanut oil to a depth of about 1/4 inch until it almost reaches the point of smoking. Remove pan from heat, and start immediately to "weave" in the eggs: Holding the first bowl about 6 inches above the edge of the skillet, dip into the egg with one hand and scoop up as much egg as can be held between the tips of the fingers. Dribble the egg into the hot oil in thin threads, weaving it into a lattice pattern. Continue the process until the egg is used up. Return the pan to moderate heat, and allow the eggs to cook until they are lightly browned on the underside. Carefully turn and brown on the other side. Remove to absorbent paper to drain, while you prepare the second batch of eggs. Add more peanut oil if necessary.

Place the omelets on a warm serving platter and spread evenly with the filling. Fold the omelets in half to completely enclose the filling, and serve them at once with a garnish of raw bean sprouts and chopped chives.

Raspberries in Red Wine

For 6 persons, clean and pick over 1 quart raspberries and sugar them to taste. Arrange in a rather shallow bowl. Add 1 cup light red wine—a Beaujolais is ideal for this particular dish—and let them stand for 1 hour before serving.

A Refreshing Summer Luncheon for 6

This meal calls for a young Chablis, well chilled.

Jambon Persillé
Caesar Salad   Melba Toast
Strawberries Romanoff

Jambon Persillé

*2 pounds cold boiled or
    baked ham
1 cup finely chopped parsley
1¹/₂ to 2 cups clarified*

*bouillon—beef or chicken,
    or half and half
1 envelope unflavored gelatin
¹/₄ cup cold water*

Remove all fat from ham, and cut in rather coarse julienne. It should be a ham with good flavor, not the run-of-the-mill boiled ham one buys in the supermarket. Canned Polish or Danish hams are excellent for this purpose. Mix some of the chopped parsley with the ham, and use the rest to line a mold. Fill the mold with the ham-parsley mixture.

Dissolve the gelatin and combine with ¹/₂ cup boiling bouillon. Stir until dissolved. Cool and combine with remaining bouillon. When it is just thick and syrupy pour over the ham and parsley. Chill in the refrigerator. Unmold on a platter, garnish with additional parsley, and serve with mustard or with Mustard Mayonnaise (see p. 337).

Caesar Salad

This famous salad is often served but seldom made correctly.

4 slices bread cut into cubes	24 or more anchovy fillets, diced
4 tablespoons butter	Juice of 1 lemon, or to taste
2 tablespoons olive oil	Salt, if needed
4 crushed garlic cloves	Freshly ground black pepper
1 or 2 heads romaine, washed,	1 egg, coddled 1 minute
chilled and dried	Parmesan cheese, freshly grated
8 tablespoons olive oil	

Sauté the croutons in butter and 2 tablespoons olive oil, and add 3 garlic cloves to the pan.

Rub a glass or china salad bowl with the remaining garlic and add the greens. Pour over them the 8 tablespoons olive oil and toss well.

Add the croutons, the anchovies and lemon juice to taste. Toss lightly and taste for salt. Add freshly ground black pepper to taste, the coddled egg and a good handful of grated cheese. Toss well and add additional cheese if desired. Serve at once.

Melba Toast

See p. 318–19.

Strawberries Romanoff

Hull 3 pints of large, ripe strawberries and place them in a rather shallow bowl. Combine 1 can (6 ounces) frozen concentrated orange juice with an equal quantity of tawny port, and pour over the berries, allowing them to soak in this marinade for several hours. Add sugar if necessary.

When ready to serve, pile the berries in a serving dish. Serve the sauce in a pitcher, and pass a bowl of whipped cream, sweetened and flavored with a little port. Decorate with chopped pistachio nuts, if you wish.

DINNERS

INFORMAL DINNERS

If you enjoy your friends around you and enjoy cooking, then the idea of entertaining informally should appeal to you. The degree of informality will depend on how well you know your guests. You may cook and serve without the necessity of extra help.

It is my great joy to invite six or eight people for an informal, simple dinner, with one or two people to serve, or with one to supervise while I do much of the serving myself. On such an occasion I am apt to offer squab, for instance; one can nibble on the bones. Or I might produce a hearty dish of corned beef. I had a group in last summer for cold corned beef and tongue and a robust salad, followed by an old-fashioned bread-and-butter pudding. It was a sensation, and I knew that this homely menu would strike the right note.

Plan your food schedule carefully, and make your table as attractive as you can, then relax. No rush should show on these occasions.

As for wines—they can be as elegant or as simple as you wish. You might drink a carafe wine all evening, or you can bring out your choicest vintages, if you are certain your guests love wine. Don't waste your best on those who would rather have beer.

A Deliciously Rich Dinner for 8

Serve a Valpolicella with dinner. After dinner—espresso.

Prosciutto and Melon
Pasta with White Truffles
Chicken with Madeira
Artichoke Salad   Italian Bread
Frozen Zabaglione
Espresso

Prosciutto and Melon

Cantaloupe or Spanish or Persian melon is best for this. Serve melon in slices, with strips of prosciutto arranged over it. Have a pepper grinder handy, and let each person pepper his dish to taste. Westphalian ham may be substituted for the prosciutto.

Pasta with White Truffles

1 pound noodles, either white   ¹/₄ pound butter
*   or green   8 ounces canned white truffles*

Boil noodles in plenty of salted water until just tender. (If you add a couple of spoonfuls of oil to the pot, the noodles will not stick together.) Drain and toss with the butter. Serve and top with freshly grated truffles, and spoon truffle liquid over pasta if you wish.

NOTE: The current (1996) price of canned white truffles is $25.00 an ounce. You may want to substitute a less impressive but less costly pasta tossed with sautéed sliced mushrooms and minced shallots and sprinkled with chopped parsley.

Chicken with Madeira (Venetian Style)

4 cloves garlic
2 sticks (8 ounces) butter
Freshly ground pepper

2 4- to 5-pound roasters
3/4 cup Madeira

Chop garlic cloves very fine, and cream with 1 stick of the butter. Add 6 to 8 turns of the pepper mill. Divide garlic butter and add half to the cavity of each chicken. Butter the outside of chickens well with remaining butter, and salt them. Place them on their sides on a rack in a shallow roasting pan, and roast at 400° for 20 minutes. Baste and turn chickens over to opposite sides. Roast another 20 minutes. Turn breast sides up and baste (add additional butter if needed). Roast another 20 minutes or until chickens are tender.

Remove to a hot platter. Drain juices from the birds into pan, remove excess fat and add Madeira. Heat sauce thoroughly, and serve with the chicken, cut into quarters.

Artichoke Salad

Combine 2 packages thawed frozen artichoke hearts with 2 heads broken romaine leaves. Dress with a vinaigrette sauce.

Frozen Zabaglione

8 egg yolks (large eggs)
2/3 cup sugar
1 tablespoon grated lemon rind
1 cup Marsala, cognac or port

1/2 envelope gelatin, dissolved in
    2 tablespoons water
3 tablespoons Grand Marnier
1 pint heavy cream, whipped

Beat egg yolks very well, and combine with sugar, lemon rind and Marsala. Continue beating over slightly boiling water until thick. Transfer pan to a bowl of ice, add dissolved gelatin and Grand Marnier and beat till cold. Fold in whipped cream, and spoon into individual dishes or a mold. Freeze several hours before serving.

An Unusual Informal Dinner for 6

Clam and Tomato Broth
Fillets of Lamb with Cèpes
Gratin of Eggplant
Crêpes Soufflés

Clam and Tomato Broth

Combine tomato juice of good quality with clam juice, in equal proportions. Add a touch of basil and salt and pepper. Heat thoroughly. Serve with a dab of salted whipped cream.

Fillets of Lamb with Cèpes

1 leg of lamb, boned
6 tablespoons butter
3 tablespoons oil
2 cloves garlic
1 teaspoon dried tarragon, or

1 tablespoon fresh chopped
tarragon
Salt and pepper
Cèpes, either fresh or canned

Cut the lamb into large cubes, about 3 inches square. Sauté in butter and oil until nicely browned. Add seasonings, and cook to the desired degree of rareness. Serve with fresh or canned cèpes drained and sautéed just enough to heat through. These are Boletus mushrooms, which grow wild in parts of the country, but you must be a mycologist to identify the edible species.

Gratin of Eggplant

1 large onion, coarsely chopped
1/2 cup oil
4 tomatoes, peeled, seeded and
   chopped or 3/4 can plum
   tomatoes

1 large eggplant, sliced (unpeeled)
1/2 teaspoon thyme
1/2 tablespoon flour
Salt and pepper
Grated Swiss cheese

Sauté the onion in oil. Add the tomatoes and let them cook for 5 to 8 minutes. Add the eggplant and the thyme and cook very slowly. You may cover for part of the cooking time. When the eggplant is tender but not mushy, sprinkle in the flour and let it blend into the sauce. Salt and pepper to taste, add the grated cheese, and run under the broiler to melt.

Serve this hot or cold.

Crêpes Soufflés (for 12 crêpes)

12 dessert Crêpes (see p. 351)
1 recipe for Grand Marnier

Soufflé (see below) or
   any other sweet soufflé

Prepare the soufflé recipe. Butter a baking sheet. Arrange 2 to 3 tablespoons soufflé mixture on 2/3 of each crêpe and fold over the remaining 1/3 very lightly. Sprinkle lightly with sugar and bake at 425° for about 5 to 8 minutes or until the soufflé mixture is set. Serve very hot on hot plates. Pass a cognac vanilla sauce: Melt 1 pint vanilla ice cream and add cognac to taste.

FOR THE GRAND MARNIER SOUFFLÉ:

3 tablespoons butter
3 tablespoons flour
1/2 cup milk, heated
1/4 cup sugar
4 egg yolks

Grated rind of 1/2 orange
1/4 cup Grand Marnier
5 egg whites, beaten stiff
   but not dry

Melt the butter over low heat, add flour and stir for 2 to 3 minutes. Add milk, remove from heat, and stir until smooth. Add sugar and egg yolks, and blend well. Return to heat for a moment or two to thicken. Stir in orange rind and Grand Marnier. Cool slightly and fold in well half of the egg whites and then the second half more lightly. Either bake in a 1 1/2-quart soufflé dish that has been buttered and well sugared, or use in crêpes as above.

An Easy but Impressive Informal Dinner for 4

Some preparation may be done ahead. You might serve a Sancerre with the crab and a Volnay with the meat course. Cognac would be pleasant after dinner.

Crabmeat Charentais
Zratys Nelson with Deep Fried Onion Rings
Bean Salad
Pears Condé

Crabmeat Charentais

6 tablespoons butter (approximately)
4 thin slices French bread
3 or 4 scallions, finely sliced
1 green pepper, finely chopped
1 tablespoon grated carrot
$1/3$ cup white wine
Salt and freshly ground

black pepper
1 teaspoon chopped tarragon leaves or $1/2$ teaspoon dried tarragon
1 pound crabmeat
$1/3$ cup cognac
Lemon slices
Chopped parsley

In skillet or chafing dish, melt butter and brown the slices of bread very quickly. Remove them to a hot platter. Add more butter if needed, and cook scallions, pepper and carrot briskly for 2 minutes. Add white wine, crab and seasonings. Toss lightly to heat crabmeat thoroughly. Heat cognac, ignite and pour flaming over the crabmeat. Blend. Spoon over toast. Garnish with lemon slices and chopped parsley.

Zratys Nelson

4 or 5 boiled potatoes
Butter
Salt and pepper
2 small cucumbers
8 mushrooms
2 tablespoons flour

8 medallions of beef, fillet or
sirloin
1 cup cream
1 tablespoon tomato paste
French fried onions (see
recipe below)

Peel and cut the potatoes in even rounds, and sauté in 3 to 4 tablespoons butter until nicely browned and crisp on the edges. Salt and pepper them. Arrange on a serving platter and keep hot.

Cut the cucumber and mushroom in thick slices and sauté in butter until the cucumbers are soft and the mushrooms slightly browned. Add the flour and mix well. Gradually add the cream, stirring constantly until thickened. Then add the tomato paste. Season to taste, and put aside to keep warm while preparing the beef.

Sauté the medallions quickly in butter until done to taste. Salt lightly. Arrange over the potatoes, and cover with cucumber-mushroom sauce. Top with Cecily Brownstone's superb Deep Fried Onion Rings.

Cecily Brownstone's Deep Fried Onion Rings

3 or 4 large Spanish onions
Ice water
1 egg, beaten
1 cup buttermilk

1 cup flour
$1/2$ teaspoon salt
$1/2$ teaspoon baking soda
Fat for deep frying

Slice the onions about $1/4$ inch thick, separate them into rings, and soak in ice water for a couple of hours. Drain, dry thoroughly, and dip in a batter made by mixing the egg with the buttermilk and adding the flour, sifted with salt and baking soda. Fry in deep fat at 375° until brown. Drain well on paper.

Bean Salad

1¹/₂ pounds young snap beans
Salted water
6 tablespoons olive oil
2 tablespoons wine vinegar

Salt and pepper
3 tablespoons chopped onion
2 tablespoons chopped parsley

Cut ends from beans, but leave them whole. Boil in salted water until tender but still crisp. Drain. Remove to a flat dish. Add oil and vinegar, and season to taste. Cool. Serve with a garnish of the onion and parsley. Add more oil and vinegar if needed.

Pears Condé

6 to 8 medium pears, peeled
and halved
2 cups sugar
1 cup water
1 teaspoon vanilla

Sweet Rice (see below)
Candied fruit
Chopped pistachio nuts
Whipped cream

Poach the pears until just tender in a syrup made by boiling together the water, sugar and vanilla. Serve warm on a border of sweet rice, and garnish with the candied fruit, nuts and whipped cream.

FOR THE SWEET RICE:

³/₄ cup uncooked rice
1¹/₂ cups boiling water
2 cups scalded milk
¹/₂ cup sugar

Pinch salt
3 tablespoons butter
1¹/₂ teaspoons vanilla
4 egg yolks, slightly beaten

Cover rice with the boiling water, and let stand for 10 minutes. Drain. Combine scalded milk with the sugar, salt, butter and vanilla. Add to the rice, and then place in a shallow baking dish. Bake 30 minutes at 325°. Remove and stir in the beaten egg yolks.

Polynesian Dinner for 6

Here is a Polynesian dinner that can be done either indoors or outdoors, using a spit. It is a pleasantly different study in flavors and would probably be best accompanied by beer or champagne. I don't think any bread is necessary with this meal, save Melba Toast (*see* p. 318–19) with the salad. To finish off the dinner, serve good coffee and perhaps one of the coffee liqueurs, or Grand Marnier.

Pacific Shrimp Appetizer
Duck Glazed with Curry and Honey
Rice Pilaff
Snow Peas and Mushrooms
Kumquat Parfait

Pacific Shrimp Appetizer

*4 to 6 heads Bibb or Limestone
    lettuce*
*1 pound tiny Pacific or Iceland
    shrimp*
*9 tablespoons oil, preferably
    olive*
3 tablespoons wine vinegar
Dash or 2 Tabasco
2 or 3 tablespoons chutney
1 teaspoon salt
*1 teaspoon freshly ground black
    pepper*

Wash Bibb well to remove sand and grit. Dry thoroughly and chill. Combine with shrimp in a salad bowl—not a wooden one! Mix the remaining ingredients and pour over salad at the last minute. Toss well.

Duck Glazed with Curry and Honey

2 4- to 5-pound ducks, cleaned	1/2 teaspoon Tabasco
2 1/2 tablespoons curry powder	1/2 cup honey
2 garlic cloves, finely chopped	1/4 cup orange juice
1 teaspoon turmeric	1/4 cup lemon juice

Rub the ducks inside and out with 1 tablespoon of the curry powder mixed with the garlic, turmeric, and Tabasco. If you are using a spit, truss, spit and balance the ducks. Roast over medium coals for about 1 1/2 hours. During the last half of roasting, baste with a mixture of the honey, orange juice, lemon juice, and the remaining curry powder. Prick the skin from time to time to release the fat.

If you are using the oven, roast on a rack at 350° for 1 1/2 hours. Baste frequently with the honey-curry mixture. Be sure to prick the skin, and raise the temperature to 475° for the last 15 to 20 minutes of cooking to crisp the skin. Serve the ducks quartered.

NOTE: These timings and temperatures should give you ducks medium done—that is, still a bit pink at the joints. If you like your duck well done, cook longer.

Rice Pilaff

2 cups uncooked rice	4 cups or so stock, broth or
2 large onions, sliced	bouillon
8 tablespoons butter	Almonds and raisins (optional)

Wash the rice and drain. Brown the sliced onions lightly in the butter and add the rice (and sliced almonds and raisins, if you wish). Cook over low heat for about 4 to 5 minutes, stirring it often to let it brown evenly. It should be just lightly colored. Heat the liquid to the boiling point and pour it over the rice to cover by a good 1 1/2 inches. Cover the pan tightly and bake in a 350° oven for 25 to 30 minutes, or until all the liquid is absorbed. Serve with plenty of butter.

NOTE: This can also be cooked on top of the stove over very low heat.

Snow Peas and Mushrooms

1 pound mushrooms
4 tablespoons butter

$^1/_2$ pound snow peas
Salt and pepper

Slice the mushrooms, and sauté very lightly in butter. Cook snow peas in salted water till just tender. Do not overcook. Combine with the mushrooms, and season to taste. Add more butter if needed.

Kumquat Parfait

1 cup preserved kumquats
(approximately)
1 pint orange ice

1 pint vanilla ice cream
$^1/_2$ pint heavy cream, whipped
6 whole preserved kumquats

Chop the 1 cup of kumquats rather coarsely. Cover the bottoms of 6 parfait glasses with orange ice, half of the chopped kumquats, and then small dips of ice cream. Add another layer of chopped kumquats, top with whipped cream, and garnish each parfait with a whole kumquat. Chill before serving.

A Southwest Dinner for 6

Serve margaritas before dinner and beer throughout the meal.

Chili con Queso
Salt and Pepper Spareribs
"Sons of Rest" Steak
Corn on the Cob
Tomatoes with Okra
Pecan Pie with Ice Cream

Chili con Queso

See p. 238.

Salt and Pepper Spareribs

Split 1 or 2 sides of spareribs down the middle so they can be managed easily with the fingers. Sprinkle liberally with coarse salt and freshly ground black pepper. Place on the rack of a broiling pan, and roast for 30 minutes at 350°. Turn the ribs and roast 30 minutes longer.

"Sons of Rest" Steak

Porterhouse steak, at least
3 inches thick
Unsalted butter
Salt and freshly ground

black pepper
1/2 cup dry sherry
Dijon mustard

Broil the steak to the rare stage (120° to 125° on a meat thermometer for very rare, 130° to 135° for rare). Then make deep diagonal cuts in it about 1 1/2 inches apart. Spread the steak with plenty of butter, pressing it into the cuts, and sprinkle with salt and pepper. Pour the sherry over the steak, and then spread the top with mustard thinned with a little water. Roast in a 450° oven for 10 to 12 minutes. Transfer to a warm platter, and with a sharp knife cut out the bone. Slice in very thin slices on the diagonal, and serve at once.

Corn on the Cob

Shuck the ears and put them flat in a deep skillet with equal parts milk and water to cover. Add 1 tablespoon sugar, and bring to a boil over rather high heat. Remove the corn when the water reaches a full, rolling boil. Serve at once with plenty of melted butter. Pass the salt and the peppermill.

Tomatoes with Okra

1 pound small okra
3 to 4 onions, peeled and
   coarsely chopped
2 cloves garlic, peeled and
   finely chopped
$^1/_2$ cup olive oil

2 cups canned Italian plum
   tomatoes
Salt and freshly ground
   black pepper
1 teaspoon ground coriander
Lemon wedges

Trim the ends from the okra, wash, and dry on paper towels. Sauté the onions and garlic in the olive oil in a large skillet, and when they are slightly brown, add the okra. Cook 3 minutes. Add the tomatoes and seasonings. Cover and simmer about 35 minutes. Serve with lemon wedges.

Pecan Pie

Pastry for a 1-crust 9-inch pie
1 cup pecan meats, either
   halves or broken pieces
2 eggs
1 cup dark corn syrup

$^1/_2$ to 1 cup brown sugar
1 teaspoon vanilla or
   2 tablespoons rum
$^1/_4$ teaspoon salt
2 to 4 tablespoons butter

Line a 9-inch pie tin with pastry and crimp the edges. Sprinkle the nut meats over the pastry. Beat the eggs in a mixing bowl, and stir in the syrup, sugar, flavoring, and salt. Pour over the nuts, and dot with butter. Bake at 450° 10 minutes, reduce the heat to 325°, and bake until the filling is almost firm in the center, about 25 to 30 minutes. Cool on a rack.

Dinner for 6

Drink a Beaujolais or Fleurie during this meal.

Terrine aux Aromates
Grilled Deviled Baby Chickens
with Sauce Béarnaise
Barley with Mushrooms
Mocha Parfait

Terrine aux Aromates

An unusual and delicious terrine that may be eaten hot or cold.

1 pound bacon
3 pounds spinach or 2 packages frozen chopped spinach
1/2 teaspoon thyme
1/2 teaspoon rosemary
3 tablespoons chopped parsley
Dash of nutmeg
1 medium onion, finely chopped
2 large or 3 small cloves garlic, finely chopped
1 tablespoon finely chopped fresh basil or 1 teaspoon dried basil

Dash of Tabasco
1 cup small pitted black and green olives—Italian or French
1 1/2 pounds coarsely ground pork, 75% lean, 25% fat
Salt and freshly ground black pepper
2 eggs
1/3 cup cognac
1/2 pound sliced uncooked ham
2 large bay leaves
Flour and water

Use a terrine that can be covered tightly. Line bottom and sides with strips of bacon. Cook the spinach just enough to wilt and chop very fine. Drain well. If frozen spinach is used, merely thaw and press water through a sieve. Do not cook. Combine with half the seasonings and half the pitted olives.

Combine chopped pork with salt, freshly ground pepper and the remaining herbs and seasonings, the eggs and the cognac. Place half the pork mixture on the bottom of the terrine, and add in layers thin slices of ham, half the spinach mixture, pork—about half the remaining amount—then ham, spinach, and finally the rest of the chopped pork. Press it down well and place the two bay leaves on top.

Cover with foil, place the cover on top and seal with flour-and-water paste. Place the terrine in a pan and bake in a 350° oven for 1½ hours.

Grilled Deviled Baby Chickens with Sauce Béarnaise

6 squab chickens, about 1 to
  1½ pounds each
½ cup soy sauce
½ cup sherry
2 tablespoons Dijon mustard
1 tablespoon Tabasco

½ cup olive oil
Melted butter
3 cups toasted bread crumbs
1½ teaspoons freshly ground
  pepper

Clean chickens, split each down the back, and marinate for 2 hours, turning often, in a mixture of soy sauce, sherry, mustard, Tabasco, and oil. Broil 6 to 8 minutes skin side down, then turn and broil another 6 minutes. Remove from oven, dip in melted butter, and roll in bread crumbs mixed with the pepper. Return to broiler for 2 minutes; watch carefully. Brush with butter, and broil another 2 minutes.

Serve with Sauce Béarnaise (see p. 335). Garnish with fresh watercress.

Barley with Mushrooms

½ pound mushrooms
4 to 5 tablespoons butter
1 large onion, peeled and
  chopped

1 cup pearl barley
2 cups broth (meat or chicken)
⅓ cup toasted slivered almonds

Wipe the mushrooms with a damp cloth and slice them. Melt the butter and sauté the onions and mushrooms until soft. Add the barley and brown it lightly. Pour into a buttered casserole. Before you pour the broth over the barley, taste it for seasoning. If it has enough, the casserole will need no additional salt or pepper. Pour 1 cup of the broth over the barley in the casserole and cover. Bake in a 350° oven for 25 to 30 minutes and then uncover and add the second cup of broth. Continue cooking until the liquid is absorbed and the barley is done. Add the toasted almond slivers just before serving.

Mocha Parfait

1/2 cup sugar	1 cup (6-ounce package)
1/2 cup water	semisweet chocolate chips
1 1/2 teaspoons instant-coffee	2 eggs
powder	1 1/2 cups heavy cream, whipped

Combine sugar, water and instant coffee in a saucepan and bring to a boil. Boil for 3 minutes. Place chocolate chips in a blender or food processor and add sugar syrup. Blend for 6 seconds. Add eggs and blend for 1 minute. Remove and fold mixture into whipped cream. Pour into ice trays and freeze until firm.

An Informal Dinner for 6, with a Viennese Touch

Stuffed Trout, Pyramide
Viennese Goulash   Spaetzle
Beets Vinaigrette   Rehruecken

Stuffed Trout, Pyramide

6 trout	1 truffle (optional)
1 carrot	4 tablespoons butter
6 mushrooms	1/4 cup cognac
2 leeks	1/4 cup port
1 stalk celery	White wine

FOR THE SAUCE:

1 cup fish bouillon	Salt and pepper
4 egg yolks	Dash of paprika
1/2 cup heavy cream	

Cut carrot, mushrooms, leeks, celery and the truffle into narrow strips the size of match sticks. (Be sure to clean the leeks thoroughly.)

Sauté in the butter for 2 minutes, then add the cognac and port. Sauté over high heat for another 2 minutes to reduce liquid to a glaze.

Split and remove backbone of the trout, and stuff each with the vegetable mixture. Poach fish in enough white wine to cover—about 5 minutes. Remove fish to hot platter while you prepare the sauce.

FOR THE SAUCE: Combine fish bouillon with the egg yolks and heavy cream. Beat over hot water until thickened. Correct the seasoning. Add a dash of paprika.

Viennese Goulash

6 onions, peeled and thinly sliced	Salt and pepper
4 tablespoons butter	1 teaspoon marjoram
3 tablespoons oil	1/2 cup tomato puree
1/4 cup vinegar	Flour
1/4 cup paprika	2 cloves garlic, chopped
3 1/2 pounds beef, cut into cubes (cross rib, chuck, arm or rump)	Chicken or beef broth
	Beurre manié
	Peel of 1 lemon
	1 tablespoon caraway seed

Simmer onions in the butter and oil until golden. Add the vinegar and paprika. Then brown the meat in this mixture, tossing it well. Add salt, pepper to taste, marjoram, and tomato puree. Simmer for 1 1/2 hours, or until liquid is practically reduced to a glaze. Sprinkle with flour, and add the garlic, and enough broth to cover. Simmer for 20 to 30 minutes. If the sauce is not thick enough, add tiny balls of beurre manié (butter and flour mixed). Whirl lemon peel and caraway in blender and add to sauce.

Spaetzle or Nockerli

2 eggs, lightly beaten	1 tablespoon melted butter
3 cups sifted flour	3/4 cup water
1 teaspoon salt	Additional butter

Mix the eggs with the flour and salt until well blended. Add melted butter. Gradually add the water, and continue beating for about 4 minutes.

Make tiny balls of this dough, and drop into a pot of briskly boiling water. The spaetzle are cooked when they rise to the surface. Drain and allow to dry, then sauté quickly in hot butter.

Beets Vinaigrette

6 to 8 beets
Water to cover
Salt

1/2 cup Vinaigrette Sauce
(see p. 338)

Cut off stems of beets, leaving about 2 inches—no less—and do not peel. Wash well, and plunge into boiling, salted water to cover. Cook covered for 20 to 30 minutes or until tender. When done, rinse in cold water and allow to cool. Slip off skins, and slice beets neatly. Cover with a vinaigrette sauce for 1 or 2 hours. Serve alone or on a bed of greens.

Rehruecken

A traditional cake baked in a ribbed mold to resemble a saddle of venison.

Butter or margarine
Dry bread crumbs
5 medium eggs, separated
2 whole medium eggs
1/2 cup sugar
1/2 teaspoon cinnamon
2 1/2 tablespoons finely chopped

citron
3/4 cup grated almonds (reserve
slivers to decorate)
1/3 cup grated unsweetened
chocolate
1/2 cup semisweet chocolate
1 tablespoon vegetable shortening

Butter two 10-inch Rehruecken molds or 1 large one, and dust with bread crumbs; or, use a melon-shaped mold.

Combine egg yolks, the 2 whole eggs, and sugar. Beat till thick and lemon colored. Add cinnamon, citron, almonds, and grated chocolate. Mix. Beat egg whites till stiff but not dry, and blend well with the first mixture. Pour into prepared pans and bake for 30 minutes in a 350°–375° oven. Allow 45 minutes for a larger cake.

Press lightly to test doneness. If cake springs back, it is done. Unmold, and let cool on a rack.

Melt semisweet chocolate and shortening over hot water, and spread over cake. Return cake to the oven, which has been cooling, and let it dry a bit. Decorate with almond slivers (to imitate lardoons in a saddle of venison).

THREE DINNERS FOR DIETERS

A Low-Calorie Dinner for 6

This is an elegant dinner with no particular richness or volume, but it will prove appetizing to those who are not dieting as well as to those who are. Furthermore, there is very little work for the cook. Serve cocktails to those who are not counting calories and Perrier or some other low-calorie drink to those who are; or serve champagne to everyone.

Melon with Lime Wedges
Lobster à la Nage
Boiled New Potatoes
Watercress   Cucumber Fingers
Cherry Tomatoes   Celery
Sherry Jelly

Lobster à la Nage

6 1 to 1½-pound lobsters	*4 cups clam broth*
2 medium onions, sliced	*1 cup white wine*
4 carrots, sliced	*2 tablespoons salt*
2 cloves garlic	*12 peppercorns*
Several sprigs of parsley	*Water*

Combine all ingredients in a deep pot, except the lobster, reserving a few sprigs of parsley for garnish. Pour in enough water to cover the lobsters when they are added. Bring to a boil and simmer for 10 minutes. Add the lobsters and return to a boil. Simmer for 18 to 20 minutes, then remove to a deep dish. Split the lobsters, crack the claws, and arrange on a platter. Garnish with parsley. Serve some of the broth separately, if you wish, and also serve an egg mustard sauce.

FOR THE EGG MUSTARD SAUCE:

3 whole hard-boiled eggs
3 hard-boiled egg yolks
1 clove garlic, minced
3 tablespoons Dijon mustard
2 tablespoons oil

1 teaspoon tarragon
$1/2$ teaspoon Tabasco
$1/2$ teaspoon freshly ground
  black pepper

Either blend the ingredients in an electric blender, or mash thoroughly with a fork, beating well to make a smooth sauce with the texture of a rather grainy mayonnaise. Correct the seasoning, if necessary, and garnish with chopped parsley.

NOTE: This sauce may be served with either hot or cold lobster.

Boiled New Potatoes

See p. 354.

Sherry Jelly

2 envelopes unflavored gelatin
1 cup cold water
Sweetener or artificial sugar

$1 1/2$ cups boiling water
$1/2$ cup sweet sherry

Sprinkle gelatin on cold water to soften. Add sweetener or artificial sugar to taste and the boiling water. Stir till thoroughly dissolved. Add sherry and pour into a mold. Chill. Serve with heavy cream to non-dieters.

This may also be made with port wine.

A Chicken Dinner for 4

Oysters on the Half Shell with Lemon
Poule au Pot
Stuffed Cabbage
Steamed Rice
Endive with Beets
Granita di Caffè

Poule au Pot

1 roasting chicken, 4 to 5 pounds	4 onions, peeled
4 carrots, scraped and cut into 1-inch lengths	2 turnips, peeled
	1 teaspoon thyme
4 leeks, trimmed and well cleaned	2 sprigs of parsley
	1½ tablespoons salt
	Freshly ground black pepper

Truss the chicken and place in a large pot with the carrots, leeks, onions, turnips, herbs, salt and a few grinds of pepper. Add water to cover, and bring to a boil. Skim off any scum and forms, then reduce the heat, and cover the pan. Poach for about 1¼ hours or until the chicken is tender and the legs can be moved easily. Do not overcook. Remove to a covered casserole with the vegetables and a little of the broth to keep warm while you prepare the Stuffed Cabbage Leaves.

Stuffed Cabbage Leaves

1 head cabbage, about 3 pounds
1 pound lean pork, ground
4 chicken livers, finely chopped
1/2 cup mushrooms finely
   chopped

1/2 cup chopped parsley
1/2 teaspoon thyme
1 teaspoon salt
1 tablespoon olive or peanut oil

Put the cabbage in a pot of boiling salted water to cover, and cook for about 15 minutes or until the leaves are tender enough to be easily separated from the head. Remove to a plate, and reserve the cooking liquid. Carefully strip off 8 leaves, lay them out flat, and cut out the coarse stem. Prepare the stuffing.

Sauté the onion, pork, livers, mushrooms, parsley, thyme and salt in the oil in a non-stick skillet for about 15 minutes over low heat, stirring from time to time. Spoon the filling into the center of the cabbage leaves, and fold to make a compact package. Place seam-side down in a large skillet. Cover with the reserved liquid, and gently poach for 30 minutes.

To serve, carve the chicken, and arrange on a platter. Surround with the Stuffed Cabbage Leaves and the vegetables. Pass the steamed rice and broth separately.

Endive and Beet Salad

The endive can be separated in leaves, quartered lengthwise or cut into strips or rounds. Leave the beets whole if they are very small. Otherwise cut into slices or julienne. Arrange on individual salad plates and sprinkle with vinaigrette sauce or combine in a bowl with vinaigrette sauce and toss.

Granita di Caffè

See p. 162. Omit the whipped cream.

A Veal Dinner for 6

Crudités
Roast Loin or Shoulder of Veal
Polenta
Snow Peas
Poached Pears with Eau de Vie de Poire

Crudités

See p. 58.

Roast Loin or Shoulder of Veal

4- to 5-pound loin roast or
  boned and rolled shoulder
  of veal
1 clove garlic
2 teaspoons tarragon

Salt and freshly ground
  black pepper
Bacon strips
White wine

Rub the veal well with garlic, tarragon, salt and pepper, and place on a rack in a shallow roasting pan. Place strips of bacon over it, and roast in a 325° oven for approximately 22 minutes per pound or until a meat thermometer registers 165°. Baste occasionally with a little white wine blended with the pan juices. Remove the bacon for the last half hour. Spoon off all fat from the pan juices and serve the juices with the veal.

Polenta

1 cup corn meal
1 cup cold water

1 teaspoon salt
3 cups boiling water

Combine the cornmeal, cold water and salt in a saucepan, and mix into a paste. Pour in the boiling water, and stir over medium heat until well blended and smooth. Transfer to the top of a double boiler, cover, and cook over simmering water for 45 minutes to 1 hour. Serve plain or with a light sprinkling of Parmesan cheese.

Snow Peas

1 to 1¹/₂ pounds snow peas   *Salted water to cover*

Trim stems and strings from the snow peas. Cook in boiling salted water to cover until just barely tender. Do not overcook.

Poached Pears with Eau de Vie de Poire

6 firm ripe pears   *Eau de Vie de Poire (white*
1¹/₂ cups sugar   *pear brandy)*
1¹/₂ cups water

Peel and core the pears, but leave them whole. Combine the sugar and water in a saucepan large enough to hold the pears, and bring to a boil. Add the pears, and poach gently for 15 to 20 minutes, turning once, until just tender. Allow to cool in the syrup. Serve the pears with a little eau de vie poured over them at the last minute.

FORMAL DINNERS

Formal dinners a few decades ago were something appalling. The yard-square double damask dinner napkins, the cut glass, the crystal, the silver, and the menu itself all combined to make an event that would floor the average young host or hostess today. The courses—there were sometimes as many as seven—ran through soup, fish, entree, roast, perhaps game, dessert, and fruit. For each course there were wines. As soon as the dessert had been cleared away, there was coffee, port or brandy, and cigars for the gentlemen in the dining room, and coffee and port for the ladies in the sitting room or drawing room. The host took his cue to join the ladies, and then conversation or cards followed for an hour or two before the party broke up, usually by midnight.

Nowadays, formal dinners are far less of a production. The basic look remains the same—a perfectly set table with fine appointments. But one is apt to have the all-purpose wine glass instead of a variety of glasses. The menu usually consists of a first course, a main course with a complementary vegetable, often a cheese course for wine lovers, or a salad, dessert and sometimes fruit. Generally two wines, or two plus champagne, are sufficient. A Madeira or sherry might be served with the soup and another wine with the main course— probably a fine Burgundy or Bordeaux. If the host is an amateur of wines, he will choose a great wine of a fabulous year to accompany the cheese course. Often there is champagne with dessert or occasionally a fine sauterne or a Beerenauslese. I frown on dry champagne with dessert but enjoy a touch of sweet wine at times.

Butter is seldom served at a formal dinner. A roll is placed on or beside the plate, and tiny hot turnovers or biscuits may be served with the opening course. If you are having a cheese course, pass French bread, preferably heated, as well as some English or American biscuits.

In the event that the hostess or the host has prepared some of the food, instructions in serving should be given to the help before the guests arrive. At an informal gathering—even a black-tie occasion—either the host or hostess may go to the kitchen to check on matters or offer assistance. At a formal dinner only an unexpected crisis in the kitchen should take host or hostess away from the guests. They should, however, help with opening wines. Fine reds should be opened several hours ahead, and certain older wines should be decanted. They should also see that white wines are not too chilled for serving, or they will lose their bouquet and flavor.

Provide legible and attractive place cards for your table, and it might be a nice touch to offer a card to each guest announcing his dinner partner. I also think it is important to do a handwritten menu; people like to know what they are eating. Two menus for one large table are ample. If you are fortunate enough to have a collection of porcelain menus (these can be written on with ink), so much the better.

As for pre-dinner drinks, I personally like to have a table set up in the living room to hold a large silver tray of bottles, decanters and ice. This is so much more elegant than a bar or a waiter who takes orders and makes drinks in the kitchen, and tricky portable bars are at the bottom of the list for a formal affair. There should also be brandies, whisky, soda and ice set up in the dining room and living room after dinner.

For detailed points of etiquette concerning a formal dinner, consult a good etiquette book. Be sure it is a sensible book, for some are inclined to be precious.

Dinner for 8 to 12

Artichoke Bottoms with Foie Gras
Chicken Kievski
Semolina Gnocchi
Braised Brussels Sprouts
Apricot Ice

Artichoke Bottoms with Foie Gras

Cook 12 large artichokes in acidulated, salted water till tender. Drain and cool. Remove leaves and chokes, and trim bottoms nicely. Fill hollows with foie gras or mousse. Top with a slice of truffle. These may be covered with an aspic.

Chicken Kievski (or Kiev)

12 flattened chicken breasts	*Flour*
Butter	*Beaten egg*
Chopped chives	*Bread crumbs*
Chopped fresh tarragon	*Oil*
Salt and pepper	

Have the butcher bone the breasts, leaving the wing bone in; or do your own boning, which is simple enough. Pound the breasts between sheets of waxed paper. Be careful not to break the flesh. The resultant piece should be rather fan-shaped.

Make small, tapered "fingers" of butter—1 for each breast. Roll butter in chives and tarragon, and chill in freezer for 30 minutes.

Roll breasts around butter, tucking in the ends of meat to make a neat package. The chicken will adhere to itself nicely. Roll in flour, dip in beaten egg, and finally roll in freshly made bread crumbs. Cook in oil to cover, heated to 360°, till golden brown. Salt and pepper. Drain on absorbent paper.

VARIATIONS:

Niçoise: Blend the butter with chopped garlic, chopped black olives, and sweet basil before chilling. Serve the chicken with an anchovy sauce, if you wish.

Alsacienne: Spread the breasts with foie gras before rolling around the butter.

Semolina Gnocchi

2 cups milk	1 cup semolina
1 teaspoon salt	1/2 cup grated Parmesan cheese
1/2 teaspoon pepper	2 eggs, beaten
Dash nutmeg	

Bring the milk to a boil, and season it with salt, pepper, and nutmeg. Slowly pour in the semolina, and stir until you have a thick mixture. Then stir in the cheese, remove from heat, and stir in the beaten eggs. Pour the mixture into a buttered dish or tin, making a layer about 1/4 inch thick.

When cooled, cut into rounds with a cutter about 1 1/2 inches in diameter, and arranged in an overlapping pattern in a fireproof dish. Pour a generous amount of melted butter over all, and brown under the grill or in the oven. A few minutes before removing, sprinkle with a handful of grated cheese. When this has melted, the gnocchi are ready.

Braised Brussels Sprouts

Choose 3 pints Brussels sprouts nicely matched for size. Melt 1 stick (1/4 pound) butter in a heavy pan, and add sprouts. Salt and pepper to taste, cover, and cook over low heat for 20 minutes. Shake pan several times during cooking. When sprouts are tender to the fork—do not overcook—add a touch of lemon juice, and cook for a moment longer.

Apricot Ice

Prepare a syrup with 1 cup sugar and 2 cups water. Boil 6 minutes and cool.

Puree 3 cups canned apricots or poached fresh apricots. Add to the syrup with a dash of lemon juice and 1/4 cup kirsch.

Pour into a mold, pack ice and salt around mold, and freeze. Or prepare in an old-fashioned freezer or any ice cream maker.

Dinner for 6 to 8

Caviar
Baron of Lamb with Sauce Niçoise
Gratin de Pommes de Terre à l'Ail
Haricots Verts
Tiny Coffee Éclairs

Caviar

It should be the best or none at all. Serve with lemon, and accompany with hot toast and sweet butter.

Iced vodka should also accompany this, or zubrowka, which is vodka flavored with sweet grass.

Baron of Baby Lamb with Sauce Niçoise

The baron consists of the two legs and part of the saddle. Rub well with salt and pepper and a bit of rosemary and garlic. Baby lamb is too delicate a flavor to stud with garlic. Roast at 325°, allowing about 12 minutes per pound, or until the meat thermometer thrust into the thickest part registers 155° to 160°. Serve at once with the pan juices and a Sauce Niçoise (*see* below).

Drink a fine Hermitage.

Sauce Niçoise

This is a version of Béarnaise sauce and is delicious for its difference.

3 garlic cloves, sliced
$1/2$ cup wine vinegar
1 teaspoon salt
$1/2$ teaspoon freshly ground
    black pepper

3 egg yolks
$1/4$ pound (1 stick) butter
Pinch of salt
2 tablespoons chopped fresh
    mint leaves

In a skillet or small saucepan place the garlic, wine vinegar, salt and pepper. Cook over a rather brisk flame until it is reduced to practically a glaze. Remove pieces of garlic, if you wish.

Prepare a basic hollandaise sauce in a double boiler: Combine the egg yolks, butter, and a pinch of salt. Let stand over warm water for $1/2$ hour. Now heat the water, and, as you do, stir ingredients with a whisk or wooden spatula until the mixture is thickened and smooth. Add the vinegar glaze and the mint. Serve warm with the lamb.

To make in a blender or food processor: Place 4 egg yolks, rather than 3, in the container with the vinegar glaze and mint. Pulse for a few seconds. Have the butter heated to the bubbling point (but do not let it brown), and pour gradually over the egg mixture while the blender or processor is on until the mixture thickens and emulsifies. Keep warm over hot, but not boiling, water.

Gratin de Pommes de Terre à l'Ail

6 Idaho potatoes, thinly sliced
4 cloves garlic, chopped
2 tablespoons parsley
1 tablespoon chives
1 teaspoon thyme

Salt and pepper
$1/2$ cup or more oil
$1/3$ cup water
1 cup grated Switzerland Swiss
    cheese

Arrange the sliced potatoes on a flat earthenware baking dish. Add garlic, parsley, chives, thyme, salt to taste and a little black pepper. Add the oil next and the water. Bake at 375° until tender. Sprinkle with grated Swiss, and return to the oven to melt the cheese.

Haricots Verts

Choose the smallest green beans available in the markets. Leave them whole, merely cutting off the ends. For eight persons cook 2 pounds tiny beans in boiling salted water until just tender. Drain. Melt 6 tablespoons butter in a heavy skillet or sauté pan and sauté the beans very gently till well saturated with butter and tender to the bite. Add additional salt and freshly ground black pepper if needed.

VARIATION: Add buttered toasted almonds, crisp bacon bits or chopped parsley and chives to the beans.

They are also good cold with olive oil, vinegar and finely chopped raw onion added.

Tiny Coffee Éclairs

Pâte à Choux (see p. 345)
Crème Pâtissière (see p. 205)
5 teaspoons instant coffee

1 package (6 ounces) semisweet
  chocolate bits
1 cup sour cream

Put pâte à choux in a pastry tube, and make small éclairs about 3 inches long. Bake and cool. Fill with coffee cream: Prepare a crème pâtissière, and flavor with 2 teaspoons of instant coffee. Glaze the éclairs with a mocha glaze: Melt chocolate over hot water, and combine with 3 teaspoons instant coffee. Stir into sour cream.

Autumn Dinner for 8

Drink a Châteauneuf-du-Pape with the squab and finish off the dinner with a good Madeira.

Mushrooms in Madeira Cream
Squab with Forcemeat
Petits Pois
Small French Rolls
Cheese
Raspberry Sherbert with Peaches

Mushrooms in Madeira Cream

2 pounds mushrooms of fairly
  even size
1/4 pound (1 stick) butter
3 tablespoons olive oil
1/3 cup Madeira
3 egg yolks
1 cup heavy cream

1 teaspoon salt
1 teaspoon freshly ground
  black pepper
Tabasco
8 or more slices fried toast
Chopped parsley

Trim stems from mushrooms, and sauté caps in butter and oil, tossing occasionally. Mushrooms should be still crisp when done; about 6 to 8 minutes cooking is ample. Season with salt, pepper, and Tabasco. Remove to a hot plate. Rinse pan with Madeira. Beat eggs lightly and mix with the cream. Add to the Madeira, and cook till the mixture begins to thicken. Remove from heat, and add mushrooms. Spoon over fried toast. Sprinkle with chopped parsley.

Squab with Forcemeat Stuffing

8 squab
12 shallots, finely chopped
Giblets
4 tablespoons butter
$1/2$ cup cognac, plus $1/3$ cup
2 cloves garlic
1 pound pork, ground
$1/2$ pound veal, ground
1 cup crumbs
2 truffles, finely chopped
$1/2$ cup finely chopped parsley

$1^1/2$ teaspoons salt
1 teaspoon thyme or rosemary
$1/2$ teaspoon Quatre Épices (see p. 331)
2 eggs
8 strips bacon
Salt and pepper
Watercress
$1^1/2$ cups Brown Sauce (see p. 332)

Sauté shallots and giblets in the butter for 3 to 4 minutes. Whirl in blender or food processor with $1/2$ cup cognac and garlic. Combine with the pork, veal, crumbs, truffles, seasonings, and eggs. Blend well. Stuff the squab, and truss them. Arrange on a rack in a shallow baking dish. Lay a strip of bacon over each breast.

Roast at 450° for 15 minutes. Reduce heat to 350°, and roast for 30 to 40 minutes more. Baste with pan juices.

When squab are done, remove bacon; salt and pepper to taste, and blaze with 1/3 cup warmed cognac. Arrange squab on a platter. Garnish with a large bunch of watercress.

Chill pan juices over ice very quickly, and remove excess fat. Combine juices with brown sauce, and heat thoroughly. Correct the seasonings. Add a drop more cognac if needed.

Petits Pois

The frozen ones that come in a plastic bag are as good as any you'll ever eat. You will need about 4 packages. Serve with an extra dollop of butter and perhaps chopped fresh tarragon, if available, or parsley.

If you cannot find the frozen variety specified, look for a good brand of canned petits pois.

Raspberry Sherbet with Peaches

Arrange balls of good raspberry sherbet in a chilled glass bowl; top with fresh peach halves that have been lightly poached in vanilla syrup. Sprinkle with eau de vie de Framboise, or kirsch. Garnish with chopped pistachio nuts.

A French Dinner for 6 to 8

Start with sherry or Madeira, nuts and tiny cucumber sandwiches. Provide spirits for those who want them. Drink a Nuits-St.-Georges with the lamb.

Consommé aux Profiteroles
Saddle of Lamb Prince Orloff
Pommes Parisienne
Endives Braisées
Fraises Kate

Consommé aux Profiteroles

Make a batch of Pâte à Choux (*see* p. 347) the day of the party. Place half of it in a pastry bag fitted with a small, plain tube. Squeeze pâte à choux into balls the size of a pea on a buttered baking sheet. Bake at 375° till they puff and brown. (Reserve the remaining pâte à choux, and bake a few large puffs for your next day's luncheon or dinner.)

The consommé may be canned, reconstituted.

5 cans beef broth	1 pound ground beef without fat
1 bay leaf	1 egg white (with shell)
1/2 teaspoon Quatre Épices (see p. 331)	1/2 cup Madeira
	Chopped parsley

Pour the cans of beef broth into a pot, and measure out and add three cans of water. Add the bay leaf, spices and meat. Bring to a boil, and simmer for 1 1/2 hours. Beat egg white lightly and add to broth along with shell. Bring to boil again, and continue boiling 5 minutes. Remove from heat, and let stand for 5 minutes. Strain through a linen cloth. Add Madeira.

Serve very hot with the tiny profiteroles and chopped parsley added.

Saddle of Lamb Prince Orloff

Saddle of young lamb
1 pint or more Sauce Soubise
(see below)

Truffles
Grated Parmesan cheese
Butter

In some places the saddle is called a "double loin." Trim the saddle well and tie it. Roast it quickly in a 450° oven for 45 minutes, and reduce to 350° for additional 25 to 30 minutes. It must be firm but rare.

Carve the fillets off the saddle in one piece. Spread the cavity with a film of sauce Soubise. Cut the fillets into scallops ½ inch thick. Brush each with sauce and reassemble, placing a thin slice of truffle between each scallop. Arrange a row of truffles on each side of the saddle, and top with additional Soubise. Sprinkle with grated Parmesan cheese, dot with butter, and run under the broiler to glaze and reheat.

FOR THE SAUCE SOUBISE:

Prepare a cream sauce with 4 tablespoons flour, 4 tablespoons butter, and 1 cup veal broth or chicken broth and ½ cup cream. Stir in ½ cup onion puree: Steam 1 cup finely chopped onion in 2 tablespoons butter in tightly covered saucepan until soft. Puree or put through the blender. Season the sauce Soubise with salt and pepper. You may add grated Gruyère cheese to this sauce for many dishes.

Pommes Parisienne

8 to 10 potatoes
1 pint oil heated to 370°

in a large skillet
Salt and pepper

Peel potatoes, and cut with a small ball-cutter. Soak potato balls in ice water for 1 hour, then dry on absorbent towels. Cook in hot fat till golden brown on the outside and soft and mealy inside. Season with salt and pepper.

Endives Braisées

12 to 14 endives
Beef broth or chicken broth
6 tablespoons butter

Salt and pepper
Chopped parsley
Marrow (optional)

Split the endives. Poach in broth to barely cover till soft. Turn once during poaching. Remove endives, and reduce broth to a glaze. Add butter, and return the endives to the pan. Salt and pepper to taste, and add a touch of chopped parsley. (Marrow also may be added.) Cook briskly for several minutes.

Fraises Kate

1 quart strawberries
Sugar
1 1/2 cups orange sections
2 cans undiluted frozen
    orange juice

2 quarts vanilla ice cream
    packed in a mold
1/3 to 1/2 cup cognac
Pistachio nuts, chopped

Sugar the berries lightly. Thaw and heat the orange juice concentrate. Unmold the ice cream on a platter, and arrange the strawberries and orange sections around it. Also garnish the top with berries and orange sections. Add cognac to the orange juice, and bring to a boil. Serve the hot sauce with the ice cream and fruit. Sprinkle all with pistachio nuts.

A Superb Formal Dinner for 8, Not Too Difficult to Prepare

Drink a Château Cheval Blanc or a Château Ausone.

Clear Green Turtle Soup with Madeira
Poppy Seed Rounds
Perfect Roast Chicken with Tarragon
Potatoes Savoyarde
Green Salad, Vintner's Style
Coffee Mousse

Clear Green Turtle Soup with Madeira

Naturally, you are not going to find a green turtle and make soup. You will buy top-quality canned turtle soup and some turtle meat; the latter is also available in cans.

2 large cans turtle soup　　　*3 cans turtle soup with meat*
1 can turtle meat or　　　*Madeira to taste*

Dice the turtle meat. Heat the soup, and flavor to taste with Madeira. Serve in cups. With the soup drink the same Madeira.

Perfect Roast Chicken with Tarragon

One of the simplest of dishes and one of the best, but it requires proper cooking.

2 or 3 large chickens	Salt and freshly ground pepper
2 lemons	6 to 8 strips bacon
A few sprigs fresh tarragon, or 1 teaspoon dried, for each chicken	1 stick or more melted butter

One-quarter of a chicken is the average serving, but you must remember that more people may want dark than white meat; or white than dark. Leftover chicken is no problem. It is excellent eaten cold, and it can be used in any number of dishes.

Wipe the outside of the chickens with a damp cloth, and dry. Remove the neck and the giblets. Clean the cavities by rubbing each with half a lemon. Pluck out any remaining pin feathers. If you can get fresh tarragon, crush a few sprigs and place into the cavity of each chicken; otherwise do the same with dried tarragon. Rub the chickens well with salt and freshly ground pepper. Then place them on a rack, turned on their sides, in a shallow roasting pan. Bard with strips of bacon. Place the giblets in the pan.

Roast at 400° for 25 minutes. Remove bacon, and turn chickens over to rest on other side. Brush well with melted butter and any fat in the pan. Roast 25 minutes more, basting once. Now place chickens on their backs. Baste well. Return to oven for 30 to 35 minutes, or until the skin is crisp and the meat is tender. Do not overcook! A little pink at the joints will never harm anyone.

Remove chickens from the oven, and let stand for 5 minutes. Cut into quarters. Serve the giblets and the pan juices, from which most of the grease has been removed. Garnish the platter with watercress.

Potatoes Savoyarde

8 to 10 potatoes	Beef broth or consommé
Butter	1 cup or more grated Gruyère
Salt and pepper	

Peel and slice potatoes very thin. Butter generously an oblong or round baking dish. Place a layer of potatoes in the dish, salt and pepper, then continue adding layers. Dot the top layer with butter. Pour in enough well-flavored beef broth or consommé to come almost to the top of the dish.

Bake at 350° for 45 minutes. Test for tenderness. If there is too much liquid left, pour off some of it. Sprinkle with the grated Gruyère, and return to oven till the cheese browns nicely and the potatoes are thoroughly cooked.

Green Salad, Vintner's Style

This should be made with walnut oil, if available. It is mainly a good, crisp green salad interestingly flavored with blanched fresh walnut halves and a dressing made partly with red wine. Sometimes shredded Gruyère is added to it.

6 heads Bibb lettuce	1 cup walnut halves
1 head romaine	1 cup shredded Gruyère (optional)
1 bunch watercress	

FOR THE DRESSING:

1 cup oil, walnut or olive	1 teaspoon salt
1/4 cup red wine	1 teaspoon freshly ground pepper
2 tablespoons vinegar	

Wash and dry the greens. Tear the larger lettuce leaves into smaller pieces. Arrange in a bowl, and add the watercress, walnut halves, and Gruyère (if you wish; remember, there is Gruyère in the potatoes savoyarde). Mix the dressing, pour over the salad at the last minute (watercress wilts easily), and toss.

Coffee Mousse

1 quart heavy cream, whipped   3 to 4 tablespoons instant coffee
1¹/₄ teaspoons ground cinnamon   1 tablespoon gelatin, dissolved
¹/₂ cup sugar   in ¹/₄ cup water

Whip the cream and add seasonings. Dissolve gelatin and melt over medium heat. Add to mixture. Freeze in a mold in freezer compartment or in an ice cream freezer.

Dinner for 8

Drinks: With soup, Madeira or sherry. With main course, Château Lascombes or another good Médoc.

Crab Soup, Margaret Jennings
Stuffed Fillet of Beef
Fondant Potatoes
Broccoli, Beurre Noir
Mincemeat Tart

Crab Soup, Margaret Jennings

1 pound crabmeat   p. 331)
¹/₂ cup milk   1 cup cream, or more
2 tablespoons butter   Salt and pepper
1 cups Sauce Béchamel (see   ¹/₃ cup Scotch whisky

Heat the crabmeat in the milk and butter. Prepare a light béchamel, and add the cream to it after it has come to the boiling point. Add the crabmeat, and again bring to a boil. Season to taste, and add more cream if the soup needs thinning. Just before serving, stir in the Scotch. Serve in heated cups with a sprinkling of finely chopped parsley.

Stuffed Fillet of Beef

8 chicken livers
Butter
Salt and freshly ground
    black pepper
6 tablespoons cognac
1 fillet of beef (5 to 6 pounds)

6 truffles
1/2 teaspoon rosemary
1 1/2 cups Sauce Espagnole (see
    p. 332) or canned beef gravy
1/2 cup Madeira

Sauté chicken livers in 3 tablespoons butter for 3 minutes, tossing to cook livers evenly. Salt and pepper lightly, and flame with half the cognac. Remove livers, and reserve pan juices.

Make an opening in the fillet with a larding needle, or have your butcher do it for you. Stuff the fillet alternately with chicken livers and truffles (reserve liquid from can). Rub the surface of the meat with butter, rosemary, salt and pepper.

Roast on a rack at 450° for 30 to 35 minutes, or until the meat reaches an inner temperature of 125°. Baste with butter, if needed, during roasting. Remove to a hot platter. Flambé with remaining cognac. Combine pan juices with juices from the sautéed livers, the truffle juice, the Sauce Espagnole, and the Madeira. Simmer 2 or 3 minutes. Correct the seasoning.

Garnish platter with watercress. Serve sauce in a sauceboat.

Fondant Potatoes

3 pounds small new potatoes
1/4 pound (1 stick) butter,

softened
Salt and pepper

You must use a heavy pan for this. Scrape potatoes, and arrange in one layer in the pan. Add butter, cover the pan, and place over medium heat for 15 minutes or so. Turn the potatoes, re-cover, and continue cooking, shaking the pan occasionally, till the potatoes are just pierceable and tender. Add salt and freshly ground pepper to taste.

Broccoli, Beurre Noir

8 medium sections broccoli
Boiling salted water

6 tablespoons butter
Dash of lemon juice

Cook the broccoli till tender but still crisp. Drain, and keep hot. Melt butter in a pan, and shake over a fairly high flame till it colors. Add a dash of lemon juice. Serve over the broccoli.

Mincemeat Tart

1 Rich Pastry recipe (see p. 347)
2 cans mincemeat
3 apples, grated but not peeled

$^1/_3$ cup cognac
1 or 2 apples, thinly sliced
Sugar
Apricot Glaze (see p. 38)

Prepare the pastry, chill, and roll to fit an oblong flan ring, a 9-inch ring, or a 9-inch pie tin. Chill again, thoroughly.

Combine mincemeat, grated apple, and cognac. Fill the pie shell with this mixture, and press it down lightly. Cover with apple slices arranged in a pattern. Sprinkle lightly with sugar. Bake at 375° for 30 to 40 minutes or until apples are soft. Remove from oven and cool. Glaze with apricot glaze. Serve warm.

Easy-to-Prepare Dinners

I have often said, when people complained about the time it takes to cook, that one can do a fine dinner for guests in an hour—an unforgettable dinner. And it *is* possible. One cannot, of course, produce a pot au feu or quenelles de brochet in that amount of time, but one can easily assemble an hors d'oeuvre and soup, a main course such as a chicken sauté, a veal scallopine or sauced tournedos, and a vegetable, salad, cheese and simple but distinguished dessert—without sitting down to the table breathless. This doesn't take magic but merely good planning and deft execution. Such meals may prove far more memorable than those which take long preparation, and they are certain to be better enjoyed by the cook.

Here are nine dinners. Some are menus in which I take great delight. All are relatively easy to prepare—and without the aid of instant foods or packaged mixes. One or two menus require greater preparation than the others but not enough to tax the willing cook.

A Very Special Steak Dinner

A Beaujolais should accompany this meal.

Steak au Poivre Flambé
Potato Galette
Fresh Asparagus, Vinaigrette
Cheese

Steak au Poivre Flambé

Choose a good porterhouse or sirloin steak about 2 inches thick. Trim excess fat from steak, and score remaining fat. About 20 minutes before cooking the steak, press 1 tablespoon cracked pepper into the meat with the heel of your hand. The pepper must be freshly cracked or ground to provide the proper flavor. To crack, use a rolling pin or a meat pounder, or give it a brief whirl in the blender. The steak may be either pan-broiled in a heavy skillet or broiled in the oven, but I suggest pan-broiling as the better method for this, although it is a smoky process.

To pan-broil: Rub a heated skillet with a little beef fat. Allow the pan to become very hot, then place the steak in the pan and sear for 3 to 4 minutes on each side. Reduce the heat slightly, and continue cooking, turning once or twice, until the meat is done to your taste (10 to 12 minutes for rare). Test by cutting near the bone with a sharp knife.

Just before removing steak to a hot platter, pour 1/3 cup cognac over steak, and flame. Pour pan juices over meat, and serve, carved in slices.

Potato Galette

See p. 356.

Fresh Asparagus, Vinaigrette

Cook asparagus in boiling salted water. I use a large skillet, in which the asparagus fits very nicely, and cook it at a fast boil. The spears should be tender but still crisp. About 6 to 8 minutes does the job. Remove asparagus, drain, and cool.

Serve with a mustard-flavored vinaigrette, made by blending the following ingredients:

3 tablespoons wine vinegar   *Salt and freshly ground pepper*
1 1/2 teaspoons Dijon mustard   *Chopped parsley*
8 tablespoons oil

Blend the vinegar and mustard before adding oil. Then salt to taste, give it a few grinds of pepper, and add the parsley.

Cheese

A good Pont l'Évêque or a ripe Brie would be in order to finish off this meal, served with French bread and biscuits.

An Italian Dinner for 4

Drink a Chianti. Look for one labeled "classico."

Antipasto
Spaghetti alla Carbonara
Green Salad
Gorgonzola and Pears

Antipasto

Buy imported Italian salami and prosciutto. Arrange on a platter with hot peppers, if you like them, and radishes, which are especially good with this combination. Serve grissini or other bread sticks, and provide coarsely ground pepper for the prosciutto.

Spaghetti alla Carbonara

1 pound spaghetti
1/2 pound thickly cut bacon
1/3 cup white wine or
  dry vermouth

2 eggs, well beaten
1/2 cup or more freshly grated
  Romano or Parmesan cheese
Freshly ground pepper

Cut bacon into dice about 1/2 inch square. Sauté till cooked through but not crisp. Remove from pan, and add wine. Cook down and keep hot. Meanwhile cook spaghetti to your taste—well done or al dente. Drain, and return to kettle. Immediately add the bacon and wine and bacon fat from the pan. Mix, then add the eggs and cheese. Toss as you would a salad. Add a few grinds of pepper. Make sure the egg adheres to the spaghetti and cooks in the hot fat; if it still looks raw, toss some more over low heat. Serve with additional cheese.

NOTE: Not authentic, I know, but I have done this dish to great acclaim with Virginia ham instead of bacon.

Gorgonzola and Pears

Select a ripe Gorgonzola, and serve with ripe fresh pears. A simple and fitting end to this meal.

A Seafood Dinner for 6

Serve white wine cassis before dinner—use a California Mountain White or a Chablis—and serve the same wine with the lobster. With the salmon drink a light Burgundy—a Beaune or a red Chassagne-Montrachet.

Cold Baby Lobster, Sauce Verte
Thin Rye Bread and Butter
Salmon Braised in Red Wine
Boiled New Potatoes
Omelet Soufflé

Cold Lobster, Sauce Verte

6 lobsters (1 pound each, or more if you wish to be generous)
Pickled walnuts
Hard-cooked eggs
Olives
2 cups mayonnaise

¹/₂ cup spinach
3 tablespoons chopped chives
3 tablespoons chopped parsley
1 teaspoon tarragon
1 tablespoon chopped mint
1 garlic clove

Cook the lobsters in boiling salted water—put them in head first—for 5 to 6 minutes after the water returns to the boiling point. Remove and cool. Split, and remove the stomach and intestinal tract; reserve the greenish-colored tomalley. Cut the meat into bite-size pieces, and crack the claws.

Arrange on serving plates. Garnish with pickled walnuts, hard-cooked eggs and olives. Two hours before serving, combine mayonnaise with the spinach, herbs and garlic, all finely chopped. Mix in the tomalley. Serve with the lobster.

Braised Salmon in Red Wine

6- to 8-pound whole salmon
2 medium onions, thinly sliced
2 stalks celery, cut in strips
1 carrot, cut in thin strips
3 sprigs parsley
1 leek, leaned and cut in strips
8 tablespoons butter

Salt
1 quart (or more) red wine
1 teaspoon thyme
1 bay leaf
18 small white onions
1 pound mushrooms

Place the sliced onions, celery, carrot, parsley and leek in the bottom of a large fish cooker or braising pan with 5 tablespoons of the butter. Cover and let cook over a medium flame until the vegetables are soft. Salt the salmon inside and out, and place it on this bed of vegetables. Add red wine to half the depth of the fish in the pan, and put in the thyme and bay leaf. Bring just to a boil. Cover the fish with a piece of cooking parchment, and place it in the oven for about 40 minutes or until the salmon is cooked through. Meanwhile, brown the small onions in 3 tablespoons of butter, and let them cook through in a covered pan. Sauté the mushrooms lightly in the remaining butter, and season to taste.

Baste the fish in the oven from time to time. When it is cooked, arrange it on a hot platter and surround it with the onions and mushrooms. Strain the sauce, and if you wish it thickened, add beurre manié (butter and flour mixed). Taste for seasoning, and serve it separately.

Boiled New Potatoes

See p. 354.

Omelet Soufflé

8 eggs
1/2 cup sugar

1/3 cup cognac or rum, plus 1/2 cup
Granulated sugar

Separate the eggs, and beat the yolks until light and lemon-colored. Gradually beat in the sugar. Add 1/3 cup of cognac or rum. Beat the egg whites until firm, and fold 1/3 of them into the yolk mixture. Then cut in the rest of the whites. This soufflé is cooked in a skillet. Select a heavy metal one with a metal handle, for it must be oven-proof. I generally use a 10-inch cast-aluminum skillet for this recipe. Heat the skillet on top of the stove, and butter it well. Sprinkle with granulated sugar. Pour the soufflé mixture into the skillet, and bake at 375° about 15 minutes. Remove it from the oven, and serve from the skillet. Sprinkle with granulated sugar, pour 1/2 cup of cognac over it and ignite. Serve at once. Makes 8 servings.

VARIATION: Omit the cognac from the basic mixture, and substitute 1/4 cup lemon juice and the grated rind of the lemon. This has a sharper flavor.

A Spring Dinner for 6

Serve Chambertin throughout this dinner. With drinks, you might serve smoked salmon on pumpernickel.

Hindquarter of Baby Lamb, Provençale
Flageolets   Tomatoes Provençale
Gruyère Soufflé
Fruit

Hindquarter of Baby Lamb, Provençale

1 hindquarter of baby lamb	¹/₂ cup olive oil
3 cloves garlic, finely chopped	1 cup white wine
Salt	1 cup pitted black olives
1 teaspoon freshly ground	(Italian or Greek)
black pepper	

Mash the chopped garlic cloves into the salt, and rub lamb well with this mixture. Then rub with the pepper and with enough of the olive oil to coat thinly. Combine the remaining oil with the white wine for basting.

Place on a rack in a shallow pan. Roast at 325°, allowing 15 minutes per pound. Baste several times during roasting with the oil and wine mixture. When the roast is done, remove to a hot platter. Skim excess fat from pan. Add olives, and cook 5 minutes. Pour this sauce over the heated Flageolets (*see* recipe below), or serve in a sauceboat.

Carve the lamb in thin slices.

Flageolets

Since flageolets are not easily found in this country except in cans, we must rely, for the most part, on those imported from France. They are very good and save you the work of starting from scratch.

For each can of beans, sauté 1 garlic clove in a tablespoon of olive oil for a few minutes, then remove the clove. Toss the beans in the hot oil, and cook just long enough to allow the beans to heat through. Correct the seasoning.

Serve with the pan juices from the roasted lamb, prepared as described above.

Tomatoes Provençale

Halve 6 good ripe tomatoes. Place 2 tablespoons olive oil in a sautéing pan. Add tomatoes, cut side down. Sauté over very low heat for 30 to 40 minutes, or until the underside has more or less caramelized. Salt and pepper to taste.

Gruyère Soufflé

Oftentimes a cheese soufflé and fruit make a superb dessert course. My dear friend Simone Prunier, of Prunier's in London, has offered this combination many times at dinner parties, with great success. The basic mixture can be made ahead and the egg white added just before the soufflé goes into the oven—as you sit down to the lamb, probably; or after your oven has reached a higher temperature, if you choose to cook it that way.

3 tablespoons butter
3 tablespoons flour
3/4 cup milk
1/2 teaspoon salt
1/2 teaspoon Tabasco
5 egg yolks
1 cup grated Gruyère cheese
6 egg whites

Make a cream sauce: Melt the butter, add flour, and cook several minutes before stirring in the milk, which has been warmed. Continue stirring till the mixture thickens. Add seasonings, and remove from heat. Cool slightly, and then stir in the egg yolks. (Warm them first by adding a few tablespoons of the mixture.) Add the cheese, and return to heat just long enough to melt the cheese; do not allow to boil. Cool. Beat egg whites till stiff but not dry. Fold 1/3 of the whites into the cheese sauce rather thoroughly, then gently fold in the remaining whites. Pour into a buttered 1 1/2-quart mold.

Bake at either 325° for 40 to 45 minutes or 400° for 25 to 30 minutes, depending on the timing of the rest of your dinner.

Serve at once. Follow with fresh fruit.

Dinner for 4

Paillard of Veal
Spinach with Cream and Nutmeg
Sliced Oranges with Grand Marnier

Paillard of Veal

This requires 4 thin slices from the leg, pounded; they should be about ⅛ inch thick. Brush the paillards with butter, and broil quickly in a very hot oven. Salt and pepper to taste, and remove to hot plates. Add a dollop of butter and a sprinkling of parsley.

Spinach with Cream and Nutmeg

2 packages frozen chopped
spinach
3 tablespoons butter
1 tablespoon flour

3 tablespoons heavy cream
⅛ teaspoon nutmeg
Salt

Thaw and drain spinach well. Chop again. Melt butter in a skillet, add flour, and stir in cream. Cook till thickened. Combine with spinach. Salt to taste and add nutmeg. Cover, and heat over very low flame, stirring once or twice; or heat in a double boiler over hot water.

Sliced Oranges with Grand Marnier

4 large or 6 medium oranges
¼ cup Grand Marnier or more

Sugar (optional)

Peel oranges, leaving no white skin on the outside. This can be done easily by using a sharp knife to peel the oranges, instead of peeling by hand. Slice oranges and arrange on plates. Sugar, if necessary. Add a little Grand Marnier to each portion.

Dinner for 4

Grilled Cheeseburgers
Mushroom-Romaine Salad
Toasted Rolls
Quick Raspberry Shortcake

Grilled Cheeseburgers

2 pounds chopped chuck or
    round
1 teaspoon salt
$^1/_2$ teaspoon freshly ground
    black pepper

$^1/_4$ teaspoon Tabasco
$^1/_2$ teaspoon mustard
1 cup loosely packed shredded
    cheddar or Gruyère cheese

Mix seasonings and cheese with beef. Form into cakes about 1$^1/_2$ inches thick. Grill or pan-broil to your taste; or ask your guests how rare they would like their meat. Do not overcook. Serve on hot plates with mustard.

Mushroom-Romaine Salad

1 large head romaine
$^1/_2$ pound raw mushrooms,
    sliced
6 to 8 scallions, finely cut
6 tablespoons oil

2 tablespoons vinegar, or to
    taste
$^1/_4$ cup chopped parsley
1 teaspoon salt
Freshly ground black pepper

Break romaine into salad bowl. Add sliced mushrooms and scallions. Blend oil, vinegar, parsley, salt and pepper. Add to salad, and toss just before serving.

Quick Raspberry Shortcake

*1 or 2 packages frozen
raspberries
4 slices Pound Cake (see*

*p. 349)
Heavy cream or sour cream*

Thaw the raspberries. Toast the pound cake on both sides. Remove to warm plates. Spoon raspberries over cake, and serve with cream. (Naturally, if they are in season, fresh raspberries, sugared, are preferable.)

Dinner for 6

A pleasant white wine—a Muscadet or Chablis—would go well with the shad roe.

*Shad Roe Poached in Butter
Boiled New Potatoes
Sautéed Zucchini with Garlic
Pineapple with Kirsch*

Shad Roe Poached in Butter

*3 good-sized pairs shad roe
1½ sticks butter
Salt and pepper*

*Chopped parsley
Lemon wedges
Toast*

Use a heavy skillet with a cover. Melt butter over medium heat, and bathe each roe in the butter. Cover pan, and cook, turning once, for 12 to 15 minutes. Remove to a hot platter. Add salt, pepper, and chopped parsley to the butter. Spoon over shad roe. Serve with lemon wedges and toast.

Boiled New Potatoes

See p. 354.

Sautéed Zucchini with Garlic

6 small zucchini
1/3 cup olive oil
2 cloves garlic, finely chopped

Salt and freshly ground pepper
Lemon juice

Cut zucchini lengthwise in three strips each. Heat olive oil, and add zucchini and garlic. Sauté quickly until zucchini are tender but still somewhat crisp. Salt and pepper to taste, and sprinkle with lemon juice.

Pineapple with Kirsch

Choose a good ripe pineapple. Slice thin and cut off peel and prickly portions. Chill, and serve with sugar and kirsch. (A knife and fork are best for eating pineapple.)

Dinner for 4

Serve a Cabernet Sauvignon.

Kidneys on the Half-Shell, Flambé
Rice with Chopped Chives and Parsley
Green Beans, Vinaigrette
Ginger Soufflé

Kidneys on the Half-Shell, Flambé

4 veal kidneys in part of their
fat

Cognac
Salt and freshly ground pepper

Set the oven to 475°. Trim some of the fat from the kidneys and roast on a rack for 25 to 30 minutes. Turn once during the roasting.

Remove to a grooved carving board or a flameproof platter. Cut the kidneys in half, and flambé with heated cognac. Salt and pepper to taste. Serve on hot plates. Spoon juices (from the board or dish) over the kidneys.

Rice with Chopped Chives and Parsley

Prepare 1 1/2 cups rice in your favorite way, then blend with butter, chopped chives and chopped parsley.

Green Beans, Vinaigrette

These may be served either hot or cold.

1 1/2 pounds green beans	1 small onion, finely chopped
Salted water	Vinaigrette Sauce (see p. 338)

Cook beans until tender but still firm. Drain. Combine with the onion and the vinaigrette sauce. If served cold, garnish with chopped parsley and onion rings.

Ginger Soufflé

3 tablespoons butter	1/2 cup sugar
3 tablespoons flour	1/2 cup finely cut preserved
3/4 cup milk, heated	ginger
Pinch salt	6 egg whites
5 egg yolks	Heavy cream, whipped

Make a cream sauce: Melt butter in a saucepan, add the flour, cook for a minute, then add the milk slowly. Stir until thickened. Cool slightly. Beat in the egg yolks and the sugar. Return to low heat for a few minutes, stirring constantly. Add ginger, and cool slightly again. Beat egg whites till stiff but not dry. Fold into cream sauce carefully, and pour into a 1 1/2-quart soufflé dish that has been buttered and sugared. Bake at 400° for 25 to 30 minutes. Serve with whipped cream.

NOTE: Prepare the soufflé before dinner, except for beating and adding the egg whites. Butter and sugar the dish; have the oven heated to the proper temperature. Then take time to clear the table and prepare it for the dessert course while the soufflé cooks.

A Very Informal but Satisfying Meal for 4 Good Friends

Moules Marinières
Toasted French Rolls
Romaine and Onion Salad
Chocolate Mousse

Moules Marinières

4 quarts mussels
1 onion, finely chopped
3 ribs celery, finely chopped
3 garlic cloves, finely chopped

2 cups white wine
¹/₂ cup chopped parsley
1 tablespoon salt

Scrub the mussels well and "beard" them with a wire brush. Place mussels, vegetables, garlic, wine and salt in a large kettle. Cover, and steam till the mussels open. Do not overcook, or they will be tough. Pour off the liquid, and strain through a linen napkin. Scoop mussels into soup plates or bowls. Add parsley to broth, heat for a minute or two, and ladle over mussels.

Toasted French rolls or French bread and butter should accompany this.

Romaine and Onion Salad

1 large or 2 small heads romaine

1 large Italian or Spanish onion
Vinaigrette Sauce (see p. 338)

Wash and dry romaine leaves, wrap in towel, and refrigerate. Peel and slice onion thinly. Place in a salad bowl with the vinaigrette sauce. Just before serving, add the romaine, broken into pieces, and toss.

Chocolate Mousse

1 6-ounce package semisweet
   chocolate bits
6 egg yolks, slightly beaten

2 tablespoons cognac
6 egg whites, beaten
Dash salt

Melt chocolate over hot water, add egg yolks and cognac, and blend well. Fold in egg whites, beaten till stiff but not dry, and the salt. Pour into individual pots or a glass dish, and chill. Make this the day before your dinner party.

DINNERS TO PREPARE IN ADVANCE

I have a predilection for rising early, and when I am preparing for a dinner party, I enjoy rising at 5:00 or 5:30 and going straight from the bath to the kitchen. I call this "cooking in the nude." It is so cool and quiet in the early hours and before midmorning one can have a whole dinner ready except for the final bits of cooking and the garnishings. You needn't get up before dawn, however, to give a dinner party. If you plan carefully, a fairly complicated menu can be assembled over a period of two or three days. Many frozen desserts may be made several days ahead; pastries and bread a week or two in advance, and frozen; crêpes, ready for filling, may be stored in the refrigerator for a week or in the freezer for a month or two. In fact, you might store away a whole buffet, providing you have enough refrigerator and freezer space, leaving only a few things to heat, dress, or garnish.

In the menus provided here, one or more courses can be prepared in advance. You will save more last-minute work if you lay out tablecloth, napkins and silver the night before, as well as serving dishes and other accessories. Ingredients for salads and garnishes can be prepared and refrigerated in plastic bags or foil. Stock your bar days in advance. If your schedule is really well thought out, you should be able to have a rest and a quick shower before the gala starts. There is nothing quite so satisfying as that lull before the first ring of the doorbell.

Dinner for 6

Seviche in Avocado Shells
Chicken Chili
Whole Hominy
Tortillas
Fresh Pineapple with Rum

Seviche in Avocado Shells

1 pound firm-fleshed whitefish,
*   boned, skinned and diced*
1 cup lemon or lime juice
3 tablespoons olive oil
1 onion, chopped
1 small can green chilies,
*   chopped*
1 tomato, chopped
1 pinch oregano
Salt and pepper to taste
3 avocados, halved and pitted

Marinate the fish in lemon or lime juice for at least 1 hour. Drain, and add the other ingredients (except avocado), mixing well. Fill the avocado halves with mixture, and serve.

Chicken Chili

2 large fowl
1 onion, stuck with cloves
Salt
Water
3 tablespoons chili powder
2 hot peppers
2 large onions, finely chopped
3 cloves garlic
1 bay leaf
3 cloves garlic, finely chopped
1 teaspoon basil
Fresh coriander
1 tin tomato paste
1 cup ripe olives
6 tablespoons fat (3 each
*   chicken fat and butter)*
Beurre manié
Sliced toasted almonds
Toasted filberts

Poach the chickens with the onion stuck with cloves, garlic, bay leaf and salt to taste.

When the chickens are tender, remove from the broth and cut meat from bones. Return carcasses to broth and cook for another 30 minutes. Add 2 tablespoons chili powder and hot peppers. Skim off excess fat. Strain broth through a linen towel. Reduce to 3 cups.

Sauté the chopped onions in fat and add garlic, remaining chili powder, herbs, and tomato paste. Add to reduced broth and add chicken. Correct seasoning and add about 1 cup ripe olives, and thicken with beurre manié (butter and flour mixed) if desired.

Serve with tortillas or with polenta. Garnish with toasted almonds and filberts.

Whole Hominy

Open and wash two large cans (about 7 cups) whole hominy. Heat with 6 tablespoons butter in a covered pan over medium heat. Salt and pepper to taste and add 1/3 cup cream.

Tortillas

Tortillas may be bought fresh in Hispanic food shops and are available frozen or canned in most supermarkets.

Fresh Pineapple with Rum

Cut off the top, and peel the pineapple, removing the prickly portions. Slice, or cut in fingers, cubes or wedges. Remove the woody core. Sugar to taste, and add 1 ounce of dark rum per serving. Chill and let mellow for at least an hour.

An Italian Dinner for 8

Here is an interesting meal for 8 persons, with very little work to do at the last minute. The peppers may be prepared several hours ahead of time and held for the final baking. The crêpes for the cannelloni may be made the day before and refrigerated; or even days before and put in the freezer. Several hours before baking, assemble the cannelloni and make the tomato sauce. Pour the sauce over just before the dish goes into the oven. Clean the dandelions well in advance, crisp in water, drain, and refrigerate wrapped in a cloth until ready to use. Also prepare the peaches a couple of hours ahead of time, and chill.

Serve Americanos (sweet vermouth and Campari) before dinner and Valpolicella with the meal.

Stuffed Green Peppers
Cannelloni with Tomato Sauce
Dandelion Salad
Fresh Peaches with Marsala

Stuffed Green Peppers

8 medium-sized green peppers	*1/2 cup currants*
2*1/2 cups croutons*	2 tablespoons chopped parsley
Oil	2 tablespoons vermouth
2 cloves garlic, finely chopped	Salt and pepper
16 anchovies, chopped	Butter
1/2 cup pine nuts	

Blanch the peppers for 8 to 10 minutes, drain, remove the tops and the seeds.

Sauté the croutons in oil with the garlic till just golden, then mix with the anchovies, pine nuts, currants, parsley and vermouth. Salt and pepper to taste (remember, the anchovies contain a good deal of salt). Stuff peppers with this mixture and place in a buttered baking dish. Top each pepper with 1 tablespoon oil. Bake in a 350° oven for 30 minutes.

The peppers may be blanched, seeded and stuffed several hours before baking.

Cannelloni with Tomato Sauce

This is an Italian version of stuffed crêpes.

16 Italian sausages
Tomato Sauce (see below)
16 Unsweetened Crêpes
  (see p. 351)

1 pound ricotta cheese
Grated Parmesan cheese
Butter

Place sausages in salted water. Bring to a boil and reduce to simmer. Poach for 12 minutes. Remove from water and when cool enough to handle, skin them and cut in long shreds.

PREPARE A TOMATO SAUCE:

2 cloves garlic
2 small onions
2 tablespoons olive oil
2¹/₂ cups canned solid

  pack tomatoes
1 teaspoon basil
Salt and pepper
1¹/₂ cans tomato paste

Chop the garlic and onion very fine. Sauté in olive oil for 3 minutes. Add the tomatoes, basil, and salt and pepper, and bring to a boil. Reduce heat and simmer for 30 minutes. Add the tomato paste, correct the seasoning, and cook for another 15 minutes, then increase the heat and let the sauce reduce a bit. Stir frequently so that the sauce does not scorch.

TO ASSEMBLE:

Spread each crêpe with ricotta cheese, sprinkle with grated Parmesan, and give it a grind from the pepper mill. Add the sausage bits, roll the crêpes, and place them in a shallow baking dish so that they barely touch each other. Pour the tomato sauce over them, and sprinkle with additional grated cheese. Bake at 375° till bubbly.

NOTE: You may vary the filling by using poached brains cut in slices, or cooked chicken, veal, pork or ham, highly seasoned.

Dandelion Salad

Dandelion greens are in the market for a great part of the year, and they are cultivated in many sections of the country.

Crisp the greens in cold water, and toss at the last moment with a good vinaigrette sauce.

Fresh Peaches with Marsala

Peel and slice 8 to 10 ripe peaches. Add sugar to taste, and flavor with 2/3 cup Marsala. Frozen peaches may be substituted.

Dinner for 4 to 6

The shrimp and salad may be assembled well ahead of time, and the dessert may also be made ahead and kept warm. For the main course: Prepare the chicken, sauce and brioche dough or pastry crust. Just before sitting down to your first course, roll out the dough, cover the baking dish, and pop it into the oven. At the same time finish up the potatoes and keep warm over hot water. With the main course serve the same wine used in the coq au vin.

Shrimp Aillade
Coq au Vin en Brioche
Fluffy Potatoes
Beet and Onion Salad
Pets de Nonne

Shrimp Aillade

1 pound cooked, shelled shrimp

For Aillade Sauce:

*12 to 14 walnut meats, finely
   chopped
3 cloves garlic, finely chopped
³/₄ cup oil*

*1 tablespoon lemon juice
¹/₂ teaspoon salt
Chopped parsley*

Blend ingredients for sauce. Mix with the shrimp and sprinkle with chopped parsley. Chill before serving.

Coq au Vin en Brioche

*4 slices salt pork, cubed
Butter
6 chicken legs and thighs or
   6 breasts
Flour
1 tablespoon oil
¹/₈ cup cognac
Bouquet garni (thyme, 1 bay*

*leaf, sprig parsley,
   peppercorns)
Red Burgundy to just cover
12 small white onions, peeled
18 mushrooms
Brioche or Plain Pastry dough
   (see pp. 344 and 347)*

Try out the salt pork in a little butter. Roll chicken pieces in flour, and brown very quickly in 4 tablespoons of butter and the oil. Blaze with cognac. Add tried-out salt pork, bouquet garni and Burgundy. Cover, and let it cook for about 40 minutes or until tender.

Sauté the onions in a little butter until nicely glazed and just cooked through. Add the mushrooms, and allow them to mix and cook with the onions.

Transfer chicken to a shallow baking dish. Add onions, mushrooms and salt pork. Strain the sauce, and correct the seasoning. Pour over the chicken. Cool. When ready to serve, cover with a thinly rolled brioche or pastry crust. Bake in a 400° oven for about 25 minutes.

Fluffy Potatoes

4 to 8 potatoes
Boiling salted water
Salt and pepper

4 tablespoons butter
4 tablespoons heated cream
(or more)

Peel potatoes, cut into halves or quarters, and cook in boiling salted water to cover. When tender, drain thoroughly and put through a ricer. Return to pan, season to taste with salt and freshly ground black pepper. Add butter, and beat thoroughly, preferably with a wire whisk. Then add cream, and beat it in well. If potatoes are not fluffy enough, beat in additional cream. Keep hot over a pan of hot water.

Beet and Onion Salad

1 can of beets or 5 cooked beets
1 Bermuda or red Italian onion

Greens
Vinaigrette Sauce (see p. 338)

Drain canned beets, or sliced cooked beets. Peel and slice the onion very thin. Arrange on a bed of greens, and dress with a good vinaigrette sauce.

Pets de Nonne or Beignets Soufflé

1 cup hot water
½ cup butter
¼ teaspoon salt
1 teaspoon sugar

1 cup plus 2 tablespoons flour
4 large or 5 small eggs
Oil for deep fryer
Granulated sugar

Pour hot water over butter, and stir till melted. Add salt and sugar, and bring to a rolling boil. Add flour, and stir vigorously until the dough leaves edges of pan and forms a ball. Remove from heat, and beat in 1 egg. Beat in remaining eggs 1 at a time till the dough is waxy and well blended.

Heat oil in a deep fryer to 370°. Drop in dough by spoonfuls, or make small balls with lightly floured hands and fry until brown and puffy. Keep beignets in a warm oven. Roll in granulated sugar and serve hot.

NOTE: These may be served with a raspberry sauce or flamed with rum and sugared.

A Provençal Dinner for 4

The daube may be prepared a day or two ahead of time and reheated. It is one of those dishes which seem to improve with age. Vegetables for the first course and fruit for the dessert may be cleaned and sliced hours ahead and kept chilled in the refrigerator. All that remains for last-minute cooking are the peppers.

With the daube drink a good Châteauneuf-du-Pape; or if you wish to be truly Provençal, you might prefer a rosé.

Crudités
Daube Provençale
Poivrons Sauté
Fruits Rafraîchis with Sables

Crudités

Prepare a Mayonnaise (*see* p. 336), and add to it 1 tablespoon Dijon mustard, a dash of Tabasco, and 3 tablespoons chopped parsley. Blend well. Serve as a sauce for the crudités. Arrange a selection of raw vegetables as attractively as possible on individual plates or on one large platter. You might combine cherry tomatoes, scallions, radishes, celery and asparagus. These may be eaten with the fingers. If you choose vegetables such as carrots, or celeriac, which can be cut in julienne strips or shredded, a fork is in order. One three-star restaurant in France serves a "bouquet of crudités" as a first course in which the vegetables are cut very fine and each is served in a different sauce. It is the most appetizing dish imaginable.

Daube Provençale

3 or 4 slices of salt pork
5 pound piece of beef, shin or
 rump
2 pig's feet or 1 calf's foot
2 bay leaves
8 cloves garlic
1 clove
1 strip orange peel

1 teaspoon rosemary
Several sprigs parsley
1 tablespoon salt
2 teaspoons freshly ground
 black pepper
Red wine (about ⁴/₅ quart)
1 pound macaroni

Place the meats and seasonings in a crock, and cover with red wine. Let stand for 24 hours. Place in a heavy braising pan or casserole— *not an iron one*—and cook at the lowest possible temperature, about 200°, for 6 hours or more, until tender.

TO SERVE HOT: Remove from heat and let stand for 20 to 25 minutes. Skim off excess fat. Remove meat to a hot platter. Strain the sauce and serve part of it blended with 1 pound macaroni cooked in boiling salted water. This is called macaronade. The rest may be served with the meats.

TO SERVE COLD: Strain the sauce, let it cool, and remove the excess fat. Slice the meat, arrange in a serving dish, and cover with the sauce. Chill, then serve in its own jelly.

Poivrons Sauté

6 tablespoons olive oil
3 cloves garlic
5 to 6 green peppers, seeded and

cut into strips 1 inch wide
Salt and pepper
Dash of vinegar

Heat the olive oil in a skillet, and add the garlic and peppers. Sauté slowly, covering part of the time, until peppers are tender but not mushy. Salt and pepper to taste, and add vinegar.

Fruits Rafraîchis with Sables

Combine fresh fruits, according to your choice and the offerings on the market—perhaps grapes, melon balls and grapefruit sections; or sliced peaches and blueberries; or pineapple cubes, strawberries and bananas. Sugar if necessary, and flavor with kirsch or Grand Marnier. Chill well before serving.

Sables

1 cup flour
1/2 cup sugar
1 egg yolk
7 tablespoons unsalted butter

1 tablespoon cold water
1/4 teaspoon salt
1 teaspoon vanilla

Sift flour and sugar together. Add egg yolk, butter cut in small pieces, water, and salt. Work the mixture quickly and blend into a ball. Add vanilla. Blend again. Chill for 30 minutes.

Roll 1/4 inch thick on a floured board. Cut with serrated cookie cutter 3 inches in diameter. Place on lightly buttered cookie sheet. Bake at 350° till delicately brown. Cool on a rack.

NOTE: The dough can be prepared in a food processor. Blend the flour, sugar salt and butter together for a few seconds, until mealy, then add the egg, water and vanilla. Blend until the dough forms a ball.

A Mexican Dinner for 6

You can have this dinner well in hand before any guests arrive. The flan should be made hours ahead so it will be thoroughly chilled. The mantequilla de pobre and salad should also be prepared in advance. Plan to put the carnitas in the oven an hour or so before your guests are due, which will allow an hour for drinking. Assemble the enchiladas last. Put them into the oven a half-hour before the Carnitas are ready to come out.

This meal calls for plenty of cold beer—Mexican, if you can find it.

Carnitas
Mantequilla de Pobre
Tostados
Swiss Enchiladas
Pepper Salad with Onions
Flan

Carnitas (Little Meats)

2 pounds lean pork (boneless   Salt and pepper to taste
   butt)

Cut the pork into 1-inch cubes, sprinkle with salt and pepper, and let stand on a rack for an hour or so. Place in a shallow baking pan in a 300° oven for about 2 hours, pouring off fat as it accumulates.

Spear with toothpicks, and serve with mantequilla de pobre and tostados.

Mantequilla de Pobre (Poor Man's Butter)

2 large tomatoes, peeled   3 tablespoons red wine vinegar
2 medium-sized avocados   1 tablespoon salad oil
12 green onions, finely cut   Salt to taste

Cut the tomatoes and avocadoes into small cubes; add onions, vinegar, oil, and salt. Toss gently until well mixed. Let stand at room temperature for about 30 minutes before serving.

Swiss Enchiladas

FOR THE STUFFING:

1 onion, chopped   1 dozen tortillas
2 tablespoons oil   Oil
1 clove garlic, crushed   3 cups hot cream
2 cups tomato puree   6 chicken bouillon cubes
2 green chilies, chopped   1/2 pound jack cheese
2 cups chopped cooked chicken   Garnish (avocado; hard-cooked
Salt   eggs; or olives, green or ripe)

Prepare the stuffing first. Sauté the onion in the 2 tablespoons of oil until soft. Then add garlic, tomato puree, chilies, and chicken. Season to taste with salt, and simmer for about 10 minutes.

Fry the tortillas in about 1 inch of hot oil. Do not let them crisp, as they are to be rolled.

Heat the cream, and in it dissolve the bouillon cubes. Dip each tortilla into this cream mixture, cover it generously with the chicken filling, and roll it up. Arrange these rolls in a baking pan, and pour the remaining cream mixture over them. Top with jack cheese, sliced or grated, and bake in a moderate oven for about 30 minutes.

Garnish with the avocado or hard-cooked eggs, sliced, or with olives. This is not a hot Mexican dish. It is mild and delicious and a certain favorite with everyone. Anything with cream in it, by the way, is called "Swiss" in Mexico.

Pepper Salad with Onions

6 green or green and red
   peppers
1 or 2 red Italian onions
2 cloves garlic

Basic Vinaigrette Sauce (see
   p. 338)
1 tablespoon fresh basil, or
   1 teaspoon dried basil

Seed the peppers and slice in rings as thin as possible. Peel onions and again slice as thin as possible. Combine and add finely chopped garlic and vinaigrette sauce seasoned with basil. Toss well, and allow to stand for an hour before serving.

Flan

This is a typical Spanish dessert, beautiful to look at and simple to make.

1³/₄ cup sugar
3 egg whites
8 egg yolks
2 12-ounce cans evaporated

milk
2 teaspoons vanilla flavoring
6 tablespoons cognac or rum

Put 1 cup of the sugar into a deep pan in which you can bake the custard. Place this over a low flame, and stir constantly until the sugar melts and turns a golden color. Tilt the pan, and allow the caramel to coat it entirely. Set this aside to cool while you make the custard.

Beat the egg whites and yolks together. Add the evaporated milk, the remaining ³/₄ cup of sugar, and vanilla flavoring. Mix well, strain into the caramel-coated pan, and place the pan in a larger pan containing hot water. Bake in a 350° oven for about an hour, or until a knife inserted in the center comes out clean. Cool slightly, and turn out on a platter while it is still warm (or else the caramel will stick to the sides).

When you are ready to serve, heat the cognac or rum slightly, pour over the flan, and ignite. Bring to the table blazing.

NOTE: Flans are best when made hours before serving and thoroughly chilled.

A Comfortable and Delicious Dinner for 6 or 8

The estofat may be done one or two days ahead and merely reheated for the party. The potatoes may be partially cooked in advance and the second half of the preparation done at the last minute. The asparagus means last-minute work, but it's easy. The dessert is best made in the morning or several hours ahead.

You might begin this dinner by serving a good dry sherry and a bowl of olives, perhaps several varieties mixed. And if you wish to serve a first course, smoked salmon or smoked sturgeon, with thinly sliced cucumbers, would be perfect. Drink a Châteauneuf-du-Pape.

Estofat de Boeuf
Glazed Potatoes
Glazed Onions
Asparagus, Vinaigrette
Les Oeufs à la Neige

Estofat de Boeuf

8 tablespoons pork drippings or goose fat	*1 pint red wine*
5 pounds rolled rump of beef	*1 pound lean and fat salt pork*
2 carrots	*2 pig's feet*
2 onions, stuck with cloves	*1 bay leaf*
4 cloves garlic	*1 teaspoon thyme*
1/2 cup cognac	*1/4 cup chopped parsley*
	Salt

Place drippings or fat in a deep kettle or braisière. Brown meat in fat on all sides over high heat. Add carrots, onion, and garlic. Place in a 450° oven uncovered for 15 minutes. Then add the cognac, wine, salt pork, pig's feet, herbs, and a small quantity of salt. Cover. Cook at 250° 4 to 5 hours, or until meat is very tender. Serve with glazed potatoes and glazed onions.

NOTE: This is also delicious when served cold, with the fat removed from the surface.

Glazed Potatoes

Boil 8 to 10 medium potatoes in their jackets until just half done. Peel, and cut in rather thick slices. Arrange in a baking dish with 1/4 pound melted butter. Sprinkle with salt and pepper, and bake at 350° for 25 to 30 minutes, tossing gently with a fork several times during the cooking. When done, the potatoes should be nicely glazed, thoroughly tender, and crisp on the edges.

Glazed Onions

18 small white onions, peeled   *1/2 teaspoon salt*
4 tablespoons butter   *1 teaspoon or more sugar*

Heat the butter in a heavy skillet, add onions, and sauté over brisk heat, rolling the pan so onions begin to brown on all sides. Sprinkle with salt and sugar and roll around well so that sugar will caramelize the onions and give them a pleasant glaze. Cover pan and steam the onions over low heat till just tender but not mushy.

Asparagus, Vinaigrette

For 8 persons, cook 5 pounds or more of asparagus, depending on size of stalks. Boil in salted water until just tender but still firm. (I find that an open skillet with enough water to cover the asparagus works as well as anything.) Drain, and serve with Vinaigrette Sauce (*see* p. 338).

Les Oeufs à la Neige

6 egg whites	6 egg yolks
1¾ cups sugar	1 teaspoon arrowroot
3 cups milk	Caramelized sugar
1 teaspoon vanilla	

Beat the egg whites very stiff, and add ¾ cup sugar, a little at a time, beating after each addition.

Heat the milk, 1 cup sugar, and vanilla to the boiling point. Keep at a feeble boil. Spoon up meringue about the size and shape of an egg and drop into the boiling milk. (You will need a second spoon to accomplish this.) Poach about 1½ minutes. Turn with a fork. Continue poaching about 2 minutes, then remove to a dry cloth to drain. When the egg white is cooked, strain the milk, and add the egg yolks, well beaten, and the arrowroot. Stir over low heat until it coats a wooden spoon. Cool in a serving bowl and float the meringue in the cream. Garnish with caramelized sugar, made by slowly heating about 1 cup sugar in a heavy-bottomed saucepan until it turns to a medium brown syrup.

A German Dinner for 8

This rather rich dinner can be prepared ahead of time, except for the potato dumplings, which may be assembled ahead but must be cooked at the last minute. The champagne kraut must also be done at the last minute to insure crispness. Prepare the pea soup in advance up to the point of adding the cream. Then reheat in a double boiler and complete the recipe.

Cream of Pea Soup
Hasenpfeffer
Potato Dumplings
Champagne Kraut
Linzer Torte

Cream of Pea Soup

5 pounds fresh peas or	Salt and pepper
3 packages frozen peas	1½ pints light cream
1 medium onion, sliced	Chopped parsley
4 tablespoons butter	Chopped chives

Cook the peas and onion in boiling salted water till just tender. Drain, and purée in a blender, food processor or food mill. Transfer to a saucepan over low heat, and stir in the butter and salt and pepper to taste. Slowly add the cream, and stir until well blended and very hot. Serve garnished with the chopped herbs.

Hasenpfeffer

2 rabbits or young hares, cut into pieces (legs and saddles)

MARINADE:

Bottle red wine	1 teaspoon thyme
3 onions, thinly sliced	Several sprigs parsley
6 shallots, chopped	Salt and pepper
1 bay leaf	12 small onions, peeled
Flour	1½ cups bouillon
4 tablespoons butter	Arrowroot
3 slices salt pork, diced	Chopped parsley
¼ cup cognac	

Combine the ingredients for the marinade, and in it marinate the pieces of rabbit for 24 to 36 hours. Remove the pieces and dry; reserve the marinade. Flour the rabbit lightly, and brown in a skillet with the butter and salt pork. Remove to a casserole large enough to hold both rabbits, or to two smaller casseroles, if need be. Flame the rabbit with cognac. Add the onions, bouillon, and enough marinade to barely cover (or you may omit the bouillon and use only the marinade).

Bake at 325° for 1½ hours.

Traditionally this sauce has currant jelly and sometimes kirsch added to it, and it is thickened with the blood and crushed liver of the rabbits. I think the flavors of the jelly and kirsch are unfortunate if you wish to enjoy a good wine with your meal; and the thickening process is obviously impossible unless you catch your own rabbit. I recommend that you thicken the sauce slightly with arrowroot and return the casserole to the oven for another 15 minutes. Taste for seasoning, and sprinkle with chopped parsley. Serve with potato dumplings.

Potato Dumplings

3 Idaho potatoes, peeled and
   boiled
2 tablespoons butter, melted
3 eggs

1 teaspoon salt
1 cup toasted bread cubes
3 tablespoons oil

Rice the potatoes, and combine with the butter, eggs and salt. Brown the bread cubes in oil, and add to the potatoes. Form mixture into smallish balls, the size of golf balls, with your hands, and cook in boiling salted water 12 to 15 minutes.

Champagne Kraut

1 head cabbage, fairly large
4 tablespoons bacon drippings

Salt and pepper
1 bottle champagne (⁴/₅ quart)

Shred the cabbage, and braise it lightly in bacon fat, tossing well. Add salt and pepper to taste, then the champagne. Cover and cook for 10 minutes. Uncover, toss well, and continue cooking till cabbage is done to your taste. I prefer mine quite crisp.

Linzer Torte

1 cup unblanched almonds or
   hazelnuts, finely grated
1½ cups sifted flour
1 cup soft butter
2 hard-cooked egg yolks,
   mashed
2 raw egg yolks
½ cup sugar
2 tablespoons dark,

   unsweetened cocoa
½ teaspoon ground cloves
¼ teaspoon cinnamon
1 teaspoon vanilla
1 teaspoon grated lemon rind
1 egg beaten with 2 teaspoons
   light cream
1½ cups thick raspberry jam

Set oven at 350°. Lightly grease a cookie sheet. Mix flour and grated almonds together in a bowl. Make a well in the center. In well, place butter, mashed hard-cooked egg yolks, raw yolks, sugar, cocoa, spices, vanilla and lemon rind. Combine these ingredients into a paste, gradually incorporating the flour and almonds to make a dough. If dough is very soft, chill it slightly.

Roll half the chilled dough between sheets of wax paper to a thickness of 1/2 inch. Using a plate or pan as a pattern, cut out a round of dough 6 inches in diameter. Place on prepared cookie sheet. Brush lightly with egg mixed with cream.

Roll out remaining half of dough into a rectangle 1/4 inch thick between sheets of wax paper. Cut into strips 1/4 inch wide. Make a border on circle with some of the strips, pressing to make certain they are set on firmly. Brush with egg.

Fill shell with 1 cup raspberry jam. Using most of remaining strips, make a lattice across top of the torte. The ends of each strip should rest on the border. Brush ends of strips with egg. Make a second border on top of first, using last of strips. Press down firmly with the tines of a fork. Chill torte (or you can freeze it for baking later).

Brush lattice and border with egg. Bake 40 to 50 minutes or until torte is lightly browned. Jam will have darkened in baking. While torte is still hot, use remaining jam for color to fill in between lattice strips.

An Easy Dinner for 6

The entire meal may be prepared hours ahead of time. The only last-minute work is adding port to the melon, heating the macaroni dish, and tossing the salad. Drink a Beaujolais.

Honeydew Melon with Port
Pasta Parisienne
Beet and Chicory Salad
Bel Paese Cheese
Italian Bread

Honeydew Melon with Port

Serve ¼ or ⅓ chilled melon to each person, depending on size of both melon and appetites. Just before serving, add 1 or 2 tablespoons port to each portion.

Pasta Parisienne

1½ pound chicken breasts
¼ pound butter
¼ cup Madeira or cognac
2 tablespoons flour
2 cups chicken broth
1 cup cream

Grated Parmesan cheese
Salt and pepper
1 cup cooked tongue
¾ cup cooked ham or prosciutto
2 canned white truffles (see Note)
1 pound ziti

Sauté the chicken breasts in 4 to 6 tablespoons butter, and toss well so they brown lightly. Cook about 10 minutes. When they are just cooked through, pour the Madeira or cognac over them. Let cook down for a few seconds, and then remove the chicken. Reserve pan juices.

Prepare a rich sauce with 2 tablespoons butter, the flour, and the chicken broth. Add pan juices, the cream, and then the grated Parmesan. Blend well. Season to taste with salt and pepper.

Cut the chicken, tongue, and ham into fine julienne; also julienne the truffles, saving half of a truffle to chop very fine. Also chop one-third of the tongue very fine.

Partially cook the ziti in boiling salted water. Drain well. Combine with the cream sauce and the strips of meat and truffle. Spoon into an ovenproof baking dish, and sprinkle with the chopped tongue, chopped truffle, and additional grated cheese.

Bake at 350° for 15 minutes.

NOTE: Or substitute ¼ pound sautéed sliced mushrooms.

Beet and Chicory Salad

1 large onion, diced
1 large cooked beet, diced
Vinaigrette Sauce (see p. 338)

1½ heads chicory (more or less, depending on size)

Combine the onion and beet in a salad bowl. Add vinaigrette sauce and let stand 30 minutes. Add chicory just before serving, and toss.

Bel Paese Cheese

Be sure to allow the cheese to warm for several hours at room temperature. Serve with good crusty Italian bread and butter.

A Hearty, Delicious Meal for 6 People Who Love Pig's Feet!

The feet may be cooked several days in advance, leaving only the final grilling. With this meal drink beer or a fruity Alsatian Gewürztraminer.

Tomato Salad
French Bread and Butter
Grilled Pig's Feet, Sauce Diable
Chip or French Fried Potatoes
Watercress
Mustards
Steamed Apples

Tomato Salad

6 ripe tomatoes, or more, depending on size	2 tablespoons chopped fresh basil or 1 teaspoon dry basil
6 tablespoons olive oil	2 tablespoons chopped parsley
2 tablespoons vinegar	Salt and pepper to taste

Scald tomatoes, or place over flame, to loosen skin. Peel. Slice very thin, and arrange on a serving dish. Spoon seasoning over the tomatoes a half-hour before serving. Crisp French bread and butter should accompany this.

Grilled Pig's Feet, Sauce Diable

6 pig's feet
6 pieces thin white cotton,
   1 yard long and 3 inches wide
6 pieces white twine

6 tablespoons pork fat
Bread crumbs
Salt and pepper

COURT BOUILLON:

1 pint white wine
2 carrots
2 cloves garlic
1 teaspoon thyme
1 bay leaf

3 sprigs parsley
2 cloves
Salt and pepper
2 quarts water

Pig's feet may be bought ready for cooking. Ask your butcher to cut them long for you, or, if you go to Italian or Chinese markets, you will often find them already cut that way. Those usually found in the markets are cut below the hock and are very short.

First combine the ingredients for the court bouillon, and allow it to boil for 30 minutes to blend the flavors. Cool.

Wash the feet and brush them well. Wrap cotton cloth around each in tight overlapping bands and tie securely. This is to prevent the skin from breaking. Now place the pig's feet in the bouillon and let simmer, covered, until tender—about 3 to 4 hours. Remove the cooked feet from the bouillon, and unwrap the cotton. Place the feet on a platter and let them cool. Reshape, and trim off any loose ends. Prepare a Sauce Diable (*see* p. 334).

When ready to grill, rub pig's feet well with pork fat, and roll in dry bread crumbs. Grill under a broiler 5 inches from heat, turning often until nicely browned, or roast in a hot oven (475°) for 10 to 15 minutes.

Serve with the Sauce Diable, watercress, a variety of mustards, and crisply cooked potatoes.

Chip or French Fried Potatoes

See p. 357.

Steamed Apples

1 stick butter
6 apples, peeled, cored, and
   cut in sixths
Vanilla

Sugar
$^1/_2$ pint heavy cream, whipped
$^1/_2$ teaspoon vanilla

Melt butter in a heavy skillet, add apples and 1 teaspoon vanilla, and cover tightly. Steam over medium heat for about 6 to 8 minutes or until tender but not mushy. Shake pan several times during cooking. Add sugar to taste. Serve apples warm with whipped cream, sweetened, and flavored with vanilla.

An Elegant but Relatively Simple French Meal for 6

The sole, its sauce, and the dessert may be made in advance. With this menu serve a Sancerre.

Melon
Paupiettes of Sole
Potatoes Persillés
Petits Pois Grandmère
Apricot and Pineapple Flan
with Almonds

Melon

Choose a ripe melon in season—you will need the cooperation of your greengrocer—and serve chilled, in slices, with lemon or lime wedges.

Paupiettes of Sole

¹/₂ pound salmon
2 eggs
¹/₂ cup chopped parsley
Salt and pepper
6 fillets of sole
White wine

1¹/₂ cups Sauce Velouté (see
p. 332)
12 mushroom caps
6 artichoke hearts, previously
cooked and trimmed
Butter

Grind the salmon, and mix with the eggs and parsley until it is smooth and pasty. Season to taste with salt and pepper, and spread on the fillets. Roll and secure with toothpicks. Poach the fillets in white wine to barely cover, basting well, until the fish is just cooked and flaky. Remove the fillets to a baking dish.

Prepare a Sauce Velouté, using 1 cup cooking liquid. Sauté the mushrooms and previously cooked and trimmed artichoke hearts in butter, and season to taste. Pour the sauce over the fish. Heat in 400° oven 20 minutes. Surround with artichoke hearts, top with the mushrooms, and garnish with the Potatoes Persillés.

Potatoes Persillés

2 pounds tiny new potatoes
6 tablespoons butter

Salt and pepper
Chopped parsley

Cut a band of skin off each potato (to allow the butter to be absorbed later), and boil in salted water till just tender. Drain, and toss with the butter, salt and pepper to taste, and about ¹/₃ cup (or to your taste) of chopped parsley.

Petits Pois Grandmère

2 packages frozen tiny peas
in butter
3 small onions, sliced

3 tablespoons butter
¹/₂ cup diced ham
Chopped parsley

Cook peas according to directions on package. Steam onions in butter till limp. Add ham, and heat for 3 minutes. Combine with the peas, and add 2 or 3 teaspoons chopped parsley.

Apricot and Pineapple Flan with Almonds

1 flan ring of Rich Pastry
  (see p. 347)
1 to 1½ cups pineapple
  preserves
⅔ cup toasted sliced almonds

2 cups cooked or canned
  apricot halves
1 cup apricot preserves for
  glaze

Prepare a flan ring as directed on p. 38. When cooled, spread the bottom with a layer of pineapple preserves. Sprinkle the pineapple with sliced toasted almonds. Then top with either poached fresh apricots or with canned apricots that have been well drained. Finally brush with Apricot Glaze (*see* p. 38).

Summer Dinners

Time was when housewives used to say on a summer's day they had to cook in the cool of the morning to have things cold for dinner. Indeed, many houses had summer kitchens, where the food was prepared to prevent the constant heat of the coal stove from raising the temperature of the living quarters. In this air-conditioned age it is possible for most people to prepare food at any hour of the day without fear of overheating the house, and it is possible to consume hot food on the hottest days. Cold food, however, continues to have a special appeal throughout the summer months, and it is a seasonal change to which I look forward with particular pleasure. I am of the opinion that most food tastes better cold anyway. A chicken roasted and allowed to cool slowly is a far more delicious dish to me than a chicken hot from the oven. Likewise, steak perfectly broiled, seasoned, cooled and sliced thin is even more succulent than steak rushed from the grill. Vegetables, too, seem to have more flavor when cold, and they lend themselves to a great variety of dressings and sauces.

It seems a good idea in any event to relieve a cold meal with at least one hot course—perhaps a hot first course or a hot dessert. If you must have a hot main course, go to the outdoor grill.

In summer, wines should be light and cooling. For the most part red wines are not so suitable as well-chilled whites and rosés. In fact, one could happily give up spirits for the summer and stay on a diet of wine.

Most cheeses are rather overpowering for summer fare. The Swiss cheeses and some of the goat cheeses are exceptions, but I believe that good red wine is so important to cheese that one should wait for a cooler season.

Summer dining can inspire all sorts of bright and amusing table settings and interesting backgrounds on the terrace or in the garden. This is the season to entertain in a relaxed and effortless fashion.

A June Dinner for 8

Drink either a West Coast dry white wine or a Sancerre from the Loire Valley.

Clam Bisque
Cold Poached Salmon
Asparagus with Sauce Vinaigrette
Rich Strawberry Shortcake

Clam Bisque

3/4 cup rice
1 1/2 quarts bottled clam juice
6 tablespoons unsalted butter
24 shucked clams
Salt and freshly ground pepper

1/4 to 1/2 teaspoon Tabasco
1 pint heavy cream
6 tablespoons cognac
Chopped fresh parsley

Cook the rice in the clam juice until very soft. Stir in the butter. Force the mixture through a fine sieve or whirl in a blender or food processor until smooth.

Finely chop 12 of the clams by hand; or place in a food processor with a little clam liquor and pulse until finely chopped.

Combine the chopped clams and rice mixture in a saucepan. Season with salt and pepper to taste and add the Tabasco. Stir in the heavy cream. Heat just to the boiling point. Add the 6 whole clams and heat just until they curl at the edges. Add the cognac and cook 2 minutes more. Ladle the soup into heated cups, putting a whole clam in each cup. Garnish with chopped parsley and serve with Melba toast.

Cold Poached Salmon

Court Bouillon
1 8-pound salmon
Cooked crabmeat
Garnish of thinly sliced

cucumbers or watercress
and cherry tomatoes
Lemon slices

FOR THE COURT BOUILLON:

9 whole cloves
3 onions, peeled
3 quarts water
1 quart white wine
1 cup wine vinegar
4 carrots, finely chopped

2 stalks celery
1 bay leaf
1 teaspoon thyme
4 to 5 sprigs parsley
1 tablespoon salt

Put 3 cloves in each of the onions. Combine all of the ingredients for the court bouillon in a pot or fish steamer large enough to hold the salmon, and bring to a boil. Reduce the heat and simmer for an hour.

Wrap the salmon in cheesecloth, leaving two long ends to serve as handles. Lower the salmon into the court bouillon and poach gently for 10 minutes per inch of thickness, measured at the thickest point. When the fish is done, remove it from the bouillon and allow it to cool. Carefully remove the skin, and trim the fish so that it looks inviting. If you are serving a whole fish, you may want to leave the head and tail on. Arrange on a large platter, and garnish with crabmeat, cucumber slices or watercress, cherry tomatoes, and lemon slices. Serve with a tarragon-flavored mayonnaise.

Asparagus with Sauce Vinaigrette

Cook asparagus by your favorite method until just done—tender but not limp. Allow to cool. Serve with a Sauce Vinaigrette. *See* p. 338.

Rich Strawberry Shortcake

FOR THE SHORTCAKE:

4 cups all-purpose flour
6 tablespoons sugar
2 teaspoons salt
5 teaspoons (1½ sticks)
    unsalted butter, chilled

and cut into bits
1½ cups heavy cream
2 tablespoons unsalted
    butter, melted and cooled

FOR THE TOPPING:

2 quarts fresh, ripe
    strawberries, washed and
    hulled

Sugar, to taste
1 pint heavy cream

For the shortcake, sift the flour, sugar, salt and baking powder together in a large bowl. Add the butter and rub it into the dry ingredients with your fingertips until most of the lumps disappear and the mixture resembles coarse meal; or pulse a few seconds in a food processor. Add the cream and mix thoroughly until a soft dough is formed. Gather it into a compact ball and place on a lightly floured board. Knead for a minute, then divide into two pieces, one a third larger than the other.

Preheat the oven to 425°. Press the larger piece of dough into a circle about ½ inch thick on a greased cookie sheet. On another sheet, press the second piece into a slightly smaller circle. Brush each with melted butter, and bake for 12 to 15 minutes or until firm to the touch and golden brown.

Coarsely chop half the strawberries, reserving the most attractive ones for the top. Spread a layer of chopped strawberries on the larger shortcake layer, sprinkle with sugar, and gently slide the top layer over the strawberries. Garnish with the whole strawberries. Pour the cream over the cake just before serving, or it can be whipped and passed separately.

A Summer Dinner for 4

Serve a chilled Beaujolais.

Double Consommé of Chicken
Cold Beef en Daube
Horseradish Cream
Rice Salad
Coffee Granita

Double Consommé of Chicken

1 fowl	*2 sprigs parsley*
3 pounds of chicken backs and	*1 teaspoon thyme*
necks	*Salt and pepper*
2 pounds of gizzards	*Nutmeg*
1 onion, stuck with 2 cloves	*3 to 4 quarts water*
1 rib celery	*2 egg whites (reserve shells)*

Cook the backs, necks and gizzards with the vegetables and seasonings in water. Simmer for 2 to 2½ hours or until the broth is strong. Add the fowl, and continue cooking until fowl is tender—about 2½ hours. Remove fowl, and reserve; dice meat for other dishes.

Strain the broth, and discard the bones, etc. Beat the egg whites slightly, and add to the broth with the shells. Bring to a boil, and simmer 20 minutes. Strain through a linen napkin or towel.

Serve in demitasse or soup cups.

Cold Beef en Daube

See recipe (p. 141) for Daube Provençale. To serve cold, strain the sauce, and let it cool. Remove excess fat. Slice the meat and arrange in a serving dish. Cover with the sauce, and let it chill. Serve in its own jelly.

Horseradish Cream

1 cup freshly grated horseradish   1 cup sour cream

Combine and chill. Or take 1 cup sour cream and add bottled horse-radish to taste.

Rice Salad

1 quart water	*¹/₂ cup converted rice*
1 bay leaf	*¹/₂ cup oil*
1 teaspoon salt	*2 to 3 tablespoons wine vinegar*
1 pinch saffron	*Freshly ground black pepper*

Bring the water to a boil. Add the bay leaf, salt, and saffron. Stir in the rice so that the water never stops boiling. Continue boiling, uncovered, until the rice is tender, about 15 minutes. Drain. Return to the pan over low heat to dry out, for 2 or 3 minutes, occasionally fluffing with a fork. Add oil, vinegar, and some freshly ground black pepper. Let it cool with this sauce. Then add:

²/₃ cup finely chopped onion	*pepper*
¹/₃ cup finely chopped seeded tomato	*¹/₄ cup raisins*
¹/₂ cup finely chopped celery	*¹/₂ cup pinenuts*
¹/₂ cup finely chopped green	*¹/₃ cup chopped parsley*

Toss well and add more oil or vinegar and seasoning to the salad if needed. Spoon into a salad bowl. Decorate with sliced eggs and tomatoes, and serve very cold.

Coffee Granita

Make 1 quart of very strong coffee—espresso or regular coffee—and let it infuse over a "warm" pad for 30 minutes. Sugar to taste and stir till sugar is dissolved. Strain through a cloth into freezing tray. Freeze for 2 hours, stirring several times in order to break up the mixture. Or briefly whirl in a food processor. It should have an icy, granular texture. Serve with whipped cream if desired. A dash of cinnamon is delicious in it.

An International Dinner for 8

You might serve tequila sours or Margaritas to begin, accompanied by tiny cocktail tamales or guacamole. Serve a white wine throughout dinner—perhaps a Muscadet or a Pinot Chardonnay.

Seviche with Scallops
Hot Tortillas or Rolls
Veal Cutlets Sicilienne
Hot Noodles with Poppyseeds
Tomatoes with Basil Dressing
Savarin with Apricot Glaze

Seviche with Scallops

2 pounds scallops
Juice of 12 limes or lemons
   (approximately)
2 garlic cloves, chopped very fine
1/4 cup chopped green onions
1/4 cup chopped green chilies
1/2 cup olive oil
1/4 cup chopped green peppers
1/4 cup chopped parsley
1/4 cup chopped cilantro, if
   available
1/4 cup chopped shallots or
   chives
1 teaspoon mustard seed
1 1/2 teaspoons salt
2 dashes Tabasco
Greens

Cover scallops with lime or lemon juice. Let stand in refrigerator 3 to 4 hours. Drain. Toss well with all of the seasonings and the olive oil. Let stand 1 hour. Line a glass dish with greens, and fill with the scallops. Serve with hot tortillas or rolls.

Veal Cutlets Sicilienne

3 large, very thin cutlets, cut across leg	2 tablespoons chopped parsley
1/4 pound salami	2 tablespoons chopped fresh basil or 2 teaspoons dried basil
1/4 pound mortadella or bologna	5 or 6 hard-cooked eggs
1/4 pound prosciutto or Virginia ham	Olive oil
1/3 cup fine bread crumbs	Salt and freshly ground black pepper
4 cloves garlic, minced	5 or 6 bacon slices
	2 cups tomato sauce

Leave veal slices in whole pieces, but remove bones. Pound veal to 1/4 inch thick. Arrange slices side by side (the long sides adjoining) so they overlap slightly. Pound overlapping areas thoroughly to press them together. On veal arrange rows of overlapping slices of salami. Top with rows of sliced mortadella or bologna and finally with sliced prosciutto or cooked ham.

Spread the surface with a mixture of the bread crumbs, 3/4 of the minced garlic, the chopped parsley, and half the basil. Down the center place a row of shelled, hard-cooked eggs. Sprinkle with olive oil and freshly ground black pepper. (The meat filling should provide enough salt for this dish; add more to taste.) Roll up very carefully and firmly, making certain the eggs stay centered. Place the roll seam side down in a baking dish and top with bacon. Pour tomato sauce around the roll, and sprinkle with the remaining garlic and basil. Bake in a 350° oven for 1 hour, basting several times with the sauce. Transfer to a hot platter, and cut in thick diagonal slices, or serve from the baking dish.

NOTE: This is exceptionally good sliced cold.

Savarin with Apricot Glaze

*1/2 cup warm water (105°
  to 115°)*
*2 packages or cakes of yeast,
  active dry or compressed*
2 1/2 cups unsifted flour
4 eggs, slightly beaten

1 tablespoon sugar
1/2 teaspoon salt
2/3 cup soft corn-oil margarine
Apricot Glaze (see p. 38)
*Fresh fruits and whipped
  cream or rum syrup*

Measure warm water into small warm bowl. Sprinkle or crumble in yeast; stir until dissolved. Add to flour in large bowl; then add eggs. Beat with spoon for 2 minutes. Cover; let rise in warm place, free from drafts, about 1/2 hour, or until bubbly and doubled in bulk. Stir down; add sugar, salt and soft margarine. Beat again until dough is elastic when dropped from spoon (about 4 minutes).

Turn into well-greased 3-quart ring mold. Again let rise in warm place, until doubled in bulk, about 30 minutes. Bake in a very hot oven (450°) 10 minutes; reduce heat to 350°, and bake 20 minutes longer, or until done. Unmold. Brush with apricot glaze. When ready to serve, fill center with fresh fruits and whipped cream or pour rum syrup over the cake.

Dinner for 4

Serve a bottle of Sancerre or a California Riesling.

Stuffed Striped Bass with Cream Sauce
Boiled New Potatoes
Spinach with Oil and Garlic
French Bread
Cheese   Apples

Stuffed Striped Bass with Cream Sauce

3-egg omelet aux fines herbes (parsley, tarragon, and chives or your choice)	Oil
	Salt and pepper
	1 cup white wine
4- to 5-pound striped bass	1 cup cream
Chopped shallots or scallions	3 egg yolks

Clean and split the striped bass.

Prepare the omelet aux fines herbes, and roll it into the fish as stuffing. Sew up the striped bass and place it on a bed of chopped shallots or onions in a well-oiled baking dish. Salt and pepper the fish, and add the wine. Bake at 400° 10 minutes per inch of thickness or about 30 to 35 minutes. Remove the fish to a hot platter and take out the string or thread that you used to secure it. Strain the pan juices, and force the onion through a fine sieve. Reduce the juices slightly and add the cream mixed with egg yolks; stir until thick, but do not let it boil. Taste for seasoning and pour the sauce around the fish.

Serve with tiny Boiled New Potatoes (*see* p. 354) and parsley.

Spinach with Oil and Garlic

2 pounds spinach   *Salt*
4 tablespoons olive oil   *Lemon juice*
3 garlic cloves, finely chopped

Wash spinach well, and drain in a colander. Heat oil slightly in a heavy skillet, and add garlic. Add spinach, and toss, as you would a salad, over medium heat till spinach is just wilted and heated through. Add salt to taste and a dash of lemon. Serve hot.

Cheese

For dessert, serve a Roquefort and a sharp cheddar cheese, along with the best apples available and French bread and butter.

Dinner for 8

Chilled champagne is the proper choice for an apéritif. With it serve nuts or small cherry tomatoes.

    A chilled white burgundy, such as Puligny-Montrachet, goes well with the sweetbreads. Serve a fine old Madeira with the dessert.

Shrimp Aillade
Sweetbreads Albert
Nutted Ala
Summer Salad
Strawberries Romanoff in
Meringue Shells

Shrimp Aillade

3 pounds tiny shrimp
Tomato wedges, hard-cooked
  eggs, black olives
4 cloves garlic, chopped
1¹/₂ cups fresh basil leaves
Salt and freshly ground
  black pepper

6 ripe tomatoes, peeled, seeded
  and chopped
1 cup olive oil
Tabasco
Lemon juice
Chopped parsley

The tiny Iceland shrimp are much better than larger shrimp for this dish. In many fine food stores in New York they come ready-cooked and frozen in blocks. The ready-cooked Pacific Coast tiny shrimp are equally good. In the South and Midwest, your best choice is the smallest fresh shrimp you can find. Poach shrimp until just done (about 2 or 3 minutes), shell and clean.

Arrange in an attractive serving dish. Garnish with tomato wedges, halved hard-cooked eggs and French or Italian black olives.

Serve with a sauceboat of aillade and toasted finger rolls. To make aillade, puree garlic and basil in a blender, or pound to a paste in a mortar. Season with salt and pepper, and mix with the chopped tomatoes. Gradually beat in oil, and add a dash of Tabasco and a little lemon juice. Let mixture stand 1 hour to mellow and blend flavors. Sprinkle with parsley. (This sauce may be made in advance.)

Sweetbreads Albert

1 leek, well washed
3 stalks celery
1 green pepper, seeded
2 small carrots, peeled
6 shallots, chopped very fine
3 tablespoons oil
Salt and pepper

2 cups white wine
4 pairs sweetbreads
1 tablespoon cornstarch
3 egg yolks
Juice of 1 lemon
Chopped parsley

Cut the leek, celery, green pepper and carrots into fine julienne strips, and sauté with shallots in oil until lightly colored. Arrange the vegetables on the bottom of a deep saucepan, season with salt and pepper to taste, and add 1 cup white wine. Arrange sweetbreads (unblanched and unwashed) on the vegetables and cover. Simmer the sweetbreads and vegetables for ¹/₂ hour over medium heat.

Remove the sweetbreads and cool them between wet towels. Drain the vegetables, and save the liquid. Measure 1 cup of the liquid, add the remaining 1 cup white wine, and the cornstarch. Place in a saucepan, and simmer until slightly thickened.

Clean the sweetbreads, add the membranes and trimmings to the drained vegetables. Puree the vegetables in an electric blender or food processor and add to the thickened white-wine broth. Beat the egg yolks lightly and add. Cook slowly, stirring constantly, until the broth thickens, but do not let it boil. Add lemon juice, and taste for seasoning.

Slice the sweetbreads and place them on a hot platter in the oven for a few minutes to heat through. Pour the sauce over them, reserving some in a sauceboat to be passed separately. Garnish the platter with chopped parsley.

Nutted Ala

Ala is the name of a cracked-wheat product—a delightful change from other cereal dishes. It is particularly complementary to sweet-breads. Follow directions on the package of ala. (For 8 persons, you may have to double the recipe.) When the ala is done, add 1 cup toasted pecan halves and 4 tablespoons melted butter. Mix well.

Summer Salad

6 scallions
1 heaping tablespoon fresh
 tarragon leaves
Salt and freshly ground
 black pepper

1 teaspoon dry mustard
Olive oil
Lemon juice
Leaf lettuce or oak leaf lettuce

Cut the scallions very fine, and chop the tarragon. Blend with salt and pepper to taste, and mustard. Add 1/2 cup olive oil and 1 teaspoon of lemon juice. Blend and let stand for one hour to mellow. Add more oil and lemon juice (to taste), and toss with the washed and dried greens at the last minute.

Strawberries Romanoff in Meringue Shells

8 individual meringue shells
2 quarts ripe strawberries
Sugar
1 6-ounce can frozen orange
   juice concentrate

1 cup port
3 tablespoons Mandarine liqueur
2 cups heavy cream, whipped
Pistachio nuts

Buy meringue shells at a good bakery, or make your own according to your favorite recipe.

Hull the berries and sugar them if needed. (Remember, the wine and the orange concentrate have sugar, as does the liqueur.) Add the orange concentrate and port and let the berries mellow in this mixture for 2 hours. Toss them carefully several times. Add the Mandarine liqueur. Whip the cream just before serving. Fill meringue shells with berries, top with whipped cream, and garnish with chopped pistachio nuts.

BUFFETS

Many people who enjoy cooking have their kitchens designed to offer an attractive background for buffet service. Guests are invited to the kitchen to collect their food and carry it back to the dining room or terrace. This technique is casual and thoroughly functional. It has saved many a host and hostess a great deal of work.

Naturally there are formal buffets, too, where magnificent *pièces montées* and lusciously arranged platters are prepared by professional chefs to feast the eye as well as the palate. They should not be so slick and professional-looking, however, that they overpower your own style or violate good taste. A buffet of this type requires the attention of well-trained waiters or caterer's assistants. I have always felt that if one brings in caterers to reproduce food that one normally finds in a deluxe restaurant, why not invite your guests to the restaurant instead?

There is one rule of buffet service frequently overlooked: Offer one course at a time. It is a most distressing sight at a large buffet party to see plates heaped indiscriminately with cold duck, molded salads, tossed salads, ham, curried prawns and sundry other things. And there should be a fresh supply of plates available.

If you are serving a dinner for six or eight, or a luncheon for ten or twelve, you may wish to lay out tables for your guests. For a larger buffet, you will have to be more casual, but do not invite more guests than you can accommodate comfortably if they are expected to use knife and fork and balance a wine glass as well. A buffet may be anything from a breakfast of juice, toast and coffee to a ball supper with a hot table, a cold table and a drink table. The rules are the same. Looks count a great deal, and the service must be efficient.

LUNCHEON BUFFETS

A Special Provençal Buffet for 8

This menu you must serve to your most intimate friends. It is devastatingly good but very special—because of the high garlic content. Anyone who does not love the flavor of garlic has no place at your table on this occasion. Drink Pernod and a Provençal Rosé.

Herb Bread
Aïoli   Cassonade

Herb Bread

1 large loaf French bread
1 small bunch parsley
8 to 10 scallions
Small bunch chives

1 sprig fresh dill
1 stick (¹/₄ pound) butter, or more
¹/₂ teaspoon salt

Split bread in half the long way. Chop the herbs and scallions, and combine with the butter and salt. Cream well. Spread mixture on each half of loaf. Press bread together again, firmly. Heat in 350° oven for 20 minutes. Cut in 1-inch slices.

Aïoli

This is a traditional Provençal sauce, delicious with hot or cold fish, cold vegetables, hot or cold meats, and cold fowl. One can make the sauce in a mortar, blender or food processor.

8 to 12 garlic cloves   *Salt to taste*
3 egg yolks   *Lemon juice to taste*
Olive oil

Mortar method: Pound the garlic in a mortar in a steady, revolving motion. Then add the egg yolks, and continue grinding. Finally, pound in olive oil, a tablespoon at a time (about 3 to 4 cups), till the mixture has the texture of a thick mayonnaise. Add salt and lemon juice to taste.

NOTE: Should the emulsion break down, remove it, clean the mortar, and start again, using 1 garlic clove, 1 egg yolk and a little oil. Then spoon in the first mixture, and continue stirring until the emulsion thickens.

Blender or food processor method: Make a heavy mayonnaise, using 3 whole eggs and 3 to 3½ cups of olive oil, or more, depending on the size of the eggs. This may be done in a blender or the food processor. Then whirl the garlic cloves in the blender or processor with 1 egg yolk and a little oil. Combine this paste with the mayonnaise.

ACCOMPANIMENTS:

1) *Salt cod*
Two pounds filleted in one piece. Soak in water to cover overnight or for 8 to 10 hours. Change the water once during the soaking. Drain, and cover with cold water. Bring to a boil, and simmer for 10 minutes or until the fish is tender. Serve hot.

2) *Boiled potatoes*
Peel and boil 10 to 12 medium-sized potatoes in salted water until just pierceable. Drain, and dry over low flame. Serve hot.

3) *A cold or hot fresh fish*
Striped bass poached in court bouillon and cooled; or poached red snapper or halibut. Serve with a garnish of sliced cucumbers.

4) *Hard-cooked eggs*
Figure on at least 1 hard-cooked egg per person. Peel them, and arrange on a serving dish.

5) *Cooked vegetables*

Scrape 10 carrots, and cook in boiling salted water till just crisply done. Wash and trim 12 smallish zucchini, and cook them in salted water till just pierceable. Poach 12 medium white onions till tender. If asparagus is in season, cook 2 pounds until tender but still firm. Boil one artichoke for each person.

6) *Snails in their shells*—2 or 3 per person

Arrange the assortment of foods on platters, and place around aïoli. Each person helps himself to the sauce and whatever he wishes to accompany it.

Cassonade

Brioche dough (1/2 recipe, p. 344)   *4 egg yolks*
1 cup brown sugar   *1 cup heavy cream*

Prepare brioche, roll out, and line a 9-inch pie tin that has been buttered. Let rise 5 to 10 minutes. Sprinkle brown sugar over bottom of the shell to cover evenly. Mix egg yolks and cream together, and pour over the sugar. Bake at 425° for 10 minutes. Reduce heat to 350°, and bake until the custard is set. Cool and serve.

A Crawfish Feast for 6

Chilled aquavit and/or cold beer are traditional with spiced crawfish. A dramatic way to present the aquavit: Freeze the bottle into a square or cylinder of ice, leaving the neck free.

Spiced Crawfish
Sliced Onion and Tomato Salad
with Cucumbers
Homemade Whole-Wheat Bread   Butter
Coeur à la Crème with Strawberries

Spiced Crawfish

These tasty shellfish are available in Louisiana, Oregon, Washington, Wisconsin, Minnesota and may sometimes be ordered from good fish merchants in other areas, who often ship by air direct to the customer. If crawfish are not available, substitute large shrimp.

2 quarts red wine (a good California bulk wine is excellent)	1 quart water
	3 bay leaves
	4 cloves garlic
1/4 cup Tabasco	6 to 8 whole allspice
2 tablespoons salt	1 teaspoon tarragon
3 sprigs parsley	6 to 8 dozen crawfish

Bring the wine, water, bay leaves, garlic, Tabasco, salt, parsley, allspice and tarragon to a boil in a deep pan. Lower the heat and simmer 10 minutes. Add the crawfish and cook 8 to 10 minutes or until just done but not mushy. Drain. (Save the bouillon; it will make the base for a fine bisque.)

Allow 12 to 16 crawfish per person and serve chilled. Provide small picks to extract the meat. They are best without sauce, but you may add a bowl of French dressing or mayonnaise for dunking if you wish.

Homemade whole-wheat bread with plenty of sweet butter is a good accompaniment.

Sliced Onion and Tomato Salad with Cucumbers

5 or 6 red onions, peeled and thinly sliced	4 cucumbers, peeled and thinly sliced
5 or 6 ripe beefsteak tomatoes, peeled and thickly sliced	1 tablespoon chopped fresh dill
	Vinaigrette Sauce (see p. 338)

Marinate the cucumber in a good vinaigrette sauce with the dill (if available) for 1 hour. Heap in center of a chilled plate. Place alternate slices of onion and tomato around the cucumbers. Serve with cruets of oil and vinegar and with salt and pepper grinders.

Homemade Whole-Wheat Bread

2 cakes or packages of yeast
1½ cups lukewarm water
1 tablespoon salt
1 teaspoon sugar

2 cups coarse whole-wheat flour
2 to 4 cups white flour
Cornmeal

Dissolve the yeast in the warm water and stir in the salt and sugar. Add the whole-wheat flour a cup at a time, beating it in with a wooden spoon; or use the dough hook on your electric mixer at low speed. Add enough white flour to make a smooth dough. Cover the dough with a towel and let stand in a warm spot to rise until double in bulk.

Turn the dough out onto a floured board and shape it into two long French-style loaves. Arrange on a baking sheet heavily sprinkled with cornmeal. Let rise for 5 minutes. Slash the tops with a knife, brush with water and start the loaves in a cold oven. Set at 400°. Place a pan of boiling water in the oven and bake bread until crusty, about 40 minutes.

Coeur à la Crème with Strawberries

2 8-ounce packages cream cheese
1 cup sour cream
Fresh strawberries or fresh

strawberry preserves
French bread or brioche loaf

Blend the cream cheese and sour cream together to a smooth paste with a fork. If the mixture is too firm, add a little heavy cream.

Line two small (or one good-sized) heart-shaped straw or reed baskets, or porcelain molds, with cheesecloth. Press the cheese mixture into the molds. Place them on a rack over a bowl in the refrigerator and let them stand for several hours.

Unmold into a chilled serving dish and surround with fresh strawberries. Serve with fresh berries or preserves and French bread or brioche.

An Hors d'Oeuvre Luncheon for 12

This delightful meal may be served outdoors or in with equal flair. Drink chilled white wines—California Chenin Blanc, Sauvignon Blanc, and Riesling—before and during the meal. Add a touch of cassis to the before-lunch version if you wish. Iced mocha is simply a blend of coffee and chocolate. You might also serve coffee- and chocolate-flavored liqueurs.

Raw Fava Beans
Radishes
Crudités with Anchovy Mayonnaise
Tian   Crabmeat Orientale
Beef Salad Parisienne
Leeks à la Grecque
Variety of Breads   Cheese
Cold Orange Soufflé   Iced Mocha

Raw Fava Beans

Fava beans (or broad beans) are in the market a good part of the summer. They come in long, broad green pods and are delicious eaten raw with salt. Simply break open the pods, slip out the beans, and dip them in a bowl of coarse salt.

Radishes

Arrange white and red radishes on crushed ice. Serve with sweet butter; or wrap each radish with an anchovy fillet fastened with a toothpick.

Crudités with Anchovy Mayonnaise

12 to 14 anchovy fillets,
    coarsely chopped
2 cloves garlic, finely chopped
1/4 cup chopped parsley
1/4 cup chopped fresh basil
1 tablespoon coarsely
    chopped capers

1 tablespoon Dijon mustard
2 cups homemade mayonnaise
Thinly sliced cucumbers, sliced
    tomatoes, sliced onion, whole
    scallions, grated carrots, grated
    raw beets or other raw
    vegetables

Combine anchovy fillets, garlic, parsley, basil, capers, mustard and mayonnaise, and taste for seasoning. Use little salt in the mayonnaise; anchovies and capers have plenty. Arrange vegetables on a platter; dunk in anchovy mayonnaise.

Tian

Olive oil
2 pounds raw spinach,
    coarsely chopped
2 pounds raw Swiss chard,
    coarsely chopped
6 to 8 finger-size zucchini,
    cut in small dice
2 medium onions, coarsely
    chopped
3 cloves garlic, finely chopped

1/2 cup finely chopped basil
    leaves
2 tablespoons dried basil
Salt to taste
1 1/2 teaspoons freshly ground
    black pepper
8 eggs, slightly beaten
1 1/2 cups grated Parmesan cheese
Bread crumbs

Cover the bottom of a large skillet with olive oil and add the spinach and Swiss chard. Cook until just wilted. Remove and drain. Press out all liquid. Add the zucchini, onion and garlic to the skillet and repeat cooking procedure.

Combine the vegetables, the fresh and dried basil, salt and pepper, and place in a lightly oiled, heavy earthenware casserole. Pour the eggs over the vegetables and top with the cheese and bread crumbs. Bake in a 350° oven until the eggs are just set and the cheese is melted and bubbly. Serve cold.

Crabmeat Orientale

3 cups cooked rice
1/2 pound raw mushrooms,
   sliced
1 cup thinly sliced water
   chestnuts
1 cup finely chopped green
   pepper
3 pimientos, finely cut
2 cups crabmeat (fresh, frozen

   or canned)
1/4 cup chopped parsley
1/4 cup chopped chives
1 cup olive oil
3 tablespoons soy sauce
3 tablespoons vinegar
1/2 teaspoon Tabasco
2 teaspoons Dijon mustard
Greens

Combine all ingredients but the greens. Toss well. Arrange on a bed of greens.

Beef Salad Parisienne

2 cups sliced, boiled, small new
   potatoes
1 cup finely cut scallions
2 cups coarsely chopped
   celery, with tops
3 cups lean boiled beef, cut
   in slices and then into
   1 1/2 inch squares
12 to 14 sliced sour pickles
1 cup cherry tomatoes
1/4 cup capers
1/2 cup green pepper strips

Greens
6 hard-cooked eggs
3 tablespoons Dijon mustard
1 cup olive oil
1 clove garlic rubbed into
   1 1/2 teaspoons salt
1 teaspoon freshly ground
   black pepper
1/3 cup vinegar
Dash of Tabasco
Pickled walnuts, sliced

Combine the potatoes, scallions, celery, beef, pickles, tomatoes, capers and green pepper strips, and toss together in a large bowl. Arrange on a bed of greens.

Shell 3 hard-cooked eggs, reserve the whites, and mash the yolks with a fork. Work in the mustard. Stir in the olive oil, garlic-flavored salt, pepper and vinegar. Add a dash or two of Tabasco, and pour this dressing over the beef salad. Garnish with 3 quartered hard-cooked eggs, the sliced pickled walnuts and the 3 egg whites, chopped.

Leeks à la Grecque

1/3 cup olive oil	1 sprig parsley
2 tablespoons wine vinegar	Good pinch of thyme
1 clove garlic, chopped	12 leeks
1/2 cup white wine	Water
1 teaspoon salt	1 tablespoon chopped parsley
1/2 teaspoon freshly ground	Dash of Tabasco
black pepper	White wine (optional)

Mix together the oil, vinegar, garlic, wine, salt, pepper, parsley and thyme, to make a sauce à la grecque. Wash the leeks and soak them well to be sure that all the grit is gone. Run them under cold water for a few minutes. Arrange the leeks in a flat pan and pour the sauce à la grecque over them. Add enough water, or white wine and water mixed, to cover. Simmer until just tender, and cool in the broth. Remove the leeks to a serving dish, and cook the broth down. Add chopped parsley and Tabasco, and pour over the leeks. Chill.

Cold Orange Soufflé

1 cup cold water	2 6-ounce cans frozen orange
2 envelopes unflavored gelatin	juice concentrate
8 eggs, separated	1 cup sugar
1/2 teaspoon salt	1 cup heavy cream, whipped

Place water in the top of a double boiler and sprinkle the gelatin over the surface to soften. Beat the egg yolks lightly and add them with the salt. Mix well. Place over boiling water and cook, stirring constantly, until the gelatin dissolves and the mixture thickens a bit, about 4 minutes.

Remove from the double boiler and stir in the orange concentrate. Chill until the mixture drops from a spoon into soft mounds. Beat egg whites until stiff but not dry. Gradually beat in the sugar and continue beating until the egg whites are stiff. Fold the whites into the orange mixture and then fold in the whipped cream.

Arrange a collar of doubled waxed paper around a 2 1/2-quart soufflé dish. The collar should come 2 inches above the top of the dish. Fasten it with gummed tape. Pour the mixture into the dish and chill until firm. Remove the collar and decorate with orange sections, if you like, before serving.

Country Sunday Lunch for 6

Serve Summer Cocktails: Fill a large wineglass with ice. Add 2 table-spoons of raspberry syrup or Framberry liqueur, 2 ounces of Lillet, 1 ounce of eau de vie de framboise or kirsch. Stir and fill the glass with Perrier water.

During the meal, drink a chilled Alsatian Riesling or Traminer. Serve chilled kirsch or framboise with the coffee.

Cervelat Salad
Cold Barbecued Loin of Pork
Horseradish Applesauce
Hot Fava Beans with Fresh Herbs
Muenster Cheese   Fresh Cherries

Cervelat Salad

6 knockwurst or Swiss-style cervelat	1 cup mayonnaise
1 medium onion, finely minced	3 tablespoons sour cream
6 sour pickles or sweet gherkins, thinly sliced	Romaine
1½ tablespoons Dijon mustard	Chopped parsley, chopped gherkins
	Hard-cooked eggs, halved

Cook the knockwurst, and cool and skin them. Slice rather thinly, and combine with the onion, sliced pickles, mustard and mayon-naise. Toss well. Add the sour cream and toss again. Arrange on a bed of romaine, and garnish with chopped parsley and chopped gherkins. Surround with halved hard-cooked eggs.

Serve with thin buttered pumpernickel.

Cold Barbecued Loin of Pork

5- to 6-pound pork loin roast
Dry mustard
Thyme
Sherry
Japanese soy sauce
3 cloves garlic, finely chopped

2 tablespoons grated fresh
  ginger, or 6 pieces of candied
  ginger cut into slivers
1 8-ounce jar apple or currant
  jelly

Have the roast boned and tied. Rub with dry mustard and thyme. Make a marinade of ½ cup sherry, ½ cup soy sauce, garlic and ginger, and pour over roast. Let the pork marinate for about 2 hours, turning it several times as it soaks. You may let it stand all night in the refrigerator and roast it early in the morning, if you wish.

To cook, remove from the marinade and arrange a meat thermometer in the thickest part of the roast. Cook at 325°, allowing about 25 minutes per pound. Baste with the marinade. When the thermometer reads 175°, the pork is done.

Melt the jelly in a heavy pan over a medium flame and when it is bubbly, add 1 tablespoon soy and 2 tablespoons sherry. Let it cook down for a minute or two, stirring constantly. Spoon over the pork and cool in a chilly room. Do not refrigerate unless the day is exceptionally hot.

Garnish the platter with sliced tomatoes, thinly sliced onions and sliced cucumbers. Serve with horseradish applesauce.

Horseradish Applesauce

Combine 2 cups applesauce and 6 tablespoons fresh grated horseradish or 4 tablespoons bottled horseradish, drained. Blend well and chill. Vary the amount of horseradish to make the sauce hotter or milder.

Hot Fava Beans with Fresh Herbs

4 pounds fava beans (broad
    beans)
6 tablespoons olive oil
1 tablespoon butter
3 cloves garlic, finely minced

1/2 cup minced onion
Salt and pepper to taste
1 tablespoon chopped parsley
2 tablespoons chopped fresh basil

Shell the beans, and cook in boiling water until just tender. Drain. Heat the oil and butter, add the garlic, onion, salt and pepper, and cook 3 minutes. Add the beans and toss well. Then add the parsley and basil, toss again, and serve at once.

NOTE: These beans may be served cold. Simply add more olive oil and a little vinegar.

A Luncheon Buffet for 6

Soupe de Poisson, Marseillaise
Toasted Buttered French Bread
Sliced Oranges, Grand Marnier

Soupe de Poisson, Marseillaise

3/4 cup olive oil
3 1/2 pounds filleted flounder,
    snapper, haddock
Salt and pepper
2 quarts water
2 large onions, chopped

1 29-ounce can Italian plum
    tomatoes
Pinch of basil
1/4 pound spaghettini
Pinch of saffron
1 cup grated Gruyère cheese

Heat 1/2 cup of the olive oil in a deep, heavy pot, and sear the fish. Reduce the heat, and cook until fish is very soft. Salt and pepper to taste, and add the water. Simmer for 1 hour.

Sauté the onions in remaining olive oil, and when soft, add the tomatoes and basil. Cook for 15 minutes. Add to the fish pot, and simmer for 30 minutes. Press fish and vegetables through a food mill, and stir back into the broth. Add the spaghettini, broken into 1- or 2-inch pieces, and saffron. Cook 12 to 15 minutes, or until spaghettini is tender. Correct the seasoning.

Serve in bowls and sprinkle with Gruyère. Have plenty of hot buttered and toasted French bread ready to accompany this hearty soup.

Sliced Oranges, Grand Marnier

Peel 6 large oranges thoroughly to eliminate all traces of skin, then slice thin and arrange in a serving dish. Sprinkle lightly with 1 tablespoon sugar, and add Grand Marnier to taste. Decorate with candied violets or chopped pistachio nuts.

DINNER BUFFETS

An Alsatian Buffet for 10

This is planned around one of the most delicious of all buffet dishes and one that guests always adore—Choucroute Garnie. It has become somewhat of a trademark for me over the years. Serve an Alsatian Riesling.

Herring and Veal Salad
Choucroute Garnie
Apple Tart

Herring and Veal Salad

4 to 5 pickled herring
2 pounds new potatoes, cooked
  in their skins
2 apples, peeled and diced
6 cooked beets, peeled and diced
2 pounds cold veal, diced
2 to 3 medium-sized onions,

  peeled and chopped
Sour cream
Mayonnaise
2 hard-boiled eggs, sliced
1 or 2 good dill pickles, cut in
  strips
Chopped parsley

Cut the herring in small dice. Peel and cut the potatoes in thin slices. Combine with the apples, beets, veal and onions. Add enough sour cream and mayonnaise to bind. Garnish with the sliced egg, pickle and chopped parsley.

Choucroute Garnie

My whole approach to this superb dish has changed over the years. I used to make it in the classic way, cooking the choucroute for hours with salt pork, sometimes pig's trotters and knuckles, and sausages. Finally, when it was done, it would be quite fatty with a flavor redolent of the various cuts of pork. Nowadays I prepare the choucroute and the garnie separately. For the choucroute: Place one or two slices of parboiled (for 10 minutes) salt pork on the bottom of a deep kettle; or use fresh pork (sometimes the salt pork is strong and gives a disagreeable flavor). Add about 5 pounds of sauerkraut, washed and drained. Next add an onion, thinly sliced, and two or three finely chopped cloves of garlic. Give this a few grinds of the pepper mill. Cover the sauerkraut with white wine and water, and bring to a boil. Reduce heat, cover, and allow to simmer atop the stove for 4 hours or bake in a 325° oven for the same time.

FOR THE GARNIE:

Ham—Bake an 8- to 10-pound ham according to your favorite method.

Loin of pork—Roast a loin of pork well, basting it with apple juice from time to time. A 5-pound roast will take about 2¼ to 2½ hours at 325°.

Sausages—Poach 2 or 3 Polish, Italian or French sausages in red wine and chopped onion for 25 to 35 minutes.

Knockwurst—10 minutes before serving, place 12 to 18 knockwurst in a pan of water and poach them.

Potatoes—Boil 18 to 20 potatoes in their jackets.

TO ASSEMBLE:

Arrange the sauerkraut on a great platter. Garnish with sliced ham, sliced pork and sliced sausages. Wreathe it with knockwurst. Serve with the boiled potatoes, mustards of all varieties, and either a good Alsatian Riesling or beer.

NOTE: To cook in the traditional way, place a large piece of salt pork into the pot with the sauerkraut. Add onions, garlic, pepper, white wine, and several pieces of pork hocks and a garlic sausage. Cook for one hour. Remove the salt pork and the sausage. Continue cooking for 2 more hours atop the stove or in the oven. Add knockwurst or other sausages, and remove when they are cooked. Roast a piece of smoked loin of pork separately. Serve with the sliced meats and boiled potatoes as above.

Apple Tart

Rich Pastry dough (see
   p. 347)
6 to 8 cooking apples
1/4 pound butter

1 teaspoon vanilla
Sugar
Apricot Glaze (see p. 38)

Make a rich pastry and roll out to fit a 9-inch pan or flan ring. Peel and core the apples and cut them into sixths. Cut two of them again into paper-thin slices, and reserve. Melt the butter in a heavy skillet, and add the apples (in sixths) and vanilla. Cover and steam over medium heat until the apples are soft but not mushy—8 to 10 minutes. Taste for sweetness, adding sugar to taste.

Sprinkle the pastry with sugar and add the cooked apples, making them level at the top. Cover with the paper-thin apple slices arranged in a pattern. Sprinkle lightly with sugar. Bake 10 minutes at 425°. Reduce heat to 350°, and bake until the pastry is nicely browned and the apples on top are cooked through. Remove from the oven and cool. Cover with an apricot glaze.

A Summer Buffet for 8

Serve either champagne or a chilled rosé throughout; the champagne, of course, will add an extra festive touch.

Cold Fillet of Beef, Japonais
Rice Salad
Liz Lucas Shrimps
Chicken Mayonnaise with Walnuts
Thinly Sliced Tomatoes with Basil Dressing
Rolls   Peaches with Bourbon
Iced Espresso

Cold Fillet of Beef, Japonais

1 large fillet of beef, 7 to 8 pounds, trimmed of all fat	*1 cup sherry*
	6 garlic cloves, chopped
1 cup Japanese soy sauce	*1 teaspoon Tabasco*
1 cup olive or peanut oil	*Dash freshly ground pepper*

Marinate the fillet in the rest of the ingredients for 24 hours, turning several times. Remove and dry. Rub with oil, and roast on a broiling rack at 475° for 25 minutes, for very rare; 28 to 30 minutes for rare. Baste with the marinade 3 or 4 times during the roasting. Allow it to cool; if possible, do not refrigerate.

Arrange on a platter with watercress and tiny cherry tomatoes.

Rice Salad

4 cups cooked rice
$^1/_2$ cup chopped onion
$^1/_2$ cup finely diced celery
$^1/_2$ cup seeded, finely diced
  cucumber

$^1/_4$ cup finely diced green pepper
Vinaigrette Sauce (see p. 338)
Chopped fresh tarragon
Chopped parsley

Combine rice, vegetables, and vinaigrette sauce, and toss well. Arrange on a handsome plate or in a salad bowl. Sprinkle with tarragon and parsley.

Liz Lucas Shrimps

3 pounds or more cooked and
  shelled shrimp
3 medium onions, thinly sliced
4 slices lemon
Chopped parsley

Salt and pepper
$^1/_4$ teaspoon Tabasco
Olive oil
3 bay leaves

Combine layers of shrimp, onion, lemon and parsley in a casserole or serving dish. Add seasonings and olive oil to cover. Top with bay leaves. Marinate for 6 to 8 hours. Serve in the casserole or dish.

Chicken Mayonnaise with Walnuts

4 cups chicken meat, cut in
  generous pieces (all white
  meat for elegance, white and
  dark for best flavor)
1 cup broken walnut meats
  (reserve about a dozen
  halves for garnish)
$1^1/_2$ to $2^1/_2$ cups mayonnaise,

preferably homemade, with
  a touch of sugar
Salt and pepper
Tabasco
Greens
Capers
Hard-cooked eggs

Combine chicken, walnuts, and mayonnaise. Taste for seasonings, adding salt and pepper, if necessary, and a dash of Tabasco. Spoon into a bowl lined with greens. Garnish with additional mayonnaise, capers, hard-cooked eggs and walnut halves.

Thinly Sliced Tomatoes

Peel tomatoes, slice thinly, and arrange on a platter. Sprinkle with salt, pepper, chopped fresh basil, and chopped parsley. Dribble oil over lightly, and add a touch of lemon juice.

Rolls

Provide a variety of hard rolls, perhaps some of rye. These will be pleasanter with the cold food if they are served warm.

Peaches with Bourbon

12 to 14 ripe peaches   *3 cups water)*
Simple syrup (3 cups sugar,   *$^{1}/_{2}$ cup bourbon*

Boil sugar and water together for 10 minutes. Peel peaches, and dip into syrup to poach till just tender. Add bourbon.
  Serve cold with or without cream.

A Pleasant Buffet for 8, Especially Suitable for Summer

Serve Vin Blanc Cassis or Champagne with the nuts and Muscadet or Riesling throughout the rest of the meal.

Salted Filberts
Salade Niçoise
Corn Bread   Coq au Riesling
Boiled New Potatoes with Parsley
Strawberry Tart

Salade Niçoise

3 cans solid-pack white tuna	8 hard-cooked eggs
Greens	Pimientos
3 cans anchovy fillets	Ripe olives
4 ripe tomatoes	Vinaigrette Sauce (see p. 338)

Open the tins of tuna, and drain off the oil. Place in center of a large platter covered with greens. Arrange anchovy fillets around the tuna. Quarter the tomatoes and the eggs. Arrange around the edges of the platter. Garnish with strips of pimiento and ripe olives. Serve with a vinaigrette sauce heavily infused with garlic and basil.

VARIATION: Also prepare thinly sliced cooked new potatoes with oil and vinegar; and cooked, crisp string beans with oil and vinegar. Arrange with the rest of the ingredients on a platter, and top with onion rings, chopped parsley and chopped fresh basil.

Corn Bread

2 cups corn meal	2 eggs
1 cup flour	1½ cups milk
3 teaspoons baking powder	½ cup melted butter
¾ teaspoon salt	

Sift the dry ingredients and combine with the well beaten eggs and milk. Blend well and finally stir in the melted butter. Pour into a shallow, well-buttered baking pan, and bake at 425° for 15 to 20 minutes or until delicately brown.

This is delicious for cocktail hors d'oeuvre when split, buttered, and sandwiched with slivers of Virginia ham.

Coq au Riesling

2 2½- to 3-pound chickens,
   quartered
Flour
6 tablespoons peanut oil
4 slices salt pork, soaked in
   water, drained, and diced
8 shallots or scallions, finely
   chopped
24 small white onions
3 carrots, cut in rounds

½ cup cognac
1½ teaspoons salt
1 teaspoon pepper
Chopped parsley
2 cloves garlic, chopped
2 cups white wine
1 pound mushroom caps
Beurre manié (flour and butter
   kneaded together)

Flour chicken quarters, and brown lightly in oil in 1 or 2 skillets.
Remove to a hot platter. Add salt pork, shallots or scallions, onions,
and carrots to peanut oil. Brown lightly. Return chicken pieces to
pan, and blaze with warmed cognac. Toss well, season with salt,
pepper, parsley, and garlic.

Add wine, and simmer for 20 minutes, covered. Add mushrooms, and turn chicken pieces. Continue cooking till mushrooms
are done, and chicken is tender. The sauce may be thickened with
beurre manié.

Serve with small Boiled New Potatoes (see p. 354) tossed in butter
and chopped parsley.

Strawberry Tart

Rich Pastry dough for 2 crusts
   (see p. 347)
1 quart or more ripe
   strawberries

2 cups (about 2 jars)
   currant or damson jelly
1 pint heavy cream
3 tablespoons sweet sherry

Line 2 9-inch pastry tins or 2 flan rings (either round or oblong)
with pastry. Fit a piece of foil inside each tin to permit you to fill it
with dry beans or peas. (This will weight down the crust and prevent
it from puffing up during the baking.) Bake at 425° for 18 to 20 minutes. Remove foil and beans. Return crust to the oven for 2 minutes
more. Allow to cool.

Arrange hulled strawberries in baked shells. Empty jelly into
saucepan, and boil for 3 minutes. Cool slightly. Spoon melted jelly
over berries to glaze.

Serve with heavy cream, whipped and flavored with sherry.

A Buffet for 8 or 10

Serve cocktails and sherry with the first course. With the main course and the cheese, serve a regional Bordeaux—a St. Émilion or a Médoc.

Anguilles au Vert
Thinly Sliced Salami
Thinly Sliced Head Cheese
Crisp Raw Vegetables
Rye Bread and Butter Sandwiches
Boned and Rolled Turkey
Beer-Glazed Ham   Boiled New Potatoes with Herbs
Rolls and Sweet Butter
Dijon Mustard   Watermelon Pickles
Cheese Board   Heavenly Crown

Have sets of plates ready for the cold dishes, the hot ones and for cheese and dessert. For your centerpiece arrange a beautiful bowl of fruit, which may be eaten with the cheese and dessert.

Anguilles au Vert

1 cup olive oil	(parsley, tarragon, chives,
3 pounds eels, cut in	basil and spinach)
1¼ inch slices and skinned	Juice of 3 lemons
1 quart broth	1 pint white wine
½ cup or more chopped herbs	Salt and pepper

Heat the oil. Sauté the pieces of eel in the hot oil for 5 minutes, turning them to cook on all sides. Add the broth, bring to a boil and cook for 5 more minutes. Add the herbs, lemon juice, wine, salt, and pepper to taste and bring once more to a boil. Turn off the heat and let stand until cool. Serves 6 to 8.

Boned and Rolled Turkey

1 10- to 12-pound boned turkey   1/2 cup finely chopped parsley
2/3 cup butter   2 cups crumbs
1 cup finely chopped onion   1 egg
1/2 cup finely chopped celery   Salt and pepper
1 tablespoon tarragon

Melt the butter in the skillet and sauté the onions and celery. Add the tarragon, parsley and crumbs. Remove from the fire and add the egg, and salt and pepper to taste. Spread this on the surface of the boned turkey, roll very tightly and tie. Brush with butter. Place on a rack in a baking pan or broiling pan and roast at 350° for 1½ to 2 hours, testing with a meat thermometer to achieve 165° internal temperature. Baste occasionally with butter.

NOTE: 1 cup of finely chopped mushrooms, chopped giblets, small sausages or chopped nuts may be added to the stuffing.

Beer-Glazed Ham

1 smoked or ready-to-eat ham   3 tablespoons prepared mustard
1 cup brown sugar   1/2 cup beer or ale

Place ham, fat side up, in shallow baking pan. Bake in a slow oven (325°). If smoked, bake 25 minutes per pound, or until meat thermometer registers 160°. If ready-to-eat, bake 14 minutes per pound, or until meat thermometer registers 130°. Forty-five minutes before ham is done, take from oven and remove rind, if necessary. Score fat surface. Mix together brown sugar and mustard; stir to a paste. Gradually add beer, stirring until blended. Brush part of mixture over ham. Continue baking, brushing frequently with remaining mixture.

Boiled New Potatoes with Herbs

Prepare Boiled New Potatoes (see p. 354) and toss with plenty of butter, chopped parsley and chopped chives.

Cheese Board

A good selection for your cheese board might include Muenster, Camembert, Liederkranz and local cheddar.

Heavenly Crown

18 ladyfingers, split lengthwise — firmly packed
1/2 cup orange juice — 1/8 teaspoon salt
1 6-ounce package semisweet — 3 egg yolks
  chocolate — 3 egg whites
1/2 pound softened cream cheese — 1 1/2 teaspoons vanilla
1 cup light brown sugar, — 1 1/2 cups heavy cream

Place ladyfingers, cut side down, in a 375° oven for 5 minutes. Cool for about 10 minutes. Brush cut sides with orange juice. Place approximately 22 pieces vertically around edge of a 9-inch spring form pan. Arrange remaining pieces on bottom of pan. Set aside.

Melt the semisweet chocolate over hot (not boiling) water. Remove from water and cool for about 10 minutes.

Meanwhile, blend together the cream cheese, 1/2 cup of the brown sugar, and the salt. Beat in the egg yolks one at a time, then stir in the cooled chocolate.

Beat the egg whites and vanilla together till stiff but not dry, then beat in gradually the remaining brown sugar, till stiff and satiny.

Fold the heavy cream into the chocolate mixture, and then fold in the beaten egg white mixture. Pour into the lined pan. Chill at least 5 hours or overnight. Yields approximately 12 servings.

An Unusual, Elegant Buffet Party for 12

This calls for champagne; as a second choice, serve a rosé.

Terrine of Duckling
Hot, Very Crisp Rolls
Country Ham with Chablis Cream Sauce
Spinach Gnocchi
Fabulous Salad
Prunes, Alice B. Toklas

Terrine of Duckling

1 Long Island duckling
1-inch strip pork skin
1 leek, well cleaned
1 sprig thyme
1 stalk celery
1 bay leaf
4 cups bouillon or stock
Water
1 pound chicken livers
1 pound lean pork
6 shallots
1 garlic clove
1 bunch chervil
5 eggs
1 tablespoon flour
$1^{1}/_{2}$ teaspoons salt
$^{1}/_{3}$ teaspoon pepper
$^{3}/_{4}$ cup cognac
1 pound tongue
Truffles
$^{1}/_{4}$ pound larding pork
1 envelope plain gelatin
$^{1}/_{4}$ cup cold water

Skin duckling. To do this, cut duck skin from neck to vent along center of breast with very sharp knife. Pull back skin, using tip of knife to help cut connective tissue where necessary. Reserve skin. Cut meat from duck bones. Reserve pieces of breast. Place bones, neck and giblets in large kettle, reserving liver. Add pork skin, the leek, thyme, celery and bay leaf to bones. Add bouillon, or chicken bouillon cubes and water. Cover and bring to boil. Let simmer for 2 hours.

Meanwhile, put duck meat (except for breast), duck liver, chicken livers and pork through food chopper, together with the shallots, garlic and chervil. Add eggs to the chopped meat one at a time, pounding in well with mortar and pestle, or use a heavy bowl and wooden spoon. Then sprinkle in the flour, salt, and pepper, which have been mixed together. Add cognac, then mix well again.

If you have a food processor, chop the meats together, then add the eggs in two batches, if necessary. Finally, add the flour, salt, pepper and cognac. Mix thoroughly.

Line the bottom of a large oval terrine, or $2\frac{1}{2}$-quart casserole, or smaller casseroles of total equivalent size, with the duck skin. Carefully pour in half of the meat and egg mixture. Arrange duck breast, strips of tongue and sliced truffles over this. Add remaining mixture. Top with thin strips of larding pork. Bake, uncovered, in slow oven, 300° for $2\frac{1}{2}$ hours or about 1 hour for 16-ounce casseroles.

When broth has been boiling slowly for about 2 hours, remove cover and turn up heat to let broth reduce to about $1\frac{1}{2}$ cups, including fat. Strain broth, then add the gelatin, which has been softened in cold water. Stir until gelatin is dissolved. When pâté is removed from oven, pour broth into casserole over pâté. Put a weight on pâté to keep it submerged in broth, and let stand for 2 hours. Remove weight, cover casserole, and refrigerate. Chill thoroughly before serving. Serve the terrine as a first course with rolls. It can be sliced or spread, as desired.

Country Ham

Real smoked country ham is available throughout the country. In and around New York there are at least six different varieties, and each requires different treatment. It is best to follow directions on the wrapping. However, most hams need final baking, even the ready-to-eat ones. Dust them well with brown sugar, crumbs, Quatre Épices (see recipe p. 331), and a little dry mustard. The baking will give the ham a glaze. You may also glaze the ham if you are serving it cold—with an Apricot Glaze (see p. 38). When serving ham, slice very thin.

Chablis Cream Sauce

4 tablespoons butter
12 shallots, finely chopped
4 tablespoons flour
1¹/₂ cups Chablis
2 tablespoons tomato paste

1 teaspoon salt
¹/₂ teaspoon freshly ground
    black pepper
1 cup heavy cream
2 egg yolks

Melt the butter in a heavy saucepan, and add the shallots. Cook until
wilted and soft. Add flour, and cook briskly for 3 minutes. Stir in
Chablis, and continue stirring till thickened. Add tomato paste and
salt and pepper. Simmer 2 to 3 minutes, then stir in cream which
has been mixed with the egg yolks. Stir till thickened, but do not
allow to boil. Correct seasoning.

Pour into a sauceboat, and serve with the ham.

Spinach Gnocchi

1¹/₂ packages frozen spinach
2 tablespoons butter
¹/₂ pound ricotta cheese
Salt and pepper

Dash of mace
2 eggs, slightly beaten
3 tablespoons flour
¹/₃ cup grated Parmesan

Cook spinach in a heavy pan till just heated through. Drain well and
chop fine. Press into a towel to drain off any remaining liquid. Combine
with butter, ricotta, salt and pepper to taste, and mace. Cook 5 minutes
or so over very low heat, stirring well. Remove from heat, and stir in
beaten eggs, flour, and Parmesan. Cool and refrigerate for 2 hours.

Form into small balls or into cylinders about 1¹/₂ inches long, and
roll in flour. Bring water to a boil in a large pot (gnocchi should not
touch during cooking) and add the gnocchi. They are done when
they rise to the surface. Remove at once and drain.

Serve with plenty of melted butter and grated Parmesan.

Fabulous Salad

It's decorative and delicious—and a conversation piece. Use a beautiful glass or china bowl to show it off.

12 heads Bibb lettuce
2½ cups canned baby beets,
   drained

1 pound small mushrooms,
   wiped clean
1 large bunch violets

Arrange the Bibb and the beets in the bowl. Slice the cleaned mushroom caps in rounds, and place over Bibb. Sprinkle with violets (sans stems).

DRESS WITH:

¾ cup olive oil
¼ cup wine vinegar
1½ teaspoons salt rubbed with

a garlic clove
1 teaspoon freshly ground
   black pepper

Toss at the last possible moment.

Prunes, Alice B. Toklas

48 large prunes, preferably
   pitted
2 fifths of port (approximately)

1 cup sugar
1 pint heavy cream, whipped
Macaroons

Soak the prunes in port to more than cover for 24 hours. Remove prunes, and add 1 cup more of port and the sugar to the wine. Place in a saucepan, add the prunes, and bring to a boil. Boil for 1 minute. Allow prunes to cool in the wine. Refrigerate for another 24 to 36 hours. Serve with whipped cream, and garnish with crumbled macaroons.

An Italian Buffet Dinner for 10

Serve a Soave or Verdicchio with the antipasto plate and Valpolicella, slightly cooled, with the main course. After dinner drink cognac with coffee.

Antipasto Plate
Green Noodles Bolognese
Tenderloin of Veal with Basil and Black Olives
Zuppa Inglese

Antipasto Plate

Salami	*Carrot Sticks*
Prosciutto	*Fennel*
Capocollo	*Scallions*
Shrimp Rémoulade	*Radishes*
Mussels Rémoulade	*Eggs Mayonnaise*
Anchovies	*Cabbage Salad*
Pickled Peppers	*Potato Salad*
Artichokes Vinaigrette	*Cotechino with White Beans*
Pickled Mushrooms	*Vinaigrette*
Pickled Beets	*Bread and Butter*
Celery	

You can make the Antipasto course as simple or as elaborate as you wish. Serve a selection from the dishes above, or the entire list. Some items, such as the pickled mushrooms or peppers, may be bought already prepared. The cotechino should be poached in water or red wine for 2 to 2½ hours and served hot with a salad of white beans—either cannellini or Great Northern—dressed with a garlic-scented Vinaigrette Sauce (*see* p. 338). Arrange the antipasto in separate dishes on your buffet table with as much eye-appeal as possible, and serve casually with cocktails or one of the Italian wines suggested.

Green Noodles Bolognese

FOR THE NOODLES:

5 or 6 cups flour

6 eggs

1/2 pound cooked spinach
well drained and puréed

Make a ring of the flour, and place eggs and spinach inside. Blend and knead very well by hand or use an electric mixer with a dough hook. Roll out several times in a pasta machine or with a rolling pin (although this takes some skill) until paper-thin. Allow to dry 15 to 20 minutes. Cut into strips about 1/4 inch wide. Or buy green pasta if you prefer.

FOR THE SAUCE:

3/4 pound chopped beef
3/4 pound chopped fat pork or
  2 slices lean salt pork
1 onion, finely chopped
1 carrot, finely chopped
1 stalk celery, chopped

1 clove garlic, chopped
1/4 cup chopped parsley
Butter
Salt and pepper
1/2 cup meat stock or bouillon
1 tablespoon tomato puree

Combine the meat and vegetables, and sauté in butter until nicely colored. Salt and pepper to taste, and add half the broth. Cook down, then add the remaining broth and the tomato puree. Cover, and cook 1 hour longer.

TO ASSEMBLE:

1 or 2 tablespoons cream   *Parmesan cheese, freshly grated*

Combine cooked noodles with the sauce, and then add the cream and Parmesan. Toss well.

Tenderloin of Veal with Basil and Black Olives

Veal tenderloin (boned loin),
  about 5 pounds, for roasting
Olive oil
3 cloves garlic, finely chopped
2 tablespoons fresh basil or

1 1/2 teaspoons dried basil
Salt and pepper
2 6-ounce cans tomato sauce
1 cup Italian or Greek olives
1/2 cup sherry or Marsala

Rub veal well with 4 tablespoons olive oil, and a bit of the garlic and basil, and salt and pepper. Place in a baking dish. Combine tomato sauce, remaining garlic and basil, and olives, and pour around veal. Add 2 tablespoons olive oil.

Roast at 325° for approximately 1 1/2 hours. Baste twice during this time. Add sherry or Marsala, and continue cooking till veal is tender.

Remove veal to a hot platter. Correct seasoning of tomato sauce. Slice veal and serve with the sauce.

Zuppa Inglese

1 1/2 pounds pound cake or a
  large Génoise (see below)
Crème Pâtissière (see below)
  or Bavarian cream
Cognac, rum, sherry or

Marsala
Chopped candied fruits—
  about 1/2 pound
Meringue

FOR THE GÉNOISE:

6 eggs
1 cup sugar
Pinch salt

1 teaspoon vanilla
1 cup sifted flour
1/2 cup clarified butter

Combine the eggs with the sugar in top of double boiler over hot, not boiling, water. Beat thoroughly for about 15 minutes with a whisk or electric beater. The mixture must be very thick, pale in color and ribbony. Flavor with salt and vanilla. Fold in the flour a little at a time, carefully. Finally fold in the clarified butter.

Pour into a long pan (11 inches by 14 inches) or into a large loaf tin, and bake at 350° for about 40 minutes, or until a cake tester comes out clean.

FOR THE CRÈME PÂTISSIÈRE:

2 cups milk
1 inch vanilla bean or
    $^1/_2$ teaspoon vanilla
$^1/_2$ cup less 1 tablespoon flour

$^1/_2$ teaspoon cornstarch
$^1/_2$ cup sugar
4 egg yolks

Heat milk with vanilla bean or vanilla. Combine flour and cornstarch and add to sugar and egg yolks, in a saucepan. Beat thoroughly. Pour a little of the hot milk into the egg mixture, and stir well. Over low heat gradually combine the 2 mixtures, stirring constantly until they are thickened, but do not let the mixture boil.

FOR THE MERINGUE:

4 egg whites

4 tablespoons granulated sugar

Beat egg whites until they form soft peaks. Gradually beat in sugar, and continue beating until glossy.

To assemble: Cut the cake into 2 or 3 layers, and add cognac, rum, sherry or Marsala to each layer. Be certain that you use enough to flavor cake properly, but not enough to cause it to disintegrate. Let stand for $^1/_2$ to 1 hour. Spread the layers with the crème patissière and sprinkle liberally with chopped candied fruits. Place the layers on top of each other, and cover with the meringue. Place in a 375° oven for 15 to 20 minutes to brown the meringue delicately. Cool the cake, and serve in slices.

BUFFET SUPPERS

A Buffet Supper for 12

This might be an after-theatre, opera or concert supper. The lamb stew can be prepared in advance and the garniture added at the last minute. The salad can be ready for tossing and the cheese board and bowl of fruit arranged. All that remains is to cook the rice.

A Beaujolais will do well throughout this supper. Beforehand offer highballs or drinks on the rocks, and perhaps pass a selection of crisp raw vegetables to munch while supper is warming.

Raw Vegetables, Dipping Sauce
Lamb Marrakech   Rice with Pinenuts
Cheese Board   French Bread
Fresh Fruit

Dipping Sauce for Raw Vegetables

Blend together

18 anchovy fillets
1 peeled lemon
3 cloves garlic

1 teaspoon black pepper
1 cup olive oil
1/2 cup parsley sprigs

Combine in blender and whirl for 1 minute. Correct seasonings.

Lamb Marrakech

7 pounds lean lamb (leg or
   shoulder), cut in 1¹/₂-inch
   cubes
1 cup peanut or olive oil
4 large onions, finely chopped
8 garlic cloves, chopped
2 tablespoons salt
2 teaspoons crushed red chili

pepper
1 teaspoon Quatre Épices
   (see p. 331)
2 teaspoons turmeric
9 or 10 tomatoes—ripe large
   ones, peeled, seeded and
   chopped
2 cups raisins soaked in sherry

FOR THE GARNITURE:

1¹/₂ cups each toasted almonds
   and filberts
Crisp fried onion rings (see

p. 81)
Chopped parsley

Brown the lamb in the oil in a large skillet, and add onion and garlic
to brown lightly. Add seasonings and tomatoes, and bring to a boil.
Cover—adding a small amount of liquid if necessary—and simmer
for 1¹/₂ hours, or transfer to a casserole and place in a 350° oven
uncovered, basting well from time to time till lamb is tender. If you
do the latter, you may have to add more liquid or cover the pan for
half the time. Add raisins and heat through. Serve with rice, and garnish with toasted nuts, onion rings and parsley.

Rice with Pinenuts

2 cups finely chopped onion
2 cups pinenuts
1¹/₂ teaspoons paprika
¹/₂ teaspoon Tabasco
1 cup olive oil

9 cups hot cooked rice
Salt and pepper
Chopped parsley
6 pimientos

Sauté onion, pinenuts, paprika and Tabasco in olive oil for 6 to 8
minutes. Toss with hot rice, using two forks. Season to taste with salt
and pepper. Garnish with chopped parsley and chopped pimiento.

A Buffet Supper for 20

This late supper may be prepared ahead in your own kitchen, or you may have it catered and sent in before you return from the theatre or other entertainment.

If this is to be a celebration, serve champagne; otherwise, you might want to offer standard drinks, and chilled white wine. With the drinks serve a platter of cold poached shrimp, lobster slices, and whole raw scallops that have been marinated as in Seviche (*see* p. 133). Along with the seafood, pass bowls of cocktail sauce and tiny hot biscuits with butter.

Cold Seafood Platter
Split Pea Soup with Sausages
Rye Toast and Butter
Cinnamon Stars
Ice Cream with Mango Macadamia Sauce

Split Pea Soup with Sausages

3 pounds split peas
1 ham butt with meat—about 4 pounds
1 onion stuck with 2 cloves
4 garlic cloves
1 bay leaf
1¹/₂ teaspoons thyme
2 or 3 ribs celery
Water (about 6 quarts)
Salt and pepper
2 tablespoons tomato paste
¹/₄ cup chopped parsley
2 or 3 Polish sausages
Croutons

Soak the peas overnight. Pick them over the next morning and combine with the ham butt, onion, garlic, bay leaf, thyme and celery. Cover with water. Bring to a boil, and boil rapidly for 30 minutes, stirring several times. Add salt to taste—about 2 tablespoons—and give several grinds of the pepper mill. Reduce the heat, cover and simmer for 3¹/₂ to 4 hours or until the soup is perfectly blended. Remove the ham, and put the soup through a sieve. Strip ham from the bones, and add small pieces to the soup. Correct seasoning, and add tomato paste. Cook down till soup has the texture of heavy cream. Just before serving add sausages heated and cut in thin slices. Garnish with chopped parsley and serve with garlic buttered croutons.

Cinnamon Stars

5 egg whites
Dash salt
2 cups sifted confectioners' sugar
2 teaspoons cinnamon

1 teaspoon grated lemon rind
1 pound unblanched almonds,
    ground

Beat egg whites with salt until they hold a soft shape, then gradually beat in the confectioners' sugar and continue beating until the mixture holds stiff peaks when you lift up the beater. Stir in cinnamon and grated lemon rind. Take about one-third of the egg white mixture and place in a separate bowl to use later on as a glaze. Fold ground almonds into remaining two-thirds of the batter and mix in thoroughly.

Take half the mixture at a time and pat it to a thickness of ³/₈ inch on a board or pastry cloth, lightly sprinkled with confectioners' sugar. If mixture seems sticky, dust the palms of your hands frequently with confectioners' sugar. Cut with a small star cutter and place on a greased cookie sheet. Brush the tops of each cookie with a generous coating of the reserved egg white mixture and bake in a preheated 300° oven for 20 minutes or until edges begin to get firm. Baking does not change the color, you will notice. Take the other half of the batter and repeat the operation. Makes approximately 5 dozen small cookies.

Mango Macadamia Syrup for Ice Cream

2 or 3 12-ounce cans preserved
    mangoes

2 cups sugar
2 cups Macadamia nuts

Bring the mangoes to a boil in a heavy saucepan, and add the sugar. Let them cook down for 8 to 10 minutes till nicely thickened. Add the Macadamia nuts and cool. Serve over ice cream with additional nuts, if you wish, and perhaps sherry-flavored whipped cream.

An Hors d'Oeuvre Supper for 10 or 12

Vegetables

TOMATO SALAD:

Scald or hold over a hot flame 4 large or 6 medium tomatoes. Peel and slice very thin. Arrange on a plate or in a ravier. Dribble 3 tablespoons oil and 1 or 2 teaspoons wine vinegar over slices, and sprinkle with chopped parsley and chopped fresh basil. Salt and pepper to taste.

CUCUMBER SALAD:

Peel 3 medium cucumbers. Split them lengthwise, and remove seeds with the aid of a spoon. Slice thinly into a soup plate. Sprinkle with 1½ tablespoons salt, and cover with another plate. Hold firmly, and shake plates well for several minutes. Let cucumbers stand for 1 hour. Rinse in cold water, and drain. Dress with oil, vinegar and freshly ground pepper—and if you wish, a little chopped fresh dill or chopped chervil.

GREEN PEPPER SALAD:

Seed three good-sized peppers, and cut them into thin shreds. Toss well with 6 tablespoons oil, 2 tablespoons wine vinegar, 1 clove garlic finely chopped, 1 teaspoon salt, and a few grinds of pepper. Allow to stand for 2 to 3 hours before serving.

CELERY SALAD:

Cut 1 bunch celery into thin, thin slices. Toss with the following dressing: 8 tablespoons olive oil, 3 tablespoons vinegar, 1 teaspoon tarragon, 1 teaspoon salt, ½ teaspoon freshly ground pepper, 2 tablespoons Dijon mustard, and 1 teaspoon dry mustard. Allow to stand for 2 to 3 hours.

ONIONS MONEGASQUE:

36 to 40 small white onions,
    of one size if possible
4 tablespoons olive oil
2/3 cup white wine
1/2 cup water
1 teaspoon salt
Sprig of fennel

1 teaspoon sugar
1/2 teaspoon thyme
1 bay leaf
Pinch of saffron
1 cup currants or
    sultana raisins

Peel onions and place in a skillet or sauteuse, and add oil, wine, water and seasonings. Simmer until onions are just crisply tender. Add saffron and currants or raisins, and cook down. Remove onions, reduce sauce, and then pour over the onions. Serve cool.

VARIATION: 1 or 2 tablespoons tomato paste may be added during cooking.

MUSHROOM SALAD:

Slice raw mushrooms very thin. To 1/2 pound sliced mushrooms add 1/2 cup Vinaigrette Sauce (*see* p. 338) and 1/4 cup finely chopped parsley.

ASPARAGUS TIPS:

Drain 2 cans white asparagus tips, and arrange in a ravier or serving dish. Garnish with chopped hard-boiled egg and chopped pimiento. Serve with a bowl of mayonnaise.

CORN SALAD:

Drain 2 cans of whole-kernel shoepeg corn, and dress with a good vinaigrette. Garnish with finely chopped green pepper and a little chopped sweet pickle.

POTATO SALAD:

See p. 359.

Fish

TUNA:

Buy tuna packed in olive oil, if possible. Serve plain in a ravier or dish.

SARDINES:

Buy extra good sardines in olive oil. Boneless and skinless ones are more elegant, and there are some delicious spiced varieties to be found in fancy food departments.

HERRING AND VEAL SALAD:

See p. 187.

See p. 187.

SMOKED FISH:

A ravier of smoked eel, salmon or whitefish; also, a layer of anchovies in a dish, garnished with chopped parsley and chopped green onion and dressed with a little olive oil and lemon juice. (Plenty of parsley is the secret of this combination.)

SHRIMP:

Cooked and shelled shrimp in an herbed mayonnaise.

LOBSTER:

If you wish to be especially generous, offer a lobster salad.

Meats and Eggs

ROLLS OF COLD BAKED HAM:

Your favorite type.

SALAMI:

Cornucopias with an herbed cream-cheese filling.

HEADCHEESE:

Homemade, if possible.

BEEF SALAD:

See p. 181.

SUMMER SAUSAGE:

Thinly sliced.

COLD BEEF ROLLS:

Rare roast beef rolled with kumquat mustard.

CERVELAT SALAD:

Peel and slice 3 cooked knockwurst. Combine with 2 cups thinly sliced boiled potatoes, 1 medium onion, chopped, 1 tablespoon capers, $1/3$ cup chopped parsley, and mayonnaise to bind.

CHICKEN:

Cold roast chicken cut in quarters. Arrange on a platter with watercress.

EGGS MAYONNAISE:

Hard-boiled eggs mashed with a good homemade mayonnaise.

EGGS IN JELLY:

Boil 12 eggs for 5 minutes. Place under cold water, then shell. Prepare jelly by softening $1/2$ envelopes gelatin in $1/4$ cup cold water. Add to 2 pints boiling consommé, and stir till dissolved. Pour a little into the bottom of 12 small round or oval molds. Allow to nearly set, then place a sprig of tarragon (if available) on jelly. Top with a slice of ham and then an egg. Cover with jelly. Let stand 1 hour or until jelly is set. Unmold.

Mexican Supper for 6

Serve tequila sours made according to the recipe for regular sours, except that tequila should be used in place of whiskey, and lime juice in place of lemon.

There are a number of good imported Mexican beers on the market. Offer a selection, well chilled, to offset the high seasoning of the food.

Serve Kahlua in hot coffee or with coffee.

Empanadas
Sole en Escabeche
Beef and Pork Chili with Eggs
Black Beans and Rice with Cracklings
Salsa Fria   Radish Salad
Fresh Mangoes

Empanadas

These delicious little turnovers may be filled with all sorts of savory tidbits. One of the best fillings is a mixture of chopped green chilies, olives and ham, bound with egg; other stuffings can be Jack cheese, chopped meats, or roast beef hash.

2¼ cups flour
¾ cup lard
1 teaspoon salt
½ teaspoon freshly ground
*   black pepper*
Dash Tabasco
Ice water
1 medium onion, chopped

2 cloves garlic, chopped fine
⅓ cup olive oil
1 pound roast beef hash
1 tablespoon chili powder
1 tablespoon chopped parsley,
*   or fresh cilantro if available*
1 egg, beaten

Blend the flour, lard, salt, pepper and Tabasco; add as little ice water as possible (about 2 tablespoons) to make a firm dough. Chill for an hour in the refrigerator. Roll out to about ⅛ inch in thickness on a floured board and cut into rounds as small or as large as you like, but large enough to hold stuffing when folded in half.

Sauté the onion and garlic in the oil. Add the hash and the rest of the ingredients and blend well. Place a spoonful of filling on one half of each round of dough. Fold the other half of the dough over the filling to make a half circle or turnover. Seal the edges with a little water and make indentations with the tines of a fork. Brush with beaten egg and bake in a 375° oven until nicely browned. This will take about 12 minutes.

Sole en Escabeche

3 tablespoons butter
3/4 cup olive oil
Flour
6 small fillets of sole
Salt, pepper
1 onion, thinly sliced and
separated into rings
1 green pepper, cut in thin rings
1 clove garlic, finely chopped

1/2 cup orange juice
Juice of 2 limes
1/4 teaspoon Tabasco
Orange slices
Lime slices
1 tablespoon orange zest
(orange part of rind, grated
or scraped)
Chopped fresh cilantro

Heat the butter and 1/4 cup of the oil. Flour the fish fillets lightly and sauté them until delicately browned on both sides and just tender. Season to taste with salt and pepper.

Arrange the fillets in a flat serving dish and top with onion rings, pepper rings and garlic. Combine the remaining 1/2 cup oil, orange juice, lime juice, Tabasco and salt and pepper to taste. Blend well and pour over the fish while it is still warm. Let stand in the refrigerator 12 to 24 hours.

To serve, garnish with orange slices, lime slices and orange zest. You may top with additional green pepper rings and chopped cilantro.

Beef and Pork Chili with Eggs

6 onions, coarsely chopped
2 cloves garlic, chopped
$1/3$ cup peanut oil
2 pounds beef chuck, cut in
  1-inch cubes
Flour
2 pounds pork loin, cut in
  1-inch cubes
1 tablespoon salt
$1^1/2$ teaspoons freshly
  ground black pepper
3 cups beef broth
(approximately)
$1/2$ cup tomato paste
$1/2$ teaspoon Tabasco
4 tablespoons chili powder
  (or to taste)
1 cup ground nuts (almonds,
  peanuts, cashews)
8 hard-cooked eggs, quartered
Chopped parsley, or cilantro
  if available
Black olives

Sauté the onions and garlic in oil, adding more oil if necessary. Dredge the beef cubes with flour and brown in the pan with the onions. Add and brown the pork cubes. Season all with the salt and pepper. Pour over enough broth to barely cover the meat. Add tomato paste and Tabasco. Simmer 1 hour.

  Stir in chili powder and continue simmering until the meat is just tender. Add ground nuts and taste for seasoning. Cook and stir until the broth thickens. Just before serving, add quartered hard-cooked eggs. Garnish with parsley and olives.

Black Beans and Rice with Cracklings

1 pound black beans
Water
4 slices rather lean salt pork
1 onion, stuck with 2 cloves
1 bay leaf
2 hot chili peppers
Salt and freshly ground
  black pepper
Tabasco
Cooked rice
Bacon cracklings
Sour cream

Soak the beans overnight. Drain and add enough fresh water to come about 2 inches above the beans. Add the salt pork, the onion, the bay leaf, hot chili peppers, salt, pepper and a dash of Tabasco. Bring to a boil, lower the heat and simmer until the beans are tender but not mushy. Remove the onion, bay leaf and hot peppers and discard. Remove the salt pork and chop rather fine. Mix the pork with the beans and taste for seasoning.

Serve this dish with cooked rice; garnish the beans and rice with cracklings. Provide a bowl of sour cream for those who like it with beans.

Salsa Fria

1 large can solid-pack tomatoes
1 can tomatillas (small green
    tomatoes)
1 can peeled green chilies,
    finely chopped
2 onions, finely chopped

10 scallions, finely chopped
Salt and freshly ground
    black pepper
1 teaspoon oregano
Chopped fresh cilantro if
    available

Chop the canned tomatoes coarsely. Peel the papery cover off the tomatillas. Blend the tomatoes, tomatillas, chilies, onions, scallions, salt and pepper to taste, oregano and a little cilantro. Chill.

Radish Salad

Slice red radishes very thin and marinate for several hours in oil, vinegar, salt and pepper. Serve on fresh crisp greens.

COCKTAIL
PARTIES

The ever popular cocktail party is an inferior form of entertaining at best, and there is a tendency to make it formal on occasion—something it was never meant to be. By all means have your house looking its best, use your best crystal and china, and have the food impeccably turned out, but don't be chi-chi. The results may be silly. Unless they are small gatherings around a tray with bottles and ice, cocktail parties should be planned so that the service is efficient and quick. Don't try to set up a professional bar in your house unless you have a barman to go with it, and you will need two if it is a largish party, and more if it is the "annual crush," which so many people use as a way to pay their social debts (and it is not really a very polite way). A large party will also need someone to tidy up from time to time. Some guests love to trail through a party leaving a wake of glasses, napkins and cigarette messes.

If you must do with a minimum of help or none at all, serve three varieties of drinks—and make good drinks—rather than attempt to offer a selection. The same holds true of cocktail food. Better to have two memorable snacks than hundreds of undistinguished canapés. In the menus provided here there is usually one item or two of substantial food. It goes without saying that the food should be attractive to look at and tasty as well.

While the cocktail party is the most popular way of entertaining it can also be the most difficult, since there is so much going on all at once. Don't make your drinks too weak, or your party won't be very lively. Neither make them too generous, or you will have a bunch of drunks on your hands. Plan four drinks per person, and have some supplies in reserve. Neither the host nor the hostess should drink unless it is something light. To give a good party you must be on the alert, though you appear to be entirely at ease. What a delight it can be to settle down later with your shoes off and have a few drinks in peace and quiet.

LARGE PARTIES

A Cocktail Party à la Helen Brown

Helen Evans Brown came one year to teach my classes the preparation of hors d'oeuvre. These were her suggestions for a party. Delicious they all are, and varied. Keep the drinks simple and offer the basic selection—Scotch, bourbon, martinis, sherry and perhaps Perrier for the nondrinkers.

Snitters
Rillettes or Rillons
Chinese Ginger and Pork Balls
Stuffed Mushrooms
Peanut Crisps

Snitters

Make tiny, open-faced sandwiches, using a variety of breads cut very thin and generously spread with sweet butter. Listed below are the delicacies you might use for fillings, together with a selection of garnishes. Be as deft and creative as you can in assembling fillings and garnishes. These can be lovely to look at, and delicious.

Fillings

Smoked Salmon	Small Shrimp
Smoked Sturgeon	Crab
Rare Beef	Lobster
Ham	Eggs
Tongue	Terrine
Veal	Cheese
Pâté	Liver Paste

Garnishes

Sliced Lemon	
Olives	Anchovies
Tomato	Parsley
Chopped Onions	Cucumber
Fried Onions	Chopped Aspic
Pickles	Scrambled Eggs
Prunes	Dill

Serve a bowl of crisp raw vegetables with the sandwiches and a mustard mayonnaise for dipping.

Rillettes or Rillons

1 pound lean pork, diced fine	*1 onion, chopped*
2 teaspoons salt	*¼ teaspoon ground cloves*
Freshly ground pepper	*¼ teaspoon thyme*
¼ teaspoon nutmeg	*1 bay leaf*
1¼ pounds pork fat, diced fine	*Water to cover*

(The difference between the two is that the rillettes are ground or pounded, the rillons left in small dice.) Mix ingredients, except bay leaf, cover with water, add bay leaf, and cook until the water has evaporated and the meat has browned. Remove bay leaf, drain off fat, and reserve. Return meat to heat and cook until crisp and brown. For rillettes, mash in a mortar or grind. Rillons are left as they are. Pack in pots, cover with reserved fat. Serve cold with toast or French bread.

Chinese Ginger and Pork Balls

1 pound ground pork
2 tablespoons minced green
    onions
1 egg
$^1/_2$ teaspoon salt

$^1/_4$ cup minced water chestnuts
1 tablespoon grated fresh ginger
1 tablespoon soy sauce
Cracker crumbs, if needed,
    to make proper consistency

Mix all ingredients, form into balls, then roll in cornstarch. Fry in deep fat (or pan fry). Serve on toothpicks.

Stuffed Mushrooms

Stuff large mushroom caps with the above mixture and sprinkle with sesame seeds. Bake in a 350° oven for 25 to 30 minutes.

Peanut Crisps

1 loaf good white bread, thinly sliced
2 cups chopped salted peanuts

1 cup peanut oil
$1^1/_4$ cups peanut butter

Cut crusts from bread and reserve. Cut each slice in half. Dry bread, including crusts, overnight in a warm, unlighted oven or other warm place. Roll crusts to make crumbs, and mix with chopped salted peanuts. Combine peanut oil and peanut butter. Dip bread in the oil–peanut butter mixture, then roll in crumb mixture. Allow to dry. These will keep for weeks.

A Cocktail Party for 20

The drinks should be simple—Scotch, bourbon, martinis, gin and tonic, sherry. Blend some martinis ahead of time and chill them.

Salted Filberts
Potted Shrimp Paste
Melba Toast Fingers
Hot Roast Loin of Smoked Pork
Rye Bread Rounds
German and French Mustard
Spiced Onions   Cherry Tomatoes
Sweet and Sour Pickles
Thin Onion Sandwiches

Salted Filberts

Pour 1 to 2 pounds filberts onto flat baking sheets. Add 1/3 cup oil to each pan. Bake at 350° till nuts are delicately toasted. Sprinkle with salt—kosher salt is excellent for this—and shake well. Cool in baking pans.

Potted Shrimp Paste

2 pounds shrimp	*1/2 pound softened butter*
Salted water	*(approximately)*
1 clove garlic	*3/4 teaspoon onion juice*
1 bay leaf	*1/2 teaspoon mace*
1/3 cup wine vinegar	*Chopped parsley*

Cook the shrimp in salted water to which you have added the garlic clove, bay leaf and wine vinegar. Three minutes after boiling should be ample. Remove shrimp, cool and clean. Chop coarsely and cream with softened butter, onion juice and mace. Add salt if necessary.

Spoon into a serving bowl, and garnish with chopped parsley and a few whole shrimp. Serve with homemade Melba Toast (*see* p. 318–19), cut in strips about an inch wide.

Hot Roast Loin of Smoked Pork

Most good butchers carry smoked loin of pork. Buy a piece weighing 4 pounds or more. Roast in a 350° oven only long enough to heat through. Serve with thin slices of rye and pumpernickel and the mustards.

NOTE: You may baste the pork with Madeira or port during cooking, if you wish.

Spiced Onions

5 pounds small white onions, peeled	1 pint wine
	1 pint wine vinegar
Salted water	1¹/₂ pounds sugar
1 large lump alum	2 bay leaves
1 quart cider vinegar	1 package pickling spices

Soak onions overnight in salted water. Drain, and pack onions in a large jar or crock with the alum. Combine the vinegar, wine, wine vinegar, sugar, bay leaves, and the spices. Heat to the boiling point, and boil for 4 minutes. Pour over the onions. Seal or cover the jar, and allow the onions to stand for 2 weeks before eating. These are thoroughly delicious.

Thin Onion Sandwiches

Cut good white bread into quite thin slices, and butter well. Salt and sprinkle with chopped parsley. Add thin onion slices, and top with another slice of buttered bread. Trim crusts, and cut into strips or "fingers." Pack in foil, and refrigerate till needed.

NOTE: Cucumber sandwiches may be made in the same manner. Simply substitute thinly sliced cucumbers for the onion.

Cocktails for 25

You will need a barman and a waiter or two for this fairly elaborate party, and, if you can manage it, have help in the kitchen as well. Serve the usual drinks, but be sure you also offer such light things as sherry or Lillet, fruit juices, and Perrier.

Salted Almonds
Salted Garlic Peanuts
Teriyaki Strips   French Bread
Bacon-Wrapped Prunes and Dates
Cheeseburger Balls
Shrimp with Green Mayonnaise
Anchovy Radishes
Foie Gras Sandwiches
Salmon-Dill Paste with Toast

Teriyaki Strips

1 quart Japanese soy sauce	1 1/2 cups sherry
1 pint olive or peanut oil	1 tablespoon salt
12 garlic cloves	1 tablespoon Tabasco
1 1/2 cups slivered preserved	6 flank steaks (any you don't
or candied ginger	use can be frozen)

Combine all the flavorings, and marinate steaks for several hours. Broil quickly—3 to 4 minutes to a side—and slice with a sharp knife in thin, diagonal slices. Serve on bread. Cook only one or two steaks at a time so they do not get cold.

Bacon-Wrapped Prunes

72 prunes   72 bacon strips
72 strips Swiss cheese

Soak the prunes in water for 1 hour. Cover and bring to a boil. Cool in the water. Drain, and remove the pits. Fill each prune with a piece of cheese, wrap in bacon, and secure with a toothpick. Broil 4 to 5 inches from heat. Serve hot.

Bacon-Wrapped Dates

72 fresh dates   72 bacon strips
Dry sherry to cover

Pit the dates, cover with dry sherry, and soak for several hours. Drain (reserve the sherry for a fruit cup later in the week), wrap with bacon, and broil till bacon is crisp. Serve hot.

Cheeseburger Balls

3 pounds lean ground chuck $1^1/_2$ teaspoons salt
3 cloves of garlic, finely chopped 1 teaspoon freshly ground
3 teaspoons Dijon mustard   black pepper
$^1/_4$ pound crumbled Roquefort   Butter and oil
   cheese

Combine all ingredients except butter and oil, form into tiny balls, and sauté in equal amounts of butter and oil. Shake the pan vigorously during sautéing so balls will roll and keep their shape. When done to your taste—do not overcook—remove to a platter, and impale each ball on a toothpick. Serve very hot—with a mustard-flavored Hollandaise, if you wish.

Shrimp with Green Mayonnaise

4 to 5 pounds (about 10 to
  15 to a pound) large shrimp
2 gallons water
1 cup vinegar
1 bottle white wine (⁴/₅ quart)

3 garlic cloves
2 bay leaves
1 teaspoon thyme
1 onion, stuck with cloves
1 sprig parsley

Clean shrimp, leaving tail shell intact. Combine liquids and seasonings, and bring to a boil. Simmer for 10 minutes, then add shrimp and cook for 3 to 4 minutes. Drain and cool. Serve on a bed of parsley with green mayonnaise.

Green Mayonnaise

1 quart mayonnaise
1 cup finely chopped raw
  spinach
2 tablespoons chopped fresh

tarragon
¹/₂ cup chopped parsley
2 tablespoons chopped chives
1 tablespoon Dijon mustard

Combine all ingredients, and blend well. Allow to stand for 2 hours before serving.

Anchovy Radishes

Clean several bunches of radishes, and crisp in cold water. Drain. Wrap an anchovy fillet around each radish and secure with a toothpick. Serve very cold.

Foie Gras Sandwiches

Butter thin slices of white bread, preferably homemade, with sweet butter. Spread with mousse of foie gras and top with another slice of bread. Cut in strips or fingers. Chill.

Salmon-Dill Paste

1 pound smoked salmon	Sour cream
1 large onion, finely chopped	Dill
2 tablespoons fresh dill	Parsley
Mayonnaise	

Dice salmon, and combine with onion and dill. Add enough mayonnaise and sour cream to bind ingredients and make a paste. Chill. Garnish with dill and parsley, and serve with pumpernickel or rye bread; or with tiny brioche, which can be purchased at some bake shops.

━━━━━━━━━━

A Cocktail Party for 30

Here is a party that embodies my approach to the cocktail hour. Instead of tray after tray of tiny morsels of food, we have a good, hearty offering. Serve the usual variety of drinks, but be sure to include some beer, champagne and chilled dry sherry.

The steak tartare should be served in a bowl surrounded with a selection of breads and crackers; or molded into a loaf and served on a chopping board. Pass the spareribs with plates and small paper napkins. Along with this, serve either a bowl of freshly shelled peas or fresh, raw asparagus tips—whichever is in season.

Steak Tartare
Glazed Spareribs
Raw Peas or Raw Asparagus Tips with
Coarse Salt and Pepper
Freshly Roasted Salted Peanuts
Knockwurst with Shallot Mustard

━━━━━━━━━━

Steak Tartare

Use top round, sirloin or tenderloin. You will need about 5 pounds. Have it ground just before you use it. Using two knives, blend into the meat in the following order:

1) 18 to 20 anchovy fillets, well chopped. After blending, mold the meat into a mound, and do so after adding each of the ingredients.

2) 1¹/₂ cups or more finely chopped onion.

3) Make a crater in the center of the mound, and add 5 egg yolks, 1¹/₂ teaspoons salt, several grinds of black pepper, and several generous dashes of Tabasco.

4) 2 tablespoons Dijon mustard, about ¹/₂ cup capers, and about ¹/₃ cup finely cut chives.

5) About ¹/₄ cup cognac.

Be sure all ingredients are thoroughly blended, then form into a loaf or loaves for serving. Sprinkle with chopped parsley if you wish. Keep chilled until ready to serve; and perhaps serve half the quantity at a time.

Glazed Spareribs

You will need about 20 pounds. Roast them, a few pounds at a time, with salt and pepper for 45 minutes in a 350° oven. This can be done well ahead of time. Cool the ribs, and cut them into individual portions.

Prepare a glazing sauce for each five pounds of spareribs:

1 cup Japanese soy sauce	5 cloves garlic, finely chopped
1¹/₂ cups tomato catsup	1 teaspoon Tabasco
1¹/₂ cups honey	

Mix all ingredients thoroughly. Place spareribs on racks over baking pans, brush well with the glaze, and roast for 10 minutes at 450° or until they are glossy and crisp. Baste several times during baking.

Knockwurst with Shallot Mustard

Buy 25 or 30 juicy knockwurst, and boil them in batches as you need them. Slice them in rounds, and serve with:

1 cup Dijon mustard	¹/₂ cup chopped shallots
1 cup Durkee dressing	or scallions
¹/₂ cup catsup	

Blend ingredients thoroughly. Add additional mustard to taste. This is even more delicious when a little chopped fresh tarragon is added.

A Large Cocktail Crush for 40

This is one of those parties which starts at about 6 or 7 o'clock and goes on till about 8:30 or 9:00 and provides enough food so that people do not need to go to dinner. I'd set up a full bar and also have some champagne and white wine with cassis. Thus you are apt to satisfy everyone. Coffee is a good idea at about 9 o'clock, with some sweet biscuits, perhaps.

Roast Beef with Mustards
Raw Vegetables in Ice
Cheese Board
Nuts
Olives

Roast Beef

I produce a full 7-rib roast and usually have it roasted by a restaurant where I dine often. It is delivered hot and served after a half hour. The chill is never in it, and it slices magnificently for sandwiches on thinly sliced dark bread and French bread. Serve a variety of mustards, as well as Burgundy mustard and mustard butter.

Burgundy Mustard

2 cups Dijon mustard
12 small sour pickles
1 small sweet pickle

1 teaspoon dried tarragon or
1½ tablespoons fresh tarragon

Chop the pickles and tarragon very fine and blend with the mustard. Garnish with finely chopped pickle.

Mustard Butter

Cream ½ pound sweet butter, and blend in 2 teaspoons dry mustard, 1 teaspoon freshly ground black pepper and a few drops lemon juice.

Raw Vegetables in Ice

Serve bowls of delicious raw vegetables in crushed ice. The usual seasonals, such as celery, carrots, scallions and radishes, can be enhanced by cauliflower flowerets, broccoli flowerets, raw asparagus, thinly sliced turnips and raw mushrooms.

Serve with the following sauce, for dunking: To ¹/₂ pint of homemade olive-oil Mayonnaise (*see* p. 336) add ¹/₂ pint sour cream and the ingredients below.

3 garlic cloves, finely chopped
2 tablespoons chopped capers
¹/₂ cup chopped parsley

1 teaspoon Tabasco
¹/₂ cup chopped chives

Cheese Board

I find that Switzerland Swiss is perfect for such a party as this. Put a large piece on a cheese board, and near it knives for cutting, crackers, water biscuits and breads.

Nuts and Olives

Salted almonds and filberts and both the Greek olives and the tiny Spanish ones are always welcome at a party. You can have bowls of these around in a number of places.

Another Large Cocktail Party for 50

Here again you should set up a full bar, including some good wine and chilled beer. The food makes this fairly buffet-ish, although it is not a full supper. This could also be turned into a late after-theatre party, at which you would serve only beer and wines.

Tiny Danish pastries and coffee may be served at the end of cock-tail time as a signal that the party is over.

Hot Corned Beef and Pastrami
Mustards   Pickles   Horseradish
Cherry Tomatoes   Sliced Onions
Scallions   Chopped Chicken Livers
Toasted Salted Walnuts   Sardine Paste
Bread, Rolls, Matzos, Biscuits
Danish Pastry   Coffee

Hot Corned Beef and Pastrami

I suggest that you order this from a good restaurant or Jewish deli-catessen. Have someone on hand to carve it for you, and carve it to order as the guests indicate their preference. Provide a wonderful selection of bread and rolls, sweet butter, a variety of mustards, thinly sliced pickles, fresh horseradish, and sliced onions.

Chopped Chicken Livers

2 pounds chicken fat	1 1/2 pounds chicken or duck
3 large or 4 medium onions,	livers
finely chopped	Salt and pepper

Chop the chicken fat in small pieces, and try out in a heavy skillet till the fat is thoroughly liquid and cracklings begin to form. Add 1/2 cup finely chopped onion, and cook till nicely browned. Strain through cheese cloth, and reserve both the fat and the cracklings. Place remaining raw onions in a heavy pot with a cover and cook in 4 tablespoons chicken fat. When the onions are soft and delicately colored, salt and pepper to taste.

Sauté the livers in the remaining chicken fat till they are just cooked through. Remove and chop rather finely. Toss in the pan with the fat, juices, onions and cracklings. Season to taste and cool. Serve in a chilled bowl with matzos and other good crackers and biscuits.

Sardine Paste

1 pound cream cheese
1 large onion, grated
1/2 cup chopped parsley
1/2 cup chopped chives
2 tablespoons or more

lemon juice
3 tins boneless and skinless
    sardines
Salt and pepper
Paprika

Mash the cheese and cream it thoroughly. Beat in the onion, chopped parsley, chives, and lemon juice. Mash the sardines and beat into the cream cheese mixture. Correct the seasoning. Sprinkle top with paprika and additional chopped parsley, and serve with wedges of lemon. This is delicious spread on crackers, biscuits or thinly sliced bread.

You may double this recipe, if desired.

Small Parties

A Simple Cocktail Party for 6 or 8

Offer an assortment of cocktails and drinks without attempting to produce everything in the bartender's handbook. You might confine yourself to martinis, daiquiris and Scotch, for example. The feature of the party will be the pâté de campagne.

Pâté de Campagne, Provençale
Fresh Toast   Anchovied Radishes
Garlic-Flavored Olives

Pâté de Campagne, Provençale

A delicious country pâté, easy to make and always welcome.

2 pounds lean pork, very coarsely chopped
2 pounds veal, chopped rather finely
1 pound ground pork liver
1 pound fresh pork siding or fat bacon, diced
6 garlic cloves, minced
3 eggs
1/2 teaspoon Quatre Épices (see p. 331)

1/3 cup cognac or whiskey
1 tablespoon basil
1 tablespoon salt (approximately)
1 teaspoon freshly ground black pepper
Bacon or salt pork (enough to line terrine)

Combine all the meats and seasonings. If you wish to test for seasoning, sauté a small piece—about 1 tablespoon—in butter till cooked through.

Line a good-sized straight-sided terrine or baking dish with salt pork or bacon. A 2½-quart soufflé dish, heavy pottery dish or a large round Pyrex dish are ideal. Fill with the mixture and form a well-rounded top. Place a few strips of bacon or salt pork over the top, and bake at 325° for 2 to 2½ hours. I always cover it with a sheet or foil for the first hour or so of cooking. It will break away from the sides a bit when done.

Remove from the oven and cool. Weight it after the first half hour of cooling. Serve from the terrine or dish in generous slices with a sharp, heavy knife. Cover tightly with foil when placed in the refrigerator.

Anchovied Radishes

Select tiny crisp radishes. Clean thoroughly and soak in ice water for an hour or so. Wrap each radish with an anchovy fillet, and secure with a toothpick.

Garlic-Flavored Olives

Buy the super-colossal California ripe olives. For 2 to 3 cups olives, add 3 tablespoons olive oil, 3 finely minced garlic cloves, and 1 tablespoon grated lemon rind. Let stand for 1 or 2 hours before serving.

Cocktails for 12 to 15, with a Mexican Flavor

Serve your favorite potables, and in addition offer tequila sours.

Chili con Queso   Breadsticks
Fritos   Celery
Fried Chicken Legs
Cheese Board   Bread and Crackers
Caviar-Stuffed Eggs

Chili con Queso

2 cloves garlic, finely chopped
1 29-ounce can Italian plum
   tomatoes
Salt and freshly ground
   black pepper
2 cans peeled green chilies,

finely chopped
1¹/₂ cups Velouté Sauce
   (see p. 332)
1 pound shredded Jack
   or cheddar cheese

Combine garlic, tomatoes, salt and pepper to taste. Cook down for 20 minutes over medium flame, stirring occasionally. Add chopped green chilies (be certain to remove the tiny seeds before chopping). Cook till thick and pasty. Add cream sauce and cheese, and place in chafing dish or electric skillet over warm heat.

Use for dipping breadsticks, fritos and celery.

Fried Chicken Legs

Buy 24 to 28 chicken legs. If you must buy thighs too, do so—use for another meal. Dredge with highly seasoned flour, using paprika, cayenne, dry mustard, salt and pepper. Fry the legs, a few at a time, according to your favorite method. Serve hot.

Cheese Board

Buy 4 or 5 varieties of cheese—perhaps Canadian cheddar, Roquefort, Switzerland Emmenthal or Gruyère, or Brie—and keep at room temperature for several hours before serving. Serve on a cheese board or a marble cheese dish with butter, and a selection of breads and English biscuits.

Caviar-Stuffed Eggs

18 to 20 eggs, hard-boiled
   and shelled
³/₄ cup or more red caviar
¹/₄ cup grated onion

Dash Tabasco
Mayonnaise, if needed
Chopped parsley

Cut eggs carefully into halves lengthwise. Remove yolks, place in a bowl and mash with the caviar and seasonings until they form a paste. Stuff the whites either with a pastry bag and rosette tube or with spoon and fork. Decorate with a dab of caviar and a touch of parsley.

An Apéritif Party for 12

Apéritifs are ideal for a group you wish to entertain very informally. Have a selection of such items as St. Raphael, Dubonnet, Byrrh, Campari, Cinzano, Cinzano Bianco, Punt y Mes, and sherry (preferably Amontillado, Manzanilla or Montilla). All of these delicious drinks should be served chilled or on the rocks, and, of course the Campari is excellent with soda or combined with sweet vermouth to make an Americano. The food should be casual, in the spirit of the party.

Pissaladière
Open-Faced Cucumber Sandwiches
Radishes Watercress

Pissaladière

This is the southern French version of pizza.

Brioche dough (see p. 344) *olive oil*
3 large onions, finely chopped *Anchovy fillets*
6 tablespoons butter or *Black Italian-style olives*

Mix one full recipe of brioche. After the first rising, punch down the dough and roll out ½ inch thick. Arrange in square or oblong baking tins. While the brioche is rising a second time, sauté the onions in butter or oil for 3 minutes. Cover and steam until they are soft and tender. Season to taste. Spread the onion over the brioche. Next arrange a lattice of anchovy fillets. Place black olives in the spaces between the fillets. Bake at 375° till the brioche is crisp and cooked through. Serve warm.

VARIATIONS: Add a spreading of tomato paste and sprinkle with finely chopped garlic and chopped fresh basil. Add thin slices of peperoni or salami.

Open-Faced Cucumber Sandwiches

24 very thin slices good white
    bread
Mayonnaise or Durkee dressing

24 slices hard-boiled egg
24 slices cucumber
24 capers or 24 rolled anchovies

Spread bread with mayonnaise or dressing. Cut in rounds with a biscuit or canapé cutter. Each round should be slightly larger than an egg or cucumber slice. Place a slice of cucumber and a slice of egg on the bread, and top with a caper or rolled anchovy. Serve as soon as possible, before bread becomes soggy.

A Champagne Party for 10 or 12

Nothing is pleasanter, to my way of thinking, than a party with good champagne and plenty of time to relax and talk. This is possible with 10 or 12 guests. Be sure there is plenty of sitting space. The food should be simple but with a quality of elegance.

Gougère
Tiny Sausage Rolls
Virginia Ham Sandwiches
Warm Salted Almonds

Gougère

Pâte à Choux (see p. 345)
1/2 cup grated Switzerland
    cheese

1/2 cup finely diced
    Switzerland cheese
1/2 teaspoon Tabasco

Make one full recipe of pâte à choux. Combine the grated and diced cheese with the choux paste and Tabasco, and fill a pastry bag, fitted with a large rosette tube. Force the paste into a ring or into individual rosettes on a buttered cookie sheet. Bake at 375° until well puffed and browned, or until the paste no longer tears. Serve warm.

Tiny Sausage Rolls

Cream Cheese Pastry or   pork sausages
    Plain Pastry (see   1 egg
      pp. 348 and 347)   3 tablespoons cream
24 to 36 well seasoned small

Make one full recipe of pastry. Poach the sausages in boiling water for 5 minutes. Drain, and cool. Roll out the pastry, and cut into squares just large enough to encase the sausages completely. Arrange on a baking sheet. Brush with egg beaten with cream. Bake at 375° until the pastry is nicely browned and crisp. Serve warm.

Virginia Ham Sandwiches

You must use a real Smithfield ham for this. You may buy slices from most good delicatessens, or you may buy a whole ham ready-cooked and ready for the table.

Spread very thin slices of white and rye bread with sweet butter. Brush ever so lightly with a good mustard, and arrange paper-thin slices of ham on the bread. Top with another buttered slice of bread, and cut into fingers or triangles.

Warm Salted Almonds

Make your own salted almonds with fine Jordan almonds and butter and salt. Either cook them slowly atop the stove in a heavy skillet, or roast them in the oven at 350° with plenty of butter and coarse salt. Do not let them overcook, or they will have a scorched flavor. I find that if I use half butter and half peanut oil it gives the nuts a most pleasant texture.

For ten persons I would toast two pounds of nuts. Any left over may be frozen or kept in an airtight container.

A Small Elegant Cocktail Party for 10

This is the type of cocktail party you give for a very close friend who loves the elegant things in life or for a visiting mogul who is tremendously important to you or to the community. In other words, it's a smash.

Fill a large silver punch bowl with ice, and in it chill bottles of champagne, vodka and zubrowka and perhaps aquavit. If guests demand other drinks, have the makings at hand, but the chilled selection in the punch bowl is appropriate for the food to be served.

Bring out small plates, knives and forks, and your best linen.

Caviar
Smoked Salmon
Foie Gras

Caviar

Be certain it is the best, and serve it in a bowl of ice with a caviar spoon or fork. Put it in charge of someone who knows how to serve it without breaking the eggs and creating havoc with your most expensive brand. With it serve lemon wedges, chopped onion and chopped egg, yolk as well as white. Keep fresh toast coming, and have dark bread, butter, and, if you wish, sour cream. You had better count on at least a kilo of caviar.

Smoked Salmon

If Scotch salmon is available, by all means serve it; if not, then certainly have the best Nova Scotia that you can find. Have someone on hand who can cut salmon beautifully in thin, longish slices and perform in the dining room. Otherwise, have it perfectly sliced beforehand. Serve capers, oil and lemon. Thinly sliced onion will appeal to many, as well. Pass the pepper grinder. Pumpernickel, hot toast and rye bread, sliced thin and buttered, are splendid with this.

Foie Gras

If you can get fresh foie gras, as is sometimes possible in New York and other cities, this will be superb. Otherwise, you will have to provide a large crock or two of the preserved goose liver. Here again it is important to have someone serve it properly. Toast and butter are necessary accompaniments.

ENTERTAINING
OUTDOORS

INDOOR–OUTDOOR COOKING

Outdoor cooking has been a staple form of cookery for centuries, but it is only since World War II that it has gained general popularity in this country. There have always been garden parties and dinners on the terrace, but there has been nothing like the mass outdoor cooking that now takes place in suburban patios and on city terraces across the nation. The appeal lies in its simplicity, the unique flavor that can be achieved, and the chance to escape from the kitchen into the open air. Furthermore, its rugged approach to cooking gives the man of the house a chance to shine. Frequently it is a cooperative enterprise, with the host tending the grill or spit while the hostess makes preparation in the kitchen. Using both indoors and outdoors this way, all sorts of variations are possible—for example, an outdoor meal with embellishments from the kitchen; an indoor meal with one course prepared on the outdoor grill and brought to the dining room; or a first course prepared outdoors and served there with drinks, while the remainder of the meal is prepared and served indoors. In any case, cooking in the open air brings a novel and informal touch to any meal. There is no more delicious way to prepare meats if the grilling is done with care. Make certain you have proper equipment, and avoid overcooking.

An Outdoor Steak Luncheon for 6 to 8

Seafood Plate, Provençale
Steak with Anchovy Butter
Hash Brown Potatoes
Pea and Mushroom Salad
Soufflé Glacé Grand Marnier

Seafood Plate, Provençale

Greens
4 lobsters, poached, split,
  claws cracked
1½ pounds cooked lump
  crabmeat
3 pounds large shrimp (10 to
  15 per pound), poached

and shelled
2 pounds bay scallops,
  marinated in lime juice
  for 1 hour
2 quarts mussels, scrubbed
  and steamed open

Place cracked ice on a large platter, decorated with greens, and arrange the seafood on the greens as attractively as possible—the lobster around the outside, a great pile of pink shrimp in the center, crabmeat on one side of the platter, and bay scallops on the other. First drain the lime juice from the scallops and mix the scallops with 1½ teaspoons salt and 2 tablespoons chopped parsley. Trim the platter with mussels on the half shell. Serve this sumptuous plate with sauce Provençale.

FOR THE SAUCE PROVENÇALE:

2½ pints homemade
  Mayonnaise, made with
  olive oil (see p. 336)
2 hard-boiled eggs, chopped
2 garlic cloves, minced

2 tablespoons chopped capers
2 tablespoons chopped parsley
2 tablespoons Dijon mustard
Salt and pepper to taste

Combine all ingredients, and allow to mellow for 2 hours before serving.

Steak with Anchovy Butter

2 large sirloin steaks,
    2½ inches thick

Salt and pepper

Rub steak well with coarse salt and freshly ground pepper. Broil over coals at medium temperature, turning several times. Increase heat at the end of cooking time if a char is desired. Slice, and add a spoon of anchovy butter to each serving.

FOR THE ANCHOVY BUTTER:

¾ pound softened butter
2 garlic cloves, minced

12 anchovy fillets, finely chopped
2 tablespoons chopped parsley

Blend butter and seasonings thoroughly. Chill for several hours before serving.

Hash Brown Potatoes

See p. 356.

Pea and Mushroom Salad

3 pounds tender fresh peas
    or 2 packages frozen small
    peas
Boiling salted water
1 tablespoon sugar

¼ cup Vinaigrette Sauce (see
    p. 338)
½ pound mushrooms, sliced
2 tablespoons fresh basil or
    1 teaspoon dried basil

Cook the peas in boiling salted water to which you have added the sugar. When just tender, drain, and add the vinaigrette sauce. Cool. Toss with the raw mushrooms, to which you have added the basil.

Soufflé Glacé Grand Marnier

5 eggs, separated
2/3 cup sugar
1 envelope unflavored gelatin
1/4 cup cold water

1/3 cup Grand Marnier
1 cup heavy cream, whipped
Macaroons
Candied cherries

Beat together the egg yolks and sugar in the top of a double boiler, and continue beating over hot (not boiling) water, until the mixture has thickened. Meanwhile let the gelatin soften in the cold water. Stir the gelatin into the egg and sugar mixture until completely dissolved. Whip the cream until firm, and put in the refrigerator. Then place the top half of the double boiler over a bowl of ice cubes or crushed ice, and beat again until the mixture is cold. Just before the gelatin has begun to set, fold in the whipped cream. Beat the egg whites until firm but not dry, and also fold into the mixture.

Spoon into a 1½-quart soufflé dish around which you have tied a collar of paper or foil, lightly brushed with vegetable oil on the inner side and extending 3 to 4 inches above the edge of the dish. Chill in the refrigerator for 4 to 6 hours. Remove the collar, and decorate the top with crushed macaroons and candied cherries.

An Indoor-Outdoor Buffet for 20

This is a delicious summer meal and one that has an unusually good blending of flavors. The roast takes long, slow cooking over the coals; the vegetables can come from the kitchen at the last minute; and the dessert can be made early in the morning. Chilled rosé is certainly the only wine to go with this food. You may want to precede it with long, cool drinks—perhaps gin and bitter lemon or tonic, garnished with a slice of lime or a sprig of mint.

Melon
Double Roast Loin of Pork with Chinese Sauce
Sautéed Peppers and Onions   Crisp Rolls
Custard Angel Food Cake   Pineapple Ice

Melon

Serve wedges of peeled honeydew or Persian melon with coarsely ground black pepper and a little salt.

Double Roast Loin of Pork with Chinese Sauce

Have two loins of pork boned and tied together, with the fat outside. Rub the roast well with salt and a touch of rosemary. Balance on the spit and roast over good coals, allowing about 25 minutes per pound. Place a pan to catch the drippings as the roast turns. It should be basted at least six or eight times during cooking with Chinese Sauce: Combine 1/2 cup soy sauce, 1/2 cup tomato catsup, 1/4 cup honey, and 3 cloves garlic finely chopped.

The pork should be roasted to 170° internal temperature and allowed to stand for 20 minutes before carving. Baste with the drippings and sauce while it is standing. Serve the basting sauce with the pork, first adding 1 1/2 tablespoons dry mustard and toasted sesame seeds to taste.

This roast is also delicious when served cold with a mustard mayonnaise and a potato salad.

Sautéed Peppers and Onions

6 to 8 large green or sweet red
  peppers
2 Italian red onions
1/2 cup olive oil

1 clove garlic
Salt and pepper
1 to 2 teaspoons wine vinegar

Remove seeds from peppers and cut into strips about 1 inch wide. Peel and slice onions moderately thin. Heat olive oil in a skillet, and add the garlic clove. Then add the peppers and sauté slowly for 20 minutes. Add the onions, and cook covered for 10 to 12 minutes. Uncover, and continue cooking till peppers and onions are just tender. Salt and pepper to taste, and add a touch of wine vinegar just before serving.

Custard Angel Food Cake

This was traditionally cooled, sliced, and spread with a custard filling; hence, the name.

1 1/4 cups sugar
1/2 cup water
8 eggs, separated
1 cup sifted cake flour

1/2 teaspoon salt
1 teaspoon cream of tartar
1 teaspoon vanilla

Combine sugar and water, and boil till it spins a thread (230° on a sugar thermometer). Beat egg yolks till very light and lemon-colored. While continuing to beat, pour hot syrup over yolks in a thin stream. The mixture should thicken noticeably. Sift the flour and salt seven or eight times, and measure. After the egg mixture has cooled to room temperature, fold in the flour.

Beat the whites till frothy, add the cream of tartar, and continue beating till the whites are stiff but not dry. Fold into the flour mixture, and add the vanilla. Pour into an ungreased tube pan, and bake at 300° for 1 1/2 to 1 3/4 hours.

This is delicious served with a dusting of powdered sugar and accompanied by a pineapple ice.

An Outdoor Dinner for 4 or 6

Here is a good, simple enough dinner enlivened by a few flourishes. Drink a young Beaujolais or a Juliénas with dinner. Have cognac with coffee after the blueberry tarts.

Figs with Bacon
Double Entrecôte with Mustard Hollandaise
Deep Fried Onion Rings
Sliced Tomatoes with Basil
Blueberry Tarts with Whipped Cream

Figs with Bacon

2 or 3 figs per person
1 slice bacon for each fig

Freshly ground black pepper

Grill bacon over coals, wrap around figs, and serve with black pepper. Or place figs in the middle of a platter and surround with crisp bacon, allowing each person to help himself. This makes a delicious combination of flavors.

Double Entrecôte with Mustard Hollandaise

Double entrecôtes are from the first three or four ribs of beef. They should be cut one or two ribs thick, and the bone should be trimmed so that the steak resembles a gargantuan French lamb chop.

Grill the entrecôtes over medium coals to the state of doneness you prefer. If it is a 1-rib steak cut full, it will take about 20 minutes for quite rare. If it is a really thick cut, allow about 25 to 30 minutes, or test by cutting near the bone with a knife. A thick 2-rib steak will serve 3 to 4, according to appetite. Serve with a brisk mustard-flavored Hollandaise.

If you have any entrecôte left over, it is even more delicious cold the next day for breakfast or lunch.

Deep Fried Onion Rings

See p. 81.

Sliced Tomatoes with Basil

Peel and slice beefsteak tomatoes. Salt and pepper them well. Prepare a dressing with:

$1/2$ cup finely chopped basil
1 red onion, coarsely chopped
1 tablespoon chopped parsley
1 teaspoon salt

1 teaspoon freshly ground
  black pepper
6 tablespoons olive oil
1 tablespoon lemon juice

Arrange tomatoes on a platter, and spoon dressing over them.

Blueberry Tarts with Whipped Cream

1 quart blueberries
¹/₂ cup water
1 cup sugar
1 teaspoon vanilla

12 tart shells or 2 pie shells
(see Plain Pastry,
p. 347)
1 pint heavy cream, whipped

Wash and pick over the blueberries. Add sugar and water, and poach gently till just softened. Add vanilla, and cool. Spoon berries into the tarts, and serve topped with whipped cream.

An Unusual Outdoor Dinner for 12 to 15

This dinner is possible for a very short season of the year, when kid is in the market. Italian butchers are apt to offer it in the spring; it is a specialty of the Easter season. Kid is deliciously tender meat, nicely flavored—and a surprise to guests. With it serve a pleasant California Zinfandel or a Pinot Noir.

Stuffed Eggs
Scallions   Radishes
Kid on a Spit   Potatoes Anna
Bibb Lettuce and Cherry Tomato Salad
French Bread
Fresh Strawberry Ice Cream

Stuffed Eggs

12 to 15 eggs, hard-boiled
and peeled
6 tablespoons softened butter
1 clove garlic, finely chopped

3 anchovies, finely cut
1 tablespoon capers
1 tablespoon chopped parsley
Mayonnaise

Cut eggs in half lengthwise or crosswise. Remove the yolks and force them through a sieve into a bowl. Add the softened butter, garlic, anchovy and capers. Blend well, add the parsley, and correct the seasoning. Finally, add mayonnaise to bind, if necessary. Force through a pastry bag with a rosette tube into the egg halves. Chill before serving, and garnish the plates or platter with radishes and scallions.

Kid on a Spit

A whole kid will weigh 12 to 15 pounds. Remove the liver, heart and kidneys. Rub the kid lightly with rosemary and garlic. Spit it well, and tie the front legs together, folding them under the body. Stretch the back legs out on the spit and tie together. Truss securely and balance. Roast over medium coals with a dripping pan in the firebox. Baste or brush with melted butter mixed with white wine and garlic.

While the kid is roasting, sauté the liver, heart and kidneys in butter. Slice very thin, and combine with 1½ cups Brown Sauce (*see* p. 332), ¼ cup Madeira, and about 2 tablespoons of chopped parsley.

When the kid is done, it should still be juicy, with the faintest blush of pink—about 150° when tested with a meat thermometer in the thickest part of the flesh. Serve with the brown sauce, which may be mixed with some of the drippings from the grill. Pass plenty of crisp rolls.

Potatoes Anna

See p. 358.

Bibb Lettuce and Cherry Tomato Salad

8 heads Bibb or Limestone lettuce	¾ cup olive oil
1½ pints cherry tomatoes	¼ cup wine vinegar
1 clove garlic	2 tablespoons fresh basil, finely chopped
1 teaspoon salt	Salt and pepper

Wash the lettuce thoroughly to rid it of sand, then drain and dry. Remove stems from cherry tomatoes, wash and drain. Combine with lettuce in a salad bowl, preferably not a wooden one. Crush the garlic clove, and rub it well into the salt. Add to the oil. Just before serving, pour oil on the salad and toss. Then add vinegar, basil and salt and pepper, and toss once again. Serve at once.

Fresh Strawberry Ice Cream

8 egg yolks	3 cups ripe, sweet strawberries
2 cups hot milk	2 tablespoons Grand Marnier
1 cup sugar	Port
1 quart heavy cream, whipped	

Beat the egg yolks lightly. Combine milk and sugar, and heat thoroughly. Pour over the egg yolks, while whisking constantly. Cook in a double boiler over hot (not boiling) water until slightly thickened. Chill, and fold in the whipped cream and 2 cups of the berries, crushed, and sweetened if necessary. Add Grand Marnier and freeze—either in your refrigerator or in an ice cream freezer. Sugar the remaining berries, flavor with a little port, and serve with the ice cream.

A Mexican-Flavored Outdoor Dinner for 8

This is somewhat plain but good, hearty fare. It can be done almost at a moment's notice and can be expanded to accommodate extra guests. Beer is the right accompaniment here.

Guacamole with Tostados
or Melba Toast
Grilled Hamburgers with Garlic Rolls
Pinto Beans with Chili and Sausage
Orange and Onion Salad
Fresh Mangoes, Cherries and Apricots

Guacamole

3 soft, ripe avocados
1 cup thinly cut green onions
2 tablespoons lime juice

$^1/_4$ teaspoon Tabasco
1 teaspoon salt

Crush avocados, and blend with the green onions. Add lime juice, Tabasco and salt. Correct the seasoning. Serve as a dip or spread with tostados or Melba toast (*see* p. 318–19).

NOTE: There are many versions of this. Some people add a little tomato paste; others, garlic. If you can get fresh coriander (cilantro) and like it, by all means add a good deal of it here. Use your imagination and your taste buds.

Grilled Hamburgers with Garlic

1 clove garlic for each pound
1 teaspoon salt for each pound
1 teaspoon freshly ground
     pepper for each pound
$^1/_2$ teaspoon Tabasco for

each pound
Chopped chuck or top
     sirloin—$^1/_2$ to $^3/_4$ pound
     per person
Butter

Mince the garlic, and combine with other seasonings. Form cakes of the meat, about 1 inch thick, and press seasoning into the side of each cake. Grill over medium coals to suit the taste of your guests. Remove from the grill, and top each hamburger with a pat of butter.

Pinto Beans with Chili and Sausage

1 pound pink pinto beans
Bay leaf
1 onion, stuck with 2 cloves
Salt to taste
$^1/_4$ pound bacon, cut thick
4 cloves garlic, finely chopped
1 cup finely chopped shallots

1 teaspoon thyme
1 teaspoon ground cumin
4 tablespoons chili powder
1 cup tomato paste
2 tablespoons wine vinegar
2 pounds pork sausages,
     preferably chorizos

Soak the beans overnight. Drain, and add fresh water to reach 1$^1/_2$ inches above the beans. Add the bay leaf, onion, and salt to taste. Bring to a boil and cook till the beans are just tender. Drain, and reserve liquid.

Meanwhile, sauté the bacon cut into small cubes. Remove and add garlic and shallots to the fat. Cook till just soft. Add the thyme, cumin, chili powder, tomato paste and vinegar, and blend with the beans, adding about 1 cup of the bean liquid. Place in a baking dish, and cover with a piece of foil. Bake at 350° for 1 hour. Add the sausages, which have been poached in water for 10 minutes. Return the baking dish to oven till the sausages are browned—about 35 to 40 minutes. Add bean liquid during cooking if necessary.

Orange and Onion Salad

2 oranges	1/2 cup orange juice
2 sweet onions	2 tablespoons lemon juice
Curly chicory or romaine	1 teaspoon salt
1/2 cup olive oil	Generous pinch of rosemary

Peel the oranges and cut into sections, removing all of the white inner peel. Peel and slice the onions very thin. Wash and dry the greens. Blend the oil, juices and seasonings, and combine with the oranges and onions. When ready to serve, add the crisped greens, and toss well.

A Seafood Dinner on the Grill for 8 to 10

Drink a brisk Pouilly-Fuissé or a Muscadet with the fish. Either choice is refreshing and delicious.

Grilled Shrimp
Toasted French Bread
Cucumber Fingers
Broiled Whole Lobster with
Herbed Butter
Cole Slaw
Blueberry Deep-Dish Pie   Ice Cream

Grilled Shrimp

The large (7 to 10 to a pound) are the best for this type of grilling. Estimate 6 to 8 per person for large appetites; 4 to 5 for lesser ones.

Split the shrimp down the back with a pair of sharp scissors and remove the vein. Marinate the shrimp in white wine, olive oil, chopped fresh dill, and salt and pepper for several hours.

Broil the shrimp in a basket grill or on skewers for 4 to 5 minutes. Serve for a first course along with drinks or with wine, and also serve cucumber fingers and toasted French loaves split in half and buttered (with or without garlic).

Broiled Whole Lobster with Herbed Butter

I prefer to use 2- to 3-pound lobsters for this treatment. Broil the lobsters whole over medium heat for 13 to 16 minutes, turning several times during the cooking. Remove from the grill, split, remove the stomach. Serve with herbed butter.

FOR THE HERBED BUTTER:

1/2 pound butter
1 tablespoon chopped shallots
  or green onions

2 tablespoons chopped parsley
Chopped fresh tarragon to taste

Combine and melt over low heat. Sometimes a little lemon juice is a pleasant addition.

Cole Slaw

1 1/2 large heads of cabbage,
  shredded
1 tablespoon celery seed

1 1/2 cups well-flavored
  mayonnaise
1 cup sour cream

Combine the ingredients and marinate for 2 to 3 hours in the refrigerator. Correct the seasoning, and toss well. Serve in a chilled glass or pottery bowl.

Blueberry Deep-Dish Pie

FOR THE PASTRY:

> 2¹/₄ cups flour   Ice water
> ¹/₂ cup butter   Salt
> ¹/₄ cup vegetable shortening

Sift flour and salt into a mound on a mixing board or marble slab. Add shortening, and quickly rub into flour with the fingers. Then add just enough ice water to hold pastry together (3 or 4 table-spoons). Pull off small bits, flatten with the heel of your hand, and form into a ball. Chill in refrigerator for 1 hour.

FOR THE FILLING:

> 2 to 2¹/₂ quarts blueberries   6 tablespoons butter
> Flour   1 egg yolk
> Sugar to taste (about 1 cup)

Butter a pie dish lightly. Pour in blueberries, keeping them higher in the center. Dust with flour, then add sugar and dot with butter. Brush with beaten egg yolk.

Roll out crust, and cover berries. Flute edges, and cut a vent in the top. Bake at 450° for 10 minutes, then reduce heat to 350° and continue to bake till crust is browned. Serve warm with maple or vanilla ice cream, or with whipped cream.

An Outdoor Dinner for 12

Serve carafes of California Mountain Red with this meal. With coffee offer a fine old bourbon or cognac.

Figs or Melon
with Prosciutto and Salami
Bread Sticks
Spitted Roast Beef   Potatoes Anna
Romaine Quarters
French Bread   Butter
Peach Shortcake with
Sherried Whipped Cream

Figs or Melon with Prosciutto and Salami

Select the best melon or figs available. If prosciutto is not available, use a Westphalian or a Virginia ham. Use a good imported salami. Serve the figs or melon on individual plates, and place a few slices of the ham and salami around the fruit. Pass the pepper grinder and plenty of breadsticks.

Spitted Roast Beef

You will need a 5- to 7-rib roast, according to the grill you are using. The roast should be rubbed with salt and pepper and then balanced on the spit. Roast over coals (without very much heat) allowing about 12 minutes per pound for rare or until your meat thermometer registers 125°. Catch the drippings in a pan, unless you have a specially designed grill that drains off the fat. Allow to rest for about 10 to 15 minutes before carving, and it should carve magnificently.

Potatoes Anna

See p. 358.

Romaine Quarters

Remove the coarse outer leaves of 3 heads of romaine lettuce, crisp in cold water, and cut into quarters. One quarter makes a serving. Offer your guests a choice of Vinaigrette Sauce (*see* p. 338), anchovy mayonnaise (*see* p. 337), or salt and pepper.

Peach Shortcake with Sherried Whipped Cream

6 to 8 ripe peaches, peeled
  and sliced
Sugar
2 cups flour
4 teaspoons baking powder
$1/2$ teaspoon salt
3 tablespoons sugar
4 tablespoons butter
$3/4$ to 1 cup heavy cream
Melted butter

Sugar peaches to taste, and set aside. Sift flour, baking powder, salt and sugar together, then work butter and cream into the dry ingredients, using fingers or fork, to make a light dough. Roll or pat out $2/3$ of the dough on a floured board to $1/2$ inch in thickness and about 9 inches in diameter. Brush with melted butter, and place on a buttered baking sheet. Dot center with additional butter. Roll out the remaining dough a little thinner and to about 7 inches in diameter. Place the smaller round on the larger, and brush with butter. For 12 guests, you had better make 2 shortcakes.

Bake at 425° for 15 to 18 minutes, or until nicely browned. Remove from oven. Separate layers. Arrange sugared peaches on lower layer, top with remaining layer, and decorate with more peaches. Serve at once with heavy cream or whipped cream flavored with sherry.

Outdoor Chef's Supper for 6

Make old-fashioneds with Jamaica rum, and skip the orange and cherry. Serve a chilled Provençal rosé with the supper and Mirabelle with the coffee.

Brochette of Giblets
Grilled Piquant Chickens
Eggplant Provençale
Raw Vegetable Plate
with Tapenade
Homemade Cassis Ice Cream

Brochette of Giblets

1 pound chicken hearts	Salt and pepper
1 pound chicken livers	1 cup red wine
1 pound chicken gizzards	1/2 cup soy sauce
Water	1/2 cup oil
1 onion	3 cloves garlic, finely chopped

Add the hearts, livers and gizzards from the chickens for the main course to the 3 pounds required here. Poach all the gizzards for 1 hour in water to cover with the onion, salt and pepper. Drain and cut in bite-size pieces. Trim and halve the livers. Combine the wine, soy sauce, oil, garlic, 1 teaspoon salt and 1/2 teaspoon freshly ground black pepper. Add the gizzards, livers and hearts, and marinate 1 or 2 hours. Drain, and dry on paper towels. String on small skewers, alternating the three kinds of giblets. Brush with the marinade and additional oil, and broil over charcoal. Serve with drinks. Toast or pita bread makes a good accompaniment.

Grilled Piquant Chickens

1 cup ground walnuts	1 teaspoon dry mustard
6 shallots, or 1 medium	Tabasco
onion, finely chopped	3 2-to 2¹/₂-pound broiling
4 tablespoons butter	chickens, cut in half
1 teaspoon salt	²/₃ cup melted butter
¹/₄ cup chopped parsley	1 teaspoon paprika

Blend the nuts, shallots, 4 tablespoons butter, salt, parsley, mustard and ¹/₂ teaspoon Tabasco to a smooth paste. Loosen the skin on the chicken breasts, and stuff the paste under the skin. Brush the bone sides of the chicken halves with a mixture of the melted butter, paprika and 3 dashes of Tabasco. Broil, bone side to the fire, for 12 to 14 minutes over medium coals. Turn and brush the skin sides with the mixture, and continue broiling until the chickens are tender. Season with salt and pepper, and serve piping hot.

Eggplant Provençale

2 eggplants, peeled	1 teaspoon freshly ground
Ice water	black pepper
¹/₄ cup olive oil	Oregano
6 ripe tomatoes, peeled,	3 cloves garlic, chopped
seeded and chopped	Buttered crumbs
1 teaspoon salt	Chopped parsley

Cut the eggplants into 3-inch slices. Soak for a few minutes in ice water. Drain, dry and brown quickly in the olive oil. Transfer the slices to a baking dish. Add more oil or butter to the pan, and cook the chopped tomatoes. Season with salt, pepper and oregano. Add to the baking dish with the chopped garlic. Top with buttered crumbs and chopped parsley, and bake in a 350° oven for 35 to 40 minutes.

You can prepare this in advance. It can stand in the warming oven while the chickens broil.

Raw Vegetable Plate

In place of a salad, arrange sliced cucumbers, sliced onions and rings or strips of green pepper on a serving plate. Add cherry tomatoes if you wish. Small raw artichokes, sliced raw turnips and carrot strips are nice additions. Serve with a bowl of tapenade for dunking.

Tapenade

1 cup bland mayonnaise
(made with 1 egg and
1 cup oil, no seasonings)
½ cup finely chopped capers
Juice and finely chopped

rind of 1 lemon
1 clove garlic, crushed
Chopped parsley
6 anchovy fillets, chopped

Blend all together thoroughly and chill in the refrigerator.

Homemade Cassis Ice Cream

2 cups black currant preserves
1 cup crème de cassis
Juice of 1 lemon
½ teaspoon vanilla

2 cups light cream
2 cups heavy cream
⅛ teaspoon salt

Put the preserves through a fine sieve, or puree in a blender or food processor with some of the cassis. Add lemon juice, the rest of the cassis and the vanilla. Mix the light and heavy cream with the salt and stir in the currant mixture. Pour into an ice cream freezer and freeze. Serve with currant preserves blended with cassis if you wish.

A Beer Supper Party for the Terrace or Beach—Serves 12

Since the theme of this gathering is beer, provide every kind of foreign and domestic beer you can find. Chill in a large tub of ice.

Sausage Tree   Hard Rolls
Coquillage   Rye Bread and Butter
Grilled Herbed Drumsticks
Grilled Flank-Steak Sandwiches
Sliced Tomatoes   Scallions
Pickles   Mustard   Salted Peanuts
Cheese Board with French and Rye Bread   Fruit

Sausage Tree

Make a metal tree with hooks for hanging the sausages, or use a real tree—a small potted one.

Buy as many different kinds of sausages as you can find. Look for salami, teawurst, cervelat, summer sausage, blutwurst, liverwurst, Braunschweiger, kielbasy, bologna, peperoni and mortadella. Buy a quarter, half or whole of each, depending on the amount you will need. Tie the sausages to hooks and hang them on the tree.

Coquillage

If you have ever been to a fine seafood bar in Europe, you undoubtedly remember the beautifully colorful displays of different kinds of shellfish arranged on seaweed or ice—the delicate pink of small shrimp, the orange and white of langoustines, the bright lobsters and langoustes, the blue-black of mussels, the pinky beige of clams, and the pale ivory of scallops.

Few foods are more tempting in summer than an assortment of seafoods served cooled, but not icy, with a choice of sauces such as plain or flavored mayonnaise, tartar sauce, or rémoulade sauce.

If you cook shrimp, remember that a white-wine court bouillon is best for these tender morsels, and that they must never be cooked for more than 4 or 5 minutes. A spicy red wine bouillon brings out the best in crawfish; and for lobster you need nothing more than plain salt and water.

Grilled Herbed Drumsticks

3/4 cup melted butter (or more if needed)
1 teaspoon tarragon
2 teaspoons chopped chives
2 tablespoons chopped parsley
Salt and freshly ground black pepper
1 dozen chicken drumsticks

Melt the butter and stir in the herbs. Dip each drumstick in the herbed butter and grill them over charcoal until done to your satisfaction. Brush the drumsticks with more of the herbed butter as they cook and turn them to brown evenly. Season to taste with salt and freshly ground black pepper.

Grilled Flank-Steak Sandwiches

2 flank steaks
1 cup dry red wine
1 clove garlic, chopped
1 onion, sliced
1 handful chopped parsley
Salt and freshly ground
black pepper
2 medium size loaves French bread
Thyme
1 clove garlic, crushed
Butter

Remove the tough outer membrane from the meat. Put the wine, chopped garlic, onion and parsley in a shallow bowl and let the meat marinate in this mixture for 2 or 3 hours. Keep it in the refrigerator and turn several times to be sure the steak is evenly bathed.

Flank steak should be at refrigerator temperature when grilled, so leave it in the marinade until the last minute. Grill it quickly over charcoal, allowing only about 4 minutes to each side. It should be crusty brown on the outside but red rare in the center. Brush with the marinade as it cooks and season to taste with salt and pepper.

Split the loaves of bread the long way and spread the halves with butter mixed with crushed garlic and a little thyme. Press the loaves together again and roll in foil. Heat these on the grill as the steak is cooking.

With a very sharp knife, slice through the steak diagonally from top to bottom, cutting it into thin strips. Remove the bread from the foil, and take off the top half of each loaf. Arrange the steak slices on the bottom halves of the loaves and replace the tops. Cut the loaves into thick slices to make tasty hot and hearty steak sandwiches.

An Outdoor Luncheon or Dinner for 10

Serve summer drinks before the meal—collinses, mint juleps, vodka and tonic, gin and tonic, and the like—and beer with the meal. With the drinks provide bowls of unshelled peanuts, pretzels, scallions, radishes, olives, pickles, and a board of various sausages, together with pumpernickel bread and several mustards.

Chuck Wagon Steak   Lentil Salad
Crisp Garlic Buttered French Bread
Sliced Tomatoes and Red Italian Onions
Cantaloupe and Watermelon with
Raspberries and Ice Cream

Chuck Wagon Steak

1 cup salad oil	1 teaspoon pepper
2 cups beer or ale	1 teaspoon dry mustard
1/4 cup lemon juice	1 teaspoon basil
2 cloves garlic, crushed	1 teaspoon oregano
1 1/2 teaspoons salt	1 teaspoon thyme
2 bay leaves	1 10-pound chuck steak*

Combine oil, beer, lemon juice and seasonings; pour over chuck steak. Refrigerate several hours or overnight. Place steak in roasting pan; brush with marinade. Roast in hot oven (425°) 2 1/2 hours for rare steak.

* You may tenderize the steak if you wish. Follow directions on the bottle of tenderizer.

Lentil Salad

2 to 3 pounds lentils
Water
1 tablespoon salt
1 onion, stuck with cloves
1 bay leaf
2 whole cloves garlic
1 cup olive oil
3/4 cup finely chopped onion

2 garlic cloves, finely chopped
1/2 cup chopped parsley
1 cup crumbled crisp bacon
Wine vinegar to taste
1/4 teaspoon Tabasco
1 teaspoon freshly ground
  black pepper
Additional olive oil, if needed

Soak lentils overnight. Drain, and cover with fresh water. Add salt, onion stuck with cloves, bay leaf and whole cloves garlic. Bring to a boil, and simmer till just tender. Drain, and while still hot add olive oil. Cool, then add remaining ingredients. Toss well, and correct the seasoning. This salad improves if it is allowed to stand for several hours. Garnish with chopped parsley and thinly sliced scallions before serving.

Sliced Tomatoes and Red Italian Onions

On a large platter arrange alternately peeled and thinly sliced tomatoes and thinly sliced red onion. Sprinkle with chopped fresh basil. Pass oil and vinegar, salt and pepper separately.

Cantaloupe and Watermelon with Raspberries and Ice Cream

Arrange halves of cantaloupe in ice, along with wedges of watermelon. Have a bowl of raspberries and powdered sugar near at hand, as well as vanilla ice cream. Your guests may fill their cantaloupe with berries alone or with both berries and ice cream.

For added variety, have a chilled bottle of kirsch on hand, and, if you can find it, a bottle of framboise, for guests who prefer to have their fruit flavored with brandy.

A Terrace Luncheon for 8

Luncheon on a terrace or in a patio is ideal on a lazy summer day when the temperature is not too warm. First, you may have apéritifs indoors or out. Light potions like white wine cassis and Americanos are recommended, except for those who are incurable Scotch or martini drinkers. With luncheon serve Muscadet or a similar light white wine; and after luncheon, kirsch, framboise or port—the first two chilled. Bring out your gayest linens and china. Place a serving table near the host or hostess to cut down on trips to the kitchen.

Double Chicken Consommé, Jellied
Cold Trout à la Turque
Sauce Verte and Green Mayonnaise
Melbaed English Muffins
Salade Rachel
Frozen Raspberry and Macaroon Mousse

Double Chicken Consommé, Jellied

2 pounds chicken necks
5 pounds chicken backs
4 quarts water
Salt
1 onion, stuck with 2 cloves
1 or 2 sprigs parsley
1 pound chicken gizzards
1 egg white and shell

6 tomatoes, peeled, seeded and chopped
Freshly ground black pepper
1 tablespoon chopped fresh basil
2 tablespoons chopped parsley
Sour cream
Chopped chives

Place chicken necks and 2 pounds of the backs in a kettle with the water, 1½ tablespoons salt, onion, and parsley. Bring to a boil, lower the heat, and simmer 2 hours. Taste for seasoning, and simmer another ½ hour. Remove from heat and strain. Return broth to kettle and add remaining backs and the gizzards. Simmer 2 hours. Strain the broth and cool. Skim off all the fat, and clarify. To do this, strain the broth through a fine linen towel. Beat an egg white until frothy, and add the white and egg shell to the broth. Return to the heat, and cook a few minutes, beating with a rotary beater. Strain again through the towel, which has first been wrung out in cold water. The egg white and shell gather all loose particles together and leave the soup perfectly clear. Pour the soup into serving cups, and chill.

Combine the tomatoes with 1 teaspoon salt, freshly ground pepper to taste, basil and chopped parsley. Spoon this mixture over the chilled soup just before serving. Pass sour cream and chopped chives.

Cold Trout à la Turque

8 good-sized trout, cleaned
White-wine Court Bouillon
  (see Poached Salmon,
  p. 60)

1 tablespoon gelatin,
  softened in 1/4 cup cold water
Dill, tarragon, or parsley
Fresh-cooked asparagus tips

Poach the trout in the court bouillon for 10 minutes per inch of thickness when the liquid returns to the boiling point. Cool. Trim the tails, and remove the skin. Arrange on a serving platter or platters. Clarify the court bouillon, if you wish. Prepare an aspic: Add gelatin to the court bouillon and chill until on point of setting. Coat the trout with it, adding any desired garnish, such as dill, tarragon or parsley. Surround with chopped, fully set aspic, tiny cooked asparagus tips. Serve with bowls of sauce verte and green mayonnaise.

Sauce Verte

1 1/2 cups walnuts
1/2 cup chopped chives
1/4 cup chopped parsley
2 tablespoons chopped tarragon

1/2 cup olive oil
Salt
Freshly ground black pepper
1 tablespoon lime or lemon juice

Chop the walnuts in a blender or food processor. Mix with the chives, parsley, tarragon, and add the oil. Season to taste with salt and pepper, and blend in the lime or lemon juice. If all the oil is absorbed by the nuts, add a little more—enough to make a smooth paste.

Green Mayonnaise

1 cup homemade
  Mayonnaise (see p. 336)
1/2 cup mixed finely

chopped herbs and greens
(parsley, tarragon,
watercress, spinach)

Mix the mayonnaise with the desired selection of chopped fresh herbs, which will lend a delicate green color and a good flavor.

Melbaed English Muffins

Slice 8 English muffins thin, as for Melba toast. Toast them, butter lavishly, and put in a warm oven to dry out and crisp a little. These make a nice change from hot bread or rolls.

Salade Rachel

1 celery root or 1 tin sliced
  celery root
2 black truffles (as large as
  you can afford)
6 artichokes, cooked
6 small new potatoes, boiled

3 pounds asparagus, cooked
  but still crisp
Romaine or Bibb lettuce
Homemade Mayonnaise
  (see p. 336)

Peel the celery root and cut into fine julienne strips. It may be used raw or blanched for 5 minutes in boiling water and then drained.

Cut the truffles in slices and then into julienne strips. Cut the artichoke bottoms away and trim them neatly. (You may use frozen artichoke hearts and cook according to the directions on the package.)

Peel and slice the potatoes; cool. Trim the stalks of the asparagus neatly; cool.

Place a bed of romaine or Bibb lettuce on a large decorative salad server, and arrange bouquets of the celery root, asparagus, sliced potatoes and artichoke bottoms or hearts on top of the greens. Garnish with the truffles, and serve with a homemade mayonnaise.

Frozen Raspberry and Macaroon Mousse

1 quart fresh raspberries
1 cup sugar
1 cup macaroon crumbs

Pinch salt
1/3 cup framboise
1 quart heavy cream, whipped

Puree the raspberries, and blend with the sugar. Add the macaroon crumbs, salt and framboise. Blend with the cream, pour into a mold and freeze until mushy. Mix well, and freeze until solid.

PICNICS

The English are the greatest of picnickers and have led the field for hundreds of years. They have hampers for the races, outdoor teas for the amusement of children, and all sorts of occasions for sitting and eating in the countryside. In France along the roads one sees families seated in collapsible chairs around a collapsible table eating and drinking with gusto. In Japan elaborate picnic boxes may be purchased to be taken to the football field or to a spot beside a placid pool. Here in America there are picnic tables along the roadside where one may set up a simple meal of sandwiches or do a barbecue.

Wherever it is done, picnicking can be one of the supreme pleasures of outdoor life. At its most elegant, it calls for the accompaniment of the best linens and crystal and china; at its simplest it needs only a bottle of wine and items purchased from the local delicatessen as one passes through town. I recall a recent picnic in France where we bought rillettes de Tours (in Tours), and elsewhere some excellent salade de museau, good bread, ripe tomatoes and cheese. A bottle of local wine and glasses and plates from the Monoprix helped to make this picnic in a heather field near Le Mans a particularly memorable one.

The color and charm of the countryside can make the most modest meal taste superb. Have a picnic at the slightest excuse. It is even fun to have a box lunch and a hot drink in the car on a wintry day, while you look out at a dazzling stretch of landscape.

A Festive Country or Beach Picnic—Without Sandwiches—for 8

Serve either martinis or Americanos for cocktails, accompanied by salted nuts. With the food have some lightly cooled Beaujolais or California Mountain Red. Also take along cognac or kirsch to go with the cake, and, of course, fill a great vacuum bottle of hot or iced coffee. To use nice crystal, attractive plates and good cutlery goes without saying.

Stuffed Tomatoes
Veal and Pork Terrine
Beef à la Mode en Gelée
Potato Salad or Green Salad
French Bread   Butter
Cheese   Fruit
Angel Food Cake

Stuffed Tomatoes

8 large ripe tomatoes
2 7-ounce tins tuna in olive oil
2 4-ounce tins anchovy fillets
* in olive oil*
2 medium onions, finely chopped

8 hard-boiled eggs
Black olives
Basil-flavored Vinaigrette
* Sauce (see p. 338)*

Cut off tops of the tomatoes evenly (reserve them), and scoop out the seeds and meat, leaving only the shell. Add pieces of tuna, a few anchovy fillets, some onion, and an egg. Top with another anchovy fillet and 2 or 3 black olives. Replace the tops of the tomatoes, and wrap each one in foil. Chill. Serve with the vinaigrette sauce and additional olives.

Veal and Pork Terrine

¹/₂ cup Madeira or sherry	1 teaspoon sage
¹/₂ cup cognac	1¹/₂ pounds veal scallopine
4 cloves garlic (2 cloves finely chopped)	Bacon
	1 pound good sausage meat
¹/₂ teaspoon Quatre Épices (see p. 331)	Salt and pepper
	1 pound ground pork and veal

Make a marinade of the Madeira, cognac, 2 whole garlic cloves, Quatre Épices and sage. Place the veal scallopine in this and soak for several hours, then pour off the marinade and reserve.

Cover the bottom of a 2¹/₂-quart terrine or casserole with bacon. Add a layer of the sausage meat, then a bit of the chopped garlic, a layer of veal scallopine and salt and pepper to taste. Continue with a layer of the ground pork and veal mixture, and repeat till the terrine is filled. Pour marinade over the meat, and cover with bacon. Top with chopped garlic. Place a piece of foil over the terrine, and cover. Set in a pan of hot water, and bake at 375° for 2 hours, adding additional hot water to pan if necessary. Cool.

Beef à la Mode en Gelée

4 pounds brisket of beef trimmed of fat	1 teaspoon thyme
	1 pig's foot, split
1 cup chopped beef suet	¹/₂ teaspoon sugar
¹/₃ cup cognac	1 cup canned beef bouillon or consommé
Salt and pepper	
2 cups white wine	6 young carrots
1 bay leaf	18 small white onions, peeled

Brown the beef very well on all sides in the melted suet. Blaze with the cognac. Salt and pepper to taste, then add the white wine, bay leaf, thyme, pig's foot, sugar and bouillon. Cover and simmer for 2 hours. Add the carrots and cook another 1¹/₂ hours. Finally add the onions, which have been first sautéed in butter and sprinkled with sugar to glaze them. Continue cooking till meat is tender.

Remove the meat after it has cooled slightly, and cut into thinnish slices. Strip the meat from the pig's foot, and slice the carrots. Place meat and vegetables in a terrine or casserole, and pour pan sauces over all. When it is quite cool, remove the fat that has risen to the surface. Wrap the terrine in foil and chill. Carry to the picnic in a portable ice chest.

Serve with Dijon mustard and either a good potato salad or a tossed green salad. Also have crisp French bread or rolls and butter.

Potato Salad

See p. 359.

Cheese

For this picnic you might take along a piece of good aged cheddar and a piece of aged Switzerland Gruyère or Emmenthal. Serve with French bread and butter. Ripe pears or apples would be a good accompaniment also.

Angel Food Cake

1¼ cups egg whites	*1 cup sifted flour*
¼ teaspoon salt	*1 tablespoon cognac*
1 teaspoon cream of tartar	*½ teaspoon either vanilla*
1½ cups sugar	*or almond*

Beat the egg whites with a large whisk or a rotary beater until they form soft peaks. Add salt and cream of tartar and beat till stiff but not dry—firm peaks and glossy surface. Add sugar, a few tablespoons at a time, and fold in gently.

Sprinkle thrice-sifted flour over the surface and fold very carefully but well. Add flavorings and fold lightly. Pour into a 10-inch unbuttered tube pan or into 2 loaf pans or 1 large loaf tin. Bake at 375° about 40 minutes or until cake will spring back when tested with finger.

Invert on a cooling rack. If there are no legs on your tube pan, rest the tube on a bottle or funnel till cool.

A Champagne Picnic for 4 or 6

Here, champagne is the apéritif and the wine. This should be a well-appointed picnic: take colorful china dinner plates, cups for the soup, additional plates for the fruit and cream cheese, cups for the coffee, and beautiful flutes or all-purpose glasses for the champagne. Also bring a portable ice box or cooler for the wine. Estimate at least half a bottle per person and perhaps some in reserve. That means 3 to 5 bottles.

Macadamia Nuts
Cold Sorrel Soup
Roast Fillet of Beef
Potato and Hearts of Palm Salad
Cherry Tomatoes
French or Italian Bread
Sweet Butter   Fresh Fruit
Cream Cheese or Roquefort
Petits Fours Squares

Macadamia Nuts

Take along a large jar of these deliciously flavored nuts to munch with your champagne as you prepare the *déjeuner sur l'herbe*.

Cold Sorrel Soup

1 large Idaho potato, peeled
   and diced
2 cups chicken broth
1½ cups finely cut fresh
   sorrel leaves

2 tablespoons butter
1 cup heavy cream
2 egg yolks
Salt to taste

Cook the diced potato in the chicken broth until very tender. Blend in a food processor or put the potato pieces through a food mill and stir back into the broth. Wilt the sorrel quickly in butter in a saucepan over medium heat. Add to the potato mixture and simmer for 10 minutes. Add the heavy cream mixed with the egg yolks, and stir over low heat until slightly thickened, but do not allow to boil. Add salt if necessary. Allow to cool thoroughly. Then chill in the refrigerator. Carry to the picnic in a vacuum jug. Garnish with chopped parsley and serve with homemade Melba Toast (*see* p. 318–19).

Roast Fillet of Beef

If your picnic spot is not too far away, roast the fillet just before you depart, and it will be cooled to the perfect state by the time you are ready to eat.

1 fillet of beef, 5 to 6 pounds,
   trimmed
4 to 5 garlic cloves
1 teaspoon salt
1 teaspoon freshly ground
   black pepper
½ teaspoon Tabasco

1 cup soy sauce (preferably Japanese)
½ cup olive oil
1 cup port wine
1 teaspoon thyme
1 bay leaf
Bacon strips

Make small gashes in the roast, and fill with the garlic cloves, cut in thin slivers. Rub well with salt, pepper and Tabasco. Marinate in the soy, olive oil, port, and herbs, turning several times.

Place on a rack in a shallow roasting pan, top with a few strips of bacon, and roast at 425° for 30 to 35 minutes. Baste with the marinade several times. A meat thermometer inserted into the heaviest part of the roast should register 125° for rare, or 120° for very rare.

Potato and Hearts of Palm Salad

12 small new potatoes
Salted water
3/4 cup olive oil
Vinegar to taste
Salt and pepper

1 large Italian red onion
Chopped parsley
1 can hearts of palm, sliced
4 hard-boiled eggs, sliced

Boil the potatoes in salted water. Drain, and slip off the skins as soon as you can handle the potatoes. Slice fairly thin, and dress with oil, vinegar, salt and pepper to taste. Cool and chill. Just before packing the picnic, add the red onion, thinly sliced, the chopped parsley, and additional oil, vinegar and seasonings, if needed. Garnish at the picnic with hearts of palm and hard-boiled eggs.

Cherry Tomatoes

Fill a large bowl with cherry tomatoes, with some watercress as a garnish. No dressing is necessary. A little salt, possibly, is the only addition required.

Petits Fours Squares

2 cups sifted flour
1/2 teaspoon baking powder
1/8 teaspoon salt
1 cup butter
2 teaspoons vanilla
1 cup light brown sugar, firmly

packed
1 3/4 cups semisweet chocolate
bits
1/2 cup finely chopped
toasted almonds

Preheat the oven to 350°. Sift together the flour, baking powder and salt. Set aside. Blend the butter and vanilla, and gradually beat in the brown sugar. Add the flour mixture, chocolate bits and almonds, and blend well. Spread evenly in an ungreased 13- by 9-inch pan. Bake for 30 minutes. Remove from the oven and cool.

For frosting: Combine 1 1/2 cups sifted confectioners' sugar, 3 tablespoons light corn syrup, 2 tablespoons milk, and 1/4 teaspoon vanilla. Spread over cake. Decorate with chocolate glaze.

Chocolate Glaze: Melt over hot (not boiling) water 1/4 cup semisweet chocolate bits and 1 1/2 teaspoons vegetable shortening. Stir till blended. Drizzle or apply with a pastry tube in thin lines, lengthwise, about 1 inch apart. Then draw the tip of a knife or a toothpick across the lines of Chocolate Glaze, again about 1 inch apart, starting from one side of the pan and returning from the opposite side. This will pull the glaze along slightly and give the decoration a "feathered" look. Let stand till the frosting is set, then cut in 1-inch squares. This will yield almost 10 dozen.

An Elegant Picnic for the Beach

Bring along quantities of chilled Almaden rosé, but if you want to be truly elegant, nothing will do but iced champagne.

Roquefort Loaf
Special Stuffed Eggs
Chicken Sandwiches
Foie Gras Sandwiches
Cherry Tomatoes
Fresh Peach Ice Cream
Sand Tarts

Roquefort Loaf

1 1/2 pounds Roquefort cheese   Cognac
1 pound (or more) cream cheese   Crushed pecans
1/2 pound butter

Blend the Roquefort, cream cheese and butter thoroughly and flavor with a little cognac. Add more cream cheese if necessary. The mixture should be quite stiff. Roll it out into a long sausage shape and then roll in crushed (not chopped) pecans. Chill the cheese roll in the refrigerator until very firm. Slice and serve with rounds of hot toast.

Special Stuffed Eggs

24 eggs
1 tin mousse de foie gras
1 tablespoon sour cream
2 tablespoons chopped parsley
1 truffle, finely chopped

Salt and freshly ground
 black pepper
Cognac
24 truffle slices (optional)

These are not the usual picnic eggs. They are very elegant, decorative and tasty.

Cook the eggs until just hard; remove the shells and cool. Cut a thin slice from the broad end of each egg to enable the eggs to stand upright on the serving dish.

Slice off the small ends of the eggs so that you can scoop out the yolks. Mash the yolks well and mix with the mousse de foie gras, sour cream, parsley, chopped truffle and salt and pepper to taste. Add enough cognac to make a good paste. Using the rosette tube of a pastry bag, force the yolk mixture back into the eggs and finish off the top of each egg with a decorative swirl. Top each with a slice of truffle and chill well. You may also glaze the eggs with aspic.

VARIATION: Mash the egg yolks and blend them with 3 tablespoons mayonnaise. Add 1 tin boneless and skinless sardines mashed, 1/2 cup finely chopped chives, 1/4 teaspoon Tabasco, 1 teaspoon lemon juice and salt and freshly ground pepper to taste. Mix thoroughly and pipe this filling into the eggs, using directions above. Top with chopped chives or parsley.

Chicken Sandwiches

There is no substitute for really good chicken sandwiches. The only trick is to make certain that you use the very best ingredients.

Personally, I believe that chicken sandwiches should always be made with good homemade bread sliced very thin. If you freeze the bread and slice it as it is thawing, you can get nice even slices. Butter well with softened sweet butter and top with plenty of thinly sliced cold chicken. Season to taste with salt and freshly ground pepper and cover with a second slice of well-buttered bread.

Trim the crusts from the sandwiches and cut them into fingersized pieces. Wrap these in foil and cover them with a damp cloth or store them in the refrigerator.

VARIATION: Spread the bread with mustard-flavored or tarragon-flavored butter.

Foie Gras Sandwiches

Spread thin slices of homemade bread with a puree of foie gras and softened butter. Remove the crusts and cut into fingersized pieces.

Fresh Peach Ice Cream

1 quart heavy cream	2 cups crushed peaches
1 cup milk	2 teaspoons vanilla
1 cup sugar	1/4 teaspoon salt

Combine the cream with the milk and rest of ingredients. Blend thoroughly to dissolve the sugar. If using an old-fashioned hand-turned freezer, pour the mixture in the freezer container, and pack the outer compartment with 1 part rock salt to 6 parts crushed ice. Turn the handle until the dasher won't turn any longer. Wipe the top clear of any salt and ice, remove the dasher, and cover the container again, with its hole plugged. Repack with ice and salt to mellow. Take the whole thing along to the picnic and serve directly from the freezer. If using any other ice cream maker, follow freezing instructions and take the ice cream to the picnic packed in dry ice.

Sand Tarts

2 1/2 sticks (10 ounces) butter	not dry
2 cups sugar	4 1/4 cups flour
3 egg yolks	Cinnamon and sugar
3 egg whites, beaten stiff but	Almonds (optional)

Cream the butter and sugar together, and add egg yolks. Beat well and add the egg whites. Then blend in the flour, and beat well. Chill dough several hours.

Roll out a little at a time (keep the rest of the dough refrigerated) as thin as possible, and cut into rounds with a cookie cutter. Place on lightly buttered baking sheets, and brush with white of egg. Sprinkle with sugar and cinnamon. Bake at 425° for 8 to 10 minutes. Place half a blanched almond on each cookie, if you wish.

A Beer Picnic for a Large Gathering

This is easy to prepare, for the most part. The essential thing is to provide for thorough cooling of the beer. Take along a few bottles of wine for those who don't happen to like beer. Of course, there should be an ample amount of coffee in thermos jugs to go with the dessert—a huge apple kuchen.

Sausage Board
Westphalian Ham
Boiled or Baked Ham
Cold Meat Loaf
Deviled Eggs   Caviar Eggs
Pungent Eggs   Cole Slaw
Senfgurken   Dill Pickles
Emmenthal Cheese
Rye Bread, Pumpernickel and Butter
Apple Kuchen

Sausage Board

Get as wide a selection of sausage as you can find, and take knives and a cutting board to the picnic. Here are some possibilities:

Summer Sausage	*Teawurst*
Blutwurst	*Yachtwurst*
Lebanon Bologna	*Cooked Bratwurst*
Lachsschinken	*Goose Liverwurst*
Kielbasy	*Tongue Sausage*
Leberwurst	*Mettwurst*
Cervelat	*Beer Sausage*

Cold Meat Loaf

Make your favorite meat loaf. Weight it down while it cools. Refrigerate. Serve sliced thin.

Deviled Eggs

Combine the hard-boiled yolks of 8 eggs with 1 small tin of boneless and skinless sardines, 1 small onion finely chopped, and 1/4 cup of parsley. Bind with mayonnaise, and fill the egg halves.

Caviar Eggs

Combine the yolks of 8 hard-boiled eggs with 3 tablespoons caviar and 3 tablespoons onion juice. Bind with sour cream. Fill egg halves and decorate with caviar.

Pungent Eggs

2 garlic cloves, finely minced
1 tablespoon curry powder
1 tablespoon butter
8 hard-boiled eggs
1 tablespoon finely chopped
  chutney
Sour cream or mayonnaise
Chopped peanuts

Cook the garlic and curry powder in butter for 3 minutes. Combine with the egg yolks and chutney, and bind with sour cream or mayonnaise. Fill the egg halves, and garnish with chopped peanuts.

Cole Slaw

1 white cabbage, finely
  shredded
1 red cabbage, finely shredded
1 small onion, finely chopped
1 tablespoon celery seed
1 1/2 cups mayonnaise
1 cup sour cream
1 teaspoon finely chopped fresh dill
Salt and pepper

Combine all ingredients, and toss well. Allow to stand for at least 2 hours in the refrigerator before serving. Garnish with additional mayonnaise and dill.

Apple Kuchen

Sweet Dough (see p. 342)
6 to 8 green apples, peeled
* and thinly sliced*

1 cup sugar
³/₄ cup butter (approximately)

Prepare a sweet dough. After the first rising, roll out, and fit into an 11- by 14-inch buttered pan. Cover with the apples, which should be pressed lightly into the dough and placed close together. Sprinkle with sugar, and dot heavily with the butter. Let rise 10 minutes. Bake at 375° till the apples are fairly soft and the dough pleasantly brown and crisp. Serve with whipped cream, if you wish; or you may spread an Apricot Glaze (*see* p. 38) on this after it cools.

CELEBRATIONS

Holiday dinners used to be staggering affairs with an overwhelming number of courses and many extra items that had been especially prepared for the occasion—cakes and pies of many flavors, all kinds of relishes, and a profusion of vegetables accompanying the main dish. It was as if one had ordered everything on the menu of a great, old-fashioned American-plan hotel.

Nowadays, save for communities far from the rush of modern life, there is not the same leisure or desire for a meal of such proportions. And the economic and sociological conditions are no longer the same. No longer available are the "hired girls" and "the generals" who cooked and cleaned and spent thirteen or fourteen hours a day attending the needs of a family. Also, families are smaller. The holiday dinner is no longer the conference table for great family conclaves. And no longer does the hostess try to outdo her relatives and friends in the production of a holiday menu.

The emphasis today is on less work in the kitchen, but we are more particular about what we eat than our forebears—many of us are calorie-conscious—and we eat considerably less. Nowadays it is a small group, usually, who sits down to a somewhat streamlined holiday dinner with good friends, good food and good wine. It is a satisfying compromise with tradition.

A New Year's Eve Party for 20

New Year's Eve can be deadly if you let it get out of hand. The secret is to start off with drinks and rather substantial snacking at about 9:30. Toward 11:30 have supper ready and timed so the pièce de résistance and wine come along at the right moment to toast the old year out and the new in. With your guests thus fortified with food, you won't have nearly the number of casualties on your hands that might be expected at the usual New Year's party. After dessert, coffee and a couple of drinks, people will be ready to go home—or on to their own merrymaking.

For the drinking period have a bar setup, with the addition of red and white wine, and champagne, of course. Here are suggestions for snacking:

Bagna Cauda with Raw Vegetables
and Bread Sticks
Sausage Board
Rye Bread   Pumpernickel
Smoked Eel   Marinated Herring
Nuts   Olives in Garlic and Lemon

Bagna Cauda

This "hot bath," literally, is made in a fondue or chafing dish and kept warm over low heat. Surround it with bowls of raw vegetables in ice and with plenty of bread sticks. Let people dunk to their heart's content. For 20 persons I would have two dishes going and enough mixture in the kitchen for replenishments.

For each dish:

1 quart olive oil
8 garlic cloves, finely cut
14 to 16 anchovy fillets,
*   finely chopped*

Salt and freshly ground
*   pepper*
1 teaspoon rosemary or
*   oregano, or 1 of each*

Combine ingredients, and heat gently over low flame. Transfer to fondue or chafing dish, and keep warm.

The vegetables for dunking might include celery, fennel, carrot sticks, turnip slices, radishes, scallions, and cauliflower buds. The crisp, cold vegetables make an unusual contrast with the bagna cauda.

It would be a good idea to have plenty of small plates and paper napkins on hand near the dunking.

Sausage Board

Provide a large cutting board, good knives and forks, and a selection of sausages—kielbasy, bologna, mortadella, salami, Thuringer, ham salami, Lebanon bologna, Braunschweiger, Yachtwurst, etc. Thinly sliced rye and pumpernickel and plenty of sweet butter go with this, and also have several types of mustard and some really good pickles—dill, sour and sweet.

Smoked Eel and Marinated Herring

For 20 persons you will need about 3 pounds of smoked eel and about 12 fillets of herring (with sour cream and onions). You might also have some smoked herring if you are fond of it.

The main part of the following supper may be assembled well in advance. In fact, the oxtail ragout improves with sitting. Only the noodles need to be cooked at the last moment.

With the ragout and the cheese drink a vin ordinaire, such as a

California Mountain Red or a French Beaujolais. Cognac, kirsch and Mirabelle should be offered with coffee.

Oxtail Ragout with Noodles
French Bread   Butter
Endive and Beet Salad
Cheese Board   Sherbets
Fruit Cake and Christmas Cookies

Oxtail Ragout with Noodles

15 to 16 pounds oxtail, cut into small joints	1 tablespoon thyme
Flour	2 tablespoons salt
1 cup chopped beef suet	1 tablespoon freshly ground black pepper
$^1/_2$ cup butter	3 cloves
6 large onions, peeled and sliced	Dash nutmeg
10 cloves garlic, finely chopped	Stock
18 carrots, cut in rounds	Red wine
6 turnips, thinly sliced	Chopped parsley
3 bay leaves	

Flour the joints lightly, and brown a few at a time in melted suet and butter, adding more fat if needed. When the joints are browned, transfer to one or two large kettles. Brown the onions and garlic lightly in the same fat. Add to the kettles, along with the carrots, turnips and seasonings. Just barely cover with 2 parts stock to 1 part red wine, bring to a boil, and boil for 5 minutes. Remove any scum that forms. Reduce the heat and simmer for 3 hours or until tender. Cool thoroughly and remove fat. Chill till ready to use.

Reheat over low flame, and thicken to taste with flour and butter kneaded together. Correct the seasoning. Just before serving, sprinkle with chopped parsley. Serve with noodles. For this party you will need about 5 pounds of noodles. Cook them in boiling salted water, adding a generous dash of oil, till just tender. Toss well with butter and grated Parmesan cheese.

Endive and Beet Salad

Use either Belgian endive cut into 1-inch lengths or chicory (curly endive, as it is called in some places). For 20 persons, you will need 5 pounds of Belgian endive or three or four heads of chicory. Combine with 5 beets, peeled and coarsely chopped.

For the dressing: 1½ cups olive oil, ½ cup wine vinegar, 1 tablespoon salt, and freshly ground black pepper to taste.

You will have to toss this salad in three or more bowls, unless you have an outsized bowl and a giant pair of tools.

Cheese Board

Buy half a Roquefort cheese, a good piece of Canadian or Vermont cheddar, and a Brie, if they are available, and perhaps a large piece of Switzerland Emmenthal. Serve bread and butter with the cheese, and plenty of red wine.

Sherbets

Buy good commercial sherbets or sorbets and store in your freezer. Raspberry, lemon and mango would make a nice selection. Serve with all your leftover Christmas fruitcakes and cookies.

A New Year's Day Dinner for 6

This used to be a more important meal than it is nowadays. Perhaps everyone attends a number of open-house parties and has neither time nor appetite for a big holiday meal. At any rate, this is a modestly festive menu and one easy to do.

Serve whatever drinks you fancy before dinner. With dinner I suggest a nice light Bordeaux—a Prieuré Lichine or a Château Beychevelle. With coffee—Grand Marnier and cognac. May you never have a worse meal!

Pâté de Campagne   Buttered Toast
Stuffed Squab Chickens
Pureed Potatoes   Tiny Peas
Fresh Pears and Cheese

Pâté de Campagne

See p. 236–37.

Stuffed Squab Chickens

6 squab chickens	2 eggs
3 cups finely cut scallions	1/2 cup chopped parsley
Butter	1 tablespoon tarragon
1 1/2 pounds sausage meat	1/2 cup cognac
4 cups crumbs	Salt and pepper

Sauté the scallions lightly in butter. Remove and, in the same pan, sauté the sausage meat, breaking it up with a fork. Combine the scallions and sausage meat with the remaining ingredients, seasoning to taste with salt and pepper.

Stuff the chickens, truss them, and butter well. Place on a rack in a shallow pan. Roast on one side for 15 minutes. Baste and turn to other side for 15 minutes more. Then place on backs and continue roasting till tender and nicely browned. Remove to a hot platter, and rinse the pan with additional cognac—about $1/3$ cup. Pour this over the birds. Garnish with parsley and watercress.

Pureed Potatoes

6 to 8 large potatoes, peeled
  and quartered
$1/2$ pound butter

$1/2$ cup heavy cream or more
$1^1/2$ teaspoons salt
Freshly ground black pepper

Cook potatoes in boiling salted water till just tender. Do not let them get watersoaked and soggy. Drain, and return to heat for 2 or 3 minutes, shaking the pan. Mash or put through a food mill. Blend with butter and cream, using a whisk. Add salt, freshly ground pepper to taste, transfer to a hot dish, and top with an additional dollop of butter.

NOTE: Some chefs say that potatoes should never be whipped—only mashed, in an up and down motion. Use your own judgment.

Tiny Peas

Use the boil-in-the-bag variety that come in a butter sauce.

Fresh Pears and Cheese

The delicious Oregon pears are at their peak at the beginning of the year. Most of us seem to get them as early as Christmas. Look for them at a good fruiterer's.

Serve ripe with Roquefort, a fine Camembert, or even with cream cheese and preserves.

A New Year's Day Open House

This is a day to cater to all different tastes. Some are nursing heads—for them we nominate cognac milk punch; some can't take a drink because of New Year's resolutions—for them tomato juice or milk; the others will drink as usual—for them champagne, Scotch, vodka, martinis or bourbon.

Tiny Pizzas Onion Sandwiches
Hors d'Oeuvre Strudel
Hot Kielbasy with Mustards
Katharine Smith's Tiny New Potatoes
Chicken Sandwiches

Tiny Pizzas

FOR THE DOUGH:

1 cake or 1 package of dry yeast
1 cup warm water
1 teaspoon sugar
1 tablespoon salt
2 tablespoons olive oil
4 cups sifted flour
(approximately)

Dissolve yeastcake or dry yeast in warm water. Add sugar, salt, olive oil, and 2 cups flour. Beat until smooth. Gradually add additional sifted flour (1½ to 2 cups) to make a firm dough. Toss on a lightly floured board, and knead until smooth and elastic. Rub with olive oil and place in a bowl in a warm place to rise until double in bulk. When dough has risen, punch down, and cut in half. Roll out to about ³/₈ inch in thickness. Cut into small rounds with a cookie or biscuit cutter, and arrange on a buttered baking sheet. I suggest you bake a half at a time.

FOR TOMATO SAUCE:

1 16-ounce can Italian plum
   tomatoes (about 2 cups)
2 cloves garlic
1¹/₂ teaspoons basil

1 can Italian tomato paste
2 tablespoons olive oil
Salt and pepper

Cook the plum tomatoes, garlic and basil over medium heat for 20 minutes. Add the tomato paste and the oil. Cook down until thick and smooth. Season to taste. Strain, if you wish.

FOR THE TOPPING:

Mozzarella or Swiss Gruyère,
   grated
Anchovy fillets
Black olives

Salami or coteghino
Sardines
Mushrooms
Grated Parmesan

Place a layer of grated mozzarella or Gruyère on the pizza, brush with tomato sauce, and sprinkle with freshly ground pepper and basil. On some pizzas place anchovy fillets and black olives; on others place thin slices of salami or coteghino; on the remaining ones place sardines or sliced cooked mushrooms. Sprinkle with grated Parmesan cheese. Brush lightly with oil. Bake at 400° until puffy and crisp on the edges.

Onion Sandwiches

Cut brioche or chalah (or in a pinch, good white bread) into thin slices, and cut these into rounds with a cutter. Peel and slice thinly about 6 or 8 small white onions. Chop finely 1 large bunch of parsley or more. Have a bowl of mayonnaise at hand. Spread the rounds of bread with mayonnaise, top half of them with slices of onion and salt them well. Top these with the remaining rounds, and press them together firmly. Roll the edges in mayonnaise and then chopped parsley. Chill in the refrigerator several hours before serving.

Hors d'Oeuvre Strudel

Strudel leaves or phyllo pastry   may be used, or a
1/2 cup butter   combination of cheese,
1 1/2 cups filling (duxelles,   and nuts, poppy seeds, etc.)
    cheese, liver, etc. Leftovers   More melted butter

Thaw strudel leaves, if frozen. Unroll on baking sheet or board. Brush well with melted butter. Spread filling. Roll and brush with additional butter. Place on buttered baking-sheet. Bake in a 375° oven for 10 to 20 minutes, depending upon filling. Cut in 1-inch slices. Serve hot.

Hot Kielbasy with Mustards

Various forms of Polish sausage may be found in almost any city in the country. Poach a large sausage for 25 to 35 minutes in a bouillon of half wine, half water, to which an onion has been added. Cut in slices, and serve hot with a variety of mustards and sliced pumpernickel.

Katharine Smith's New Potatoes

Choose the smallest new potatoes you can find. Scrub well, and boil with jackets on in salted water till just tender. With a small ball cutter, scoop out a hole in each potato, and fill with sour cream mixed with fresh dill or chives. Serve hot with coarse salt. These are to be eaten with the fingers. They are incredibly delicious.

Chicken Sandwiches

And I mean *chicken*! Too many people make turkey sandwiches, which are all right too, but there is an incomparable flavor to the fine white meat of chicken, thinly sliced and placed between slices of well-buttered bread with only the addition of a bit of salt and mayonnaise.

For this party poach four large roasting chickens. Reserve the dark meat for a chicken salad or chicken crêpes later on in the week. Allow the white meat to cool—do not refrigerate—and slice thin. Spread good white or whole wheat bread, preferably homemade, with sweet butter, and add slices of chicken. Salt lightly, and brush with mayonnaise. Trim sandwiches and pack in foil, waxed paper, or plastic till ready to cut and use. Keep cool with a wet towel rather than refrigerate.

St. Patrick's Day Party

This is a party in two parts. The first part is for a largish group—maybe just back from the parade—with drinks and snacks of sausage rolls and ham on soda bread. The second part is a dinner for six special guests you ask to linger on. For the opening celebration serve Irish Whiskey Sours, Irish whiskey on the rocks or Black Velvets (half champagne, half stout). Serve stout or beer with the meal.

Sausage Rolls
Thinly Sliced Ham on Buttered Soda Bread
Timbales of Smoked Haddock Mousse
Corned Beef
Potatoes in their Jackets
Braised Cabbage in White Wine
Hot Mustard · Pickled Onions
Irish Whiskey Trifle

Sausage Rolls

2 pounds boneless fatty pork
   shoulder, trimmed of
   connective tissue and cut
   into 1-inch pieces
1/2 pound pork loin, cut into
   1-inch pieces
3 1/2 teaspoons coarse salt
Freshly ground black pepper
1 tablespoon finely chopped

fresh sage
1/2 teaspoon anise seed
3 large garlic cloves, finely
   chopped
3 tablespoons ice water
Sausage casings
Puff pastry (see p. 348–49)
2 eggs, beaten with
   2 teaspoons water

Grind the pork shoulder and loin, using a food processor and metal blade or a food grinder and medium disk. Mix the ground meats with the seasonings and ice water. Put the mixture into the sausage casings and form into thin links about 1 1/2 inches long.

Brown the links lightly in a skillet and drain. Roll the puff pastry 1/8 inch thick and cut into 1½-inch squares. Encase each sausage link in a square of pastry, leaving the ends open. Brush with the egg wash.

Place the rolls on lightly greased baking sheets about ½ inch apart and bake at 350° for 12 to 15 minutes until golden brown.

Timbales of Smoked Haddock Mousse

1 pound smoked haddock fillets	1½ ounces unflavored gelatin
Milk	¼ cup cold water
1 tablespoon unsalted butter	2 cups heavy cream
2 tablespoons béchamel sauce	

Place the haddock in a saucepan, add milk to cover and the butter, and poach gently for 15 minutes or until the fish flakes. Drain and purée in a food processor or blender, or put through a food mill. Mix with the béchamel sauce.

Soften the gelatin in the water in a small saucepan, stirring over low heat until dissolved. Thoroughly mix the gelatin into the haddock purée.

Whip the cream until it is nearly thick, then mix it gradually and thoroughly into the purée with a wooden spatula. Pour the mixture into six 1-cup molds and chill until firm and set.

Corned Beef and Potatoes

4 to 5 pounds corned beef	6 carrots, scraped
(preferably brisket)	6 to 8 new potatoes in
6 small white onions	their jackets
6 to 8 small turnips, peeled	

Wash the corned beef, place it in a kettle of cold water, and bring to a boil. Skim any scum that rises. Reduce the heat and simmer, covered, 2½ to 3 hours. Add the onions and turnips and cook 30 minutes more. Add the carrots and potatoes and simmer for another 15 minutes or until cooked. Transfer the meat to a hot platter and surround with the vegetables. Serve with hot mustard or horseradish.

Braised Cabbage in White Wine

1 2- to 3-pound head of cabbage
4 tablespoons unsalted butter,
   bacon fat, or pork drippings
1 teaspoon salt
1 teaspoon freshly ground

black pepper
2 teaspoons chopped fresh
   dill or 1 teaspoon dry dill weed
1/2 cup dry white wine

Clean, shred and soak the cabbage in water to cover for 40 minutes to 1 hour. Drain well. Melt the fat in a heavy skillet. Add the cabbage and sear over medium-high heat, tossing it with two wooden spoons. When it is lightly browned, reduce the heat, and add the seasonings. Add the wine, cover, and simmer till just tender. Uncover, raise the heat and cook down for 2 minutes. Taste for seasoning. Spoon into a heated serving dish.

Irish Whiskey Trifle

10 to 12 ladyfingers
Irish whiskey (about 1/2 cup)
1/2 cup raspberry preserves
2 1/2 cups chilled Crème

Anglaise (recipe follows)
1 cup heavy cream
2 tablespoons superfine sugar
1/3 cup chopped pistachio nuts

Line the bottom of a 9-inch serving bowl or soufflé dish with the ladyfingers. Liberally sprinkle them with the whiskey, but do not make soggy. Let stand for 15 minutes.

Spread the ladyfingers with a thick layer of raspberry preserves. Cover with the Crème Anglaise and chill for 3 or 4 hours.

Just before serving, whip the cream in a chilled bowl until it stands in soft peaks, then beat in the sugar and 1 or 2 tablespoons Irish whiskey. Cover the surface of the Crème Anglaise with the whipped cream, smoothing it evenly with a rubber spatula. Sprinkle the chopped nuts over the top. Serve chilled, but do not let stand in the refrigerator for more than 30 minutes or it will become soggy.

Crème Anglaise

4 large egg yolks	*1 cup milk*
¹/₄ cup sugar	*1 cup heavy cream*
Pinch salt	*2 teaspoons vanilla extract*

Combine the egg yolks, sugar and salt in a heavy saucepan or top of a double boiler and beat together with a wire whisk or wooden spatula until pale and creamy. In another pan scald the milk. Gradually stir the hot milk into the egg mixture. Cook over medium-low heat or—if using a double-boiler—over hot water, stirring continuously until the custard thickens enough to lightly coat a spoon. This may take as long as 20 minutes. The mixture should not be allowed to boil. Remove from the heat and cool. Stir in the heavy cream and vanilla. Pour into a chilled bowl and cool. Crème Anglaise can be served warm, at room temperature or chilled.

An Easter Breakfast for 10 or 12

I feel that a festive event calls for good strong drinks. Nothing is better in the morning than the enlivening vodka drinks—Bloody Marys and Screwdrivers. With the drinks serve a plate of thinly sliced prosciutto and another of bread sticks. Those with sesame seeds are superb. Let your guests roll their own—a slice of prosciutto around each bread stick. Also, colored Easter eggs help to set the theme and make excellent snacks. Have radishes, too—the harbinger of spring.

Drink a delicious rosé with this breakfast.

Bread Sticks with Prosciutto
Easter Eggs   Radishes
Shenandoah Fried Chicken   Cream Gravy
Boiled New Potatoes   Asparagus, Vinaigrette
Hot French Bread   Sweet Butter
Strawberry Preserves   Buckwheat Honey
Fruit Basket

Shenandoah Fried Chicken

12 chicken legs and thighs	seasoned with salt and pepper
12 gizzards	1/4 pound butter
Hearts	2 cups vegetable shortening
Flour	or 1 1/2 cups olive oil
2 eggs, beaten with	4 tablespoons flour
3 tablespoons water	2 cups cream
Coarsely rolled cracker crumbs,	Salt and pepper

I prefer the legs and thighs for this dish, for they are so much more juicy. The gizzards and hearts are for those who love them as much as I. Flour all parts well, dip into beaten egg, and then roll in cracker crumbs. Chill for 30 minutes to 1 hour, being careful to press the seasoned crumbs firmly into the chicken.

Melt the butter and vegetable shortening or olive oil in a heavy skillet or two. The fat should be about 1 inch deep. Add pieces of chicken, gizzards and hearts. Cook over fairly brisk heat till nicely browned, then turn and brown on other side. Reduce the heat, and continue cooking for about 15 to 18 minutes. Cover the pan for some of the cooking. Remove chicken pieces to absorbent paper placed on a baking sheet, and heat in a 250° oven for a few minutes while you make the cream gravy.

Cream Gravy

Pour off all the fat from the skillet, save 3 tablespoons. Add flour and blend well. Scrape in all bits of delicious crumbs that stick to the pan. Finally stir in cream, and continue stirring until the sauce thickens nicely. Season with salt and freshly ground black pepper, and allow to simmer for a few minutes. Pour into a sauceboat, and serve with chicken.

Boiled New Potatoes

See p. 354.

Asparagus, Vinaigrette

Cook 4 pounds or more of asparagus in boiling salted water till just tender and still crisp. (I find a large skillet works perfectly for this.) Drain and serve warm with Vinaigrette Sauce (see p. 338).

A Derby Day Lunch or Picnic for 6

Mint Juleps
Kentucky Fried Chicken
White Bean Salad
Beaten Biscuits
Mustard & Onion Relish
Ginger Cakes

Mint Juleps

Any Derby party calls for the traditional opener of mint juleps, a concoction so delectable it ought to be the national drink.

FOR EACH DRINK:

6 small fresh mint leaves
plus 1 sprig fresh mint
1 1/2 teaspoons confectioners'
or superfine sugar

1 tablespoon cold water
Shaved or finely crushed ice
4 ounces Kentucky bourbon

Place the mint leaves, sugar and water in an 8-ounce highball glass or, more traditionally, a silver mint julep mug. With a bar muddler, crush the mint, then stir until the sugar dissolves.

Pack the glass tightly almost to the top with shaved or crushed ice and pour in the bourbon. With a long-handled bar spoon, use a chopping motion to mix the ice and whiskey together. Dry the outside of the glass or mug and chill the julep in the refrigerator for at least 1 hour or in the freezer for about 30 minutes until the outside of the glass or mug is covered with frost.

To serve, remove the mint julep from the refrigerator with paper napkins or towels, taking care not to wipe off the frost. Garnish the drink with the sprig of mint, insert a straw, and serve at once.

Kentucky Fried Chicken

2 to 4 pounds lard
Two 2¹/₂- to 3-pound chickens,
   cut into 16 serving pieces
3 teaspoons salt

Freshly ground black pepper
2 eggs, lightly beaten and
   combined with 1 cup milk
1¹/₂ cups all-purpose flour

Preheat the oven to its lowest setting, then line a large shallow baking dish with paper towels and place it in the center of the oven.

Melt 2 pounds of the lard over high heat in a deep fryer or large, heavy saucepan. When melted, it should be 1¹/₂ to 2 inches deep. Add more lard if necessary. Heat the lard to a temperature of 375° on a deep-fry thermometer or until very hot but not smoking.

Pat the pieces of chicken dry with paper towels and season with salt and pepper. Immerse the chicken pieces one at a time in the egg and milk mixture, then dip in flour to coat lightly and evenly.

Fry the thighs and drumsticks for about 12 minutes, turning them frequently with tongs, until browned on all sides. As they brown, transfer to the paper-lined dish in the oven to keep warm. Then fry the wings and breast pieces, which will take 7 or 8 minutes.

White Bean Salad

2 cups white pea beans
1 bay leaf
1 onion, peeled and stuck
   with 2 cloves
1 clove garlic, peeled
1¹/₂ teaspoons salt
¹/₂ teaspoon freshly ground
   black pepper

1 cup finely chopped
   green pepper
¹/₂ cup finely chopped parsley
¹/₂ cup finely chopped celery
¹/₂ cup finely chopped scallions
1 to 1¹/₂ cups Sauce Vinaigrette
   (see p. 338)
Romaine lettuce

Pick over the beans and discard any that are damaged and any bits of pod or stone. Place in a deep kettle, add more than enough water to cover, and bring to a boil. Cover and let stand for 1 hour. Add the bay leaf, onion, garlic and salt and pepper, and bring to a boil again. Cover, reduce the heat, and simmer until the beans are tender but not mushy, adding water if necessary. Unprocessed beans will take 1 to 3 hours; quick-cooking beans, about ¹/₂ hour.

Drain the beans and discard the onion, garlic and bay leaf. Cool. Mix with the green pepper, parsley, celery, scallions, and vinaigrette. Serve in a bowl lined with romaine lettuce.

Beaten Biscuits

This southern specialty really does take a beating—the dough is walloped for as long as twenty-five minutes—to achieve its proper texture. You can cheat and make a fair version in the food processor, but it won't equal the honest biscuit produced with hand and hammer.

2 cups unbleached all-purpose
   flour
1 teaspoon salt

4 ounces unsalted butter, cut
   into pieces
1/2 cup ice water

Preheat the oven to 350°. With the metal blade in place, put the flour and salt in the container of a food processor. Pulse the machine twice to aerate the flour. Add the butter and pulse a few times until the mixture has the texture of cornmeal. With the machine running pour ice water through the feed tube in a steady stream. Process until the mixture forms a ball and for an additional 2 minutes.

Carefully remove the dough. Roll out on a lightly floured board to a rectangle 1/8 inch thick. Fold in half to form 2 layers. Cut through both layers with a 1 1/2-inch round fluted cutter.

Place biscuits on ungreased cookie sheets and bake for 25 to 30 minutes or until golden brown. Remove from the oven and split immediately. If the centers are soft, return split biscuits to the oven for an additional 3 or 4 minutes. Makes 36.

Ginger Cakes

2 cups sifted all-purpose flour
1 cup brown sugar, firmly
   packed
1 tablespoon ground ginger

1 teaspoon baking soda
1/2 pound unsalted butter,
   cut into 1-tablespoon pieces

Mix the flour, sugar, ginger and baking soda thoroughly, then blend with the butter until the mixture is crumbly. Press it into 8-inch-square cake pans to make a 1/2-inch thick layer. Bake at 325° for 45 minutes to 1 hour until lightly browned. While still warm, cut into finger-length pieces about 1 inch wide. Remove with a spatula, and when cool store in a covered tin. Makes about 50 cookies.

A Country Wedding Buffet for 20

There shouldn't be a caterer in sight for this wedding reception, which should be pretty, simple, and genuine. Homemade food. Garden flowers. The meal should come out of your own kitchen. And the bride's cake is not the usual elaborate concoction, but a delicate cake made with egg whites and baked in either round tins or sheet tins. Adorn the cake or the serving platter with fresh flowers.

Serve white wine with the meal and end with champagne, or champagne can flow throughout the festivities.

Country Pâté
Homemade Rolls
Lobster Salad with Shrimp Garnish
Cucumber Salad
Hard Rolls
Homemade Vanilla Ice Cream with Fresh Berries
Bride's Cake

Country Pâté

See Pâté de Campagne, p. 236–37. You will need to make at least two of these loaves.

Lobster Salad

22 to 25 pounds live lobsters
3 cups finely cut celery hearts
2 quarts mayonnaise
24 large cooked shrimp

Boston lettuce
1/2 cup finely chopped fresh
  tarragon
1 cup finely chopped parsley

Cook the lobsters (or have them cooked for you by your local fish-monger) and allow to cool. Remove the meat in large chunks. Combine the lobster meat and celery in a large mixing bowl. Add just enough mayonnaise to bind the salad together. It should not be soupy. Transfer the salad to the center of a large serving platter, garnish with the shrimp and lettuce, and sprinkle with the herbs. Makes 20 servings.

Cucumber Salad

This makes 2 quarts. You will probably need to increase it by half.

1 cup cider or white wine
  vinegar
4 tablespoons water
1 teaspoon salt
1/3 cup sugar

1/2 teaspoon freshly ground
  black pepper
1/4 cup chopped fresh dill
8 cups thinly sliced English
  cucumbers, unpeeled

Combine the vinegar, water, salt, sugar, pepper, and dill in a large bowl. Add the cucumbers, and stir to coat with the dressing. Cover with plastic wrap, and let stand for at least 3 hours before serving.

Hard Rolls

2 packages active dry yeast
1 teaspoon sugar
2 cups warm water (100° to
  115°)
1 tablespoon coarse salt
1 cup hard-wheat flour

4 to 5 cups soft-wheat flour
  (available in health food
  stores)
Cornmeal
2/3 cup ice water mixed
  with 1 tablespoon salt

Combine the yeast with the sugar and warm water in a large bowl, and let stand until bubbly. Mix the coarse salt with the hard-wheat flour and add to the yeast mixture. Stir in the soft-wheat flour, 1 cup at a time, until you have a firm dough. Remove to a lightly floured board and knead about 10 minutes, adding flour as necessary, until no longer sticky. Place in an oiled bowl and turn to coat the surface of the dough. Cover and let rise in a cool place for about 2 hours or until doubled in bulk.

Punch down the dough. Turn out on a floured board and knead for about 2 minutes. Cut the dough into 24 pieces and form into balls. Place on baking sheets that have been sprinkled with cornmeal. Slash the tops of the dough. Cover and let rise about 30 minutes, until doubled in size.

Preheat the oven to 400°. Place four small custard cups filled with boiling water on the corners of the oven rack. Bake the rolls for 25 to 30 minutes, brushing the tops with salted ice water every 5 minutes, until rolls are nicely browned and sound hollow when tapped. Remove a rack to cool.

Homemade Vanilla Ice Cream with Berries

This makes about 2 quarts. You will need to make two batches and double the amount of berries, sugar and kirsch.

6 egg yolks	extract
1¹/₃ cups sugar	1 pint raspberries
¹/₈ teaspoon salt	1 pint strawberries, hulled
2 cups milk	and halved
1 quart heavy cream	¹/₄ cup kirsch
1¹/₂ to 2 tablespoons vanilla	

Combine the egg yolks, 1 cup sugar, and salt in a heavy saucepan or the top of a double boiler and beat together with a wire whisk or wooden spatula until well mixed. In another pan scald the milk. Gradually pour the hot milk into the egg mixture, stirring constantly. Cook over medium heat—or, if in a double boiler, over hot water—stirring constantly until the custard thickens enough to coat a wooden spoon. Do not allow to boil. Remove from the heat and cool. Stir in the heavy cream and vanilla extract. Place in the container of an ice cream freezer and freeze, following the manufacturer's directions.

Place the raspberries and strawberries in a bowl and sprinkle with the remaining ¹/₃ cup sugar and kirsch. Serve the ice cream topped with the berries.

Bride's Cake

Makes one 9½-inch four-layer cake.

FOR THE CAKE:

4½ cups all-purpose flour
1½ teaspoons baking powder
½ teaspoon salt
1½ pounds unsalted butter

3 cups sugar
12 large eggs, separated
3 tablespoons lemon juice
Zest of 1 lemon

FOR THE FILLING:

1½ pounds dried apricots
4 cups water

1 cup sugar
⅓ cup kirsch

FOR THE FROSTING:

1½ cups sugar
⅔ cup water
⅛ teaspoon cream of tartar

3 egg whites, stiffly beaten
⅛ teaspoon salt
1 teaspoon vanilla extract

FOR THE CAKE:

Butter and flour an 8½ × 2-inch and a 9½ × 2-inch cake pan lined with wax paper.

Sift the flour onto wax paper, then spoon it gently into a measuring cup. Spoon the flour back into the sifter, add the baking powder and salt, and sift twice more, each time spooning it very gently into the sifter.

Using an electric mixer, cream the butter until it is very light and fluffy. Then beat in 1 cup of the sugar. Beat in the egg yolks until the mixture is light and lemon-colored, then add the lemon juice and zest. Gradually fold in the sifted flour mixture. In a separate bowl beat the whites with a wire whisk until they hold soft peaks. Very gradually whisk the remaining 2 cups sugar into the whites. Gently fold into the batter until completely smooth, but do not overmix.

Divide the batter between the two cake pans. Bake in a 350° oven for 1 hour. Check the smaller cake after 45 minutes; it is done when the edges of the cake begin to pull away from the sides of the pan.

Remove the cakes from the oven and cool on a rack for 15 to 30 minutes. Loosen the sides very gently and invert the cakes onto racks to finish cooling.

For the filling: In a medium-size saucepan soak the apricots in the water for 1 hour. Add the sugar and bring to a boil, stirring until the sugar has dissolved. Boil for 30 to 45 minutes until the mixture is slightly thickened. Cool. Put in a blender or food processor, add the kirsch and process to make a smooth purée.

Slice the cakes in half horizontally. Place the bottom of the larger cake on a platter and spread with $1/3$ of the apricot filling. Add the top layer and spread the center with another $1/3$ of the filling, leaving about an inch of the circumference untouched; it will be frosted. Add the bottom half of the smaller cake and spread with the last $1/3$ of the apricot filling. Place the remaining layer on top.

For the boiled frosting: In a saucepan combine the sugar, water, and cream of tartar. Bring the mixture slowly to a boil, stirring once or twice to dissolve the sugar. Cover and boil 3 minutes, then uncover and boil to the soft-ball stage (240° to 245° on a candy thermometer). Remove the pan from the heat. Beat the egg whites in an electric mixer at medium to high speed until stiff, and pour the syrup in a thin stream into the whites as you continue beating. Add the salt and vanilla, and beat until the frosting cools a bit and is firm enough to spread. If too firm, beat in about $1/4$ teaspoon boiling water.

Spread the frosting on the sides and top of the cake, fluffing it into peaks with a spatula or back of a spoon. Decorate with a cluster of fresh garden flowers.

A Fourth of July Picnic

This is a far cry from the old-time picnics with the traditional fried chicken, homemade potato salad and all the provender of the early 1910's and '20's. Here, we are going to be unorthodox and elegant.

If you begin with chilled champagne, continue with it throughout the meal. Or serve a white wine cassis followed with a very young Beaujolais, lightly chilled. With the drinks serve small frankfurters (if you have a means of heating them) and crisp rolls. Or serve a fine bologna and liverwurst and crisp rolls. Pass hot mustard and salad mustard.

Tiny Frankfurters and Crisp Rolls
Cold Lobster with Spicy Mayonnaise
Glazed Fillet of Beef
Rice Salad   Vegetable Salad
Cherry Tomatoes
Pumpernickel Bread and Butter Sandwiches
Homemade Bread with Garlic Butter
Glenna McGinnis Lane Cake
Fresh Strawberries or Raspberries with Kirsch

Cold Lobster

Poach a 1- to 1½-pound lobster for each person. Cool, and pack in a portable ice box. At the picnic, split each lobster with a large knife. Provide nutcrackers for the claws.

Spicy Mayonnaise

1 pint homemade Mayonnaise
  (see p. 336)
1/2 cup sour cream
1 cup chopped green onions
1 tablespoon tomato paste

1 tablespoon Worcestershire
  sauce
1 teaspoon Tabasco
1/4 cup chopped parsley

Blend together and let stand for an hour or two before using.

Glazed Fillet of Beef

Marinate for several hours or overnight a whole fillet, well trimmed and fat removed, in 1 cup Japanese soy sauce, 1/3 cup olive oil, 4 finely chopped garlic cloves, 1/2 cup sherry. Turn several times.

Roast on a rack in a 425° oven, basting with the marinade from time to time, for about 28 to 30 minutes. Cool, and tote to picnic in foil. If you are not driving too far, do not even chill it.

Rice Salad

Combine 4 cups cooked rice with 1/2 cup olive oil, 2 tablespoons wine vinegar, and salt and freshly ground pepper to taste. Toss well and garnish with 1/3 cup finely chopped pimiento and a tablespoon chopped basil. Keep in portable ice box.

Vegetable Salad

Wrap up peeled and sliced beefsteak tomatoes, peeled and sliced cucumbers, crisp cooked whole green beans, sliced cooked beets, grated raw carrot, raw sweet peas and greens of your choice. Arrange on a plate or in a bowl at picnic spot, and toss with a jar of Vinaigrette Sauce (see p. 338) at the last minute. Or arrange on a platter, and serve the sauce separately. This is the preferred way.

Glenna McGinnis Lane Cake

1³/₄ cups butter
3³/₄ cups granulated sugar
1 teaspoon vanilla
3¹/₄ cups sifted all-purpose
    flour
3¹/₂ teaspoons double-acting
    baking powder
1¹/₄ teaspoons salt
1 cup milk
8 egg whites, beaten till stiff

but not dry
12 egg yolks
¹/₂ cup rye or bourbon whiskey
1¹/₂ cups coarsely chopped
    pecans
1¹/₂ cups chopped seeded raisins
1¹/₂ cups shredded fresh coconut
1¹/₂ cups quartered candied
    cherries

Grease four round layer pans (1 inch deep, 9 inches in diameter) with a little butter, and line bottoms with waxed paper cut to fit. If you have only 2 pans, simply bake 2 layers at a time.

With an electric mixer or a large spoon beat 1 cup butter in a large bowl until fluffy. Gradually add 2 cups sugar, beating after each addition until fluffy. Add vanilla, and beat until mixture is as light as whipped cream.

Sift, then lightly spoon 3¹/₄ cups flour in a measuring cup. Level top with spatula. Put into a sifter, add baking powder and ³/₄ teaspoon salt. Sift onto a large piece of waxed paper. Add to butter mixture, alternating with the milk, beating in small amounts at a time. Fold in beaten egg whites carefully, and distribute evenly.

Divide batter among 4 pans and spread to sides with a spatula. Place on two oven racks so that one pan is not directly beneath another—one rack set in the middle of the oven, the other about 2 inches below. Bake in a 350° oven 25 minutes or until the cake shrinks from the sides of pan and springs back to light pressure of the finger. Let pans stand on cake racks 10 minutes. Carefully loosen edges and turn out upside down on racks. Slowly peel off waxed paper. Cool before frosting.

Put egg yolks in top part of a double boiler, and beat slightly with rotary beater. Add 1³/₄ cups sugar, ¹/₂ teaspoon salt, and ³/₄ cup butter. Cook over simmering water, stirring constantly until sugar is dissolved, butter melts, and mixture is slightly thickened. Do not overcook or eggs will become scrambled. Remove from heat, and add rye or bourbon, beating for 1 minute with rotary beater. Add nuts, raisins, coconut and cherries. Mix, and cool.

Spread frosting between layers and on top and sides. After an hour, if any has dripped off, spread it back on sides. Repeat if necessary. Cover with cake cover or loosely with foil, and store to ripen in a cool place for several days. The cake will keep well in storage for several weeks. If it is to be frozen, wrap in vapor-proof wrapping, and store. It will keep indefinitely.

My Own Version of Thanksgiving Dinner

I bow to tradition inasmuch as I usually have a turkey, but the meal is relatively simple. I always serve champagne, accompanied by nuts and celery or other raw vegetables, or perhaps olives flavored with olive oil and finely chopped garlic.

You may serve champagne or your favorite cocktails, as you wish. With the caviar or smoked salmon, serve either chilled vodka or champagne; and with the turkey and cheese courses, a fine Bordeaux—a Lascombes or a Château Haut Brion. You may also offer a sweet sauterne for the dessert. If you are so steeped in tradition that you must have cranberries with your turkey, have them, but be warned that they will impair the taste of wine. Drink kirsch, framboise or cognac.

Caviar or Smoked Salmon
Buttered Pumpernickel or Rye
Turkey with Tarragon Crumb and
Spiced Sausage Stuffing
Pan Sauce with Giblets
Mashed Yellow Turnips with Butter
Salad   Cheese   Rich Pumpkin Pie

Tarragon Crumb Stuffing for a 12-Pound Turkey

2½ quarts (10 cups) freshly
    made bread crumbs
2 cups finely chopped scallions
    or shallots
¾ pound butter
1 tablespoon or more

tarragon, to taste
½ cup chopped parsley
2 teaspoons salt
1 teaspoon freshly ground
    black pepper

Make the crumbs in a blender or food processor, or grate them. French or Italian bread is recommended, and you may use part whole wheat if you wish. Place the scallions or shallots in a pan with the butter, and heat just enough to melt the butter. Mix with the crumbs, add the seasonings, and toss well. Taste for salt. If the stuffing is too dry, add a little sherry, cognac or turkey broth.

Stuff the larger cavity, place a piece of folded foil in the vent, and secure the vent with skewers or sew it. You will have more than enough stuffing for a bird of this size. Any extra can be baked in a separate pan.

Spiced Sausage Stuffing (for the neck vent)

First remove the neck, leaving the skin intact.

2½ pounds lean ground pork
1 clove garlic, finely chopped
¼ cup finely chopped parsley
1 teaspoon or more of salt
½ teaspoon Tabasco

¼ teaspoon nutmeg
1 teaspoon freshly ground
    black pepper
1 teaspoon thyme
1 tablespoon cognac

Combine ingredients, blend well, and fill the neck cavity. Mold into shape, and sew or skewer the skin to the bird.

To Roast the Turkey

I like to use a rack placed in a shallow pan. Tie the legs securely or run a larding needle through the thighs with string attached and then tie this around the legs. Rub turkey well with butter, and sprinkle with salt and pepper. Place breast side down on the rack, and cover lightly with a piece of foil. Roast at 325° for 1 hour. Turn on one side, baste, and continue roasting another 45 minutes. Turn on opposite side, and repeat. Remove foil, turn turkey breast side up, and baste well. Continue roasting till done—45 minutes to 1 hour. Baste 2 or 3 times more during this last period. If there are not enough pan juices for basting, combine ¼ pound melted butter with ½ cup white wine.

It is difficult to tell when a turkey is perfectly done, because turkeys vary so in structure and tenderness. A standard test is to see if the legs and thighs move up and down freely. For a more accurate test insert a meat thermometer into the thickest part of one thigh without touching the bone. The interior temperature should be about 170°.

Allow the turkey to settle in a warm place for 15 to 20 minutes before carving.

To serve:

Remove the strings and skewers from the turkey, and place on a hot platter large enough to allow for carving. Garnish discreetly with watercress; the carver needs all the space he can find. The carver's implements should include a sharp carving knife; a small, sharp boning knife for the legs, thighs, and wings; spoons for the stuffing; a large fork for holding the bird; and a serving fork. A small extra platter for the legs, thighs, and wings is valuable also.

Pan Sauce with Giblets

You may either use the pan drippings in reasonable quantity, or you may pour off all but 2 tablespoons, adding 1½ cups giblet broth, together with the giblets, chopped. If you do the latter, cook down for 4 minutes, correct the seasoning and thicken with butter and flour kneaded together. Add 2 tablespoons Madeira or cognac.

Mashed Yellow Turnips with Butter

For 6 persons peel and slice 2 medium or one very large yellow turnip—called rutabaga or swede, according to the part of the country in which you live. Cook in boiling salted water till tender. Drain and mash with ¼ pound butter. Add salt and freshly ground pepper to taste.

NOTE: If you must have mashed potatoes, that is your privilege. For my starch, I prefer the dressing.

Salad

Serve a simple romaine or Bibb lettuce salad with a basic Vinaigrette Sauce (*see* p. 338).

Cheese

Select 2 or 3 cheeses of varying types and serve with toasted French bread or rolls.

Rich Pumpkin Pie

Plain Pastry for 2 9-inch shells (see p. 347)	*²/₃ cup sugar*
2 cups mashed pumpkin— canned is ideal	*1 teaspoon cinnamon*
	¹/₄ teaspoon ground cloves
6 eggs	*¹/₂ cup finely cut preserved or candied ginger*
2 cups heavy cream	*¹/₂ cup cognac*
¹/₄ teaspoon salt	*¹/₄ teaspoon mace*

Fill shells with foil and beans and bake at 425° for 12 minutes. Remove foil and beans.

Place pumpkin in a bowl and make a well in center. Add lightly beaten eggs combined with heavy cream, seasonings and chopped ginger. Blend thoroughly. Correct the seasoning—you may want a spicier pie. Pour into the partially baked pie shells, and bake at 375° till custard is just set.

I prefer to serve this pie on the warm side with cognac-flavored and sweetened whipped cream.

A Christmas Eve Supper

This can be a delightfully informal meal to be partaken of by the family, invited guests, and close friends who drop in unannounced to leave a gift or to say Merry Christmas. Provide a selection of favorite drinks, including champagne. Eschew if you can Tom and Jerries and eggnogs, which to me are unpalatable concoctions that ruin the appetite. For the food, I like a rather international menu.

With the food serve chilled champagne and white wine (perhaps a Pouilly-Fumé) or a California Mountain Red or Pinot Chardonnay. Also offer beer and soft drinks.

Smoked-Fish Platter
Smithfield Ham   Roast Turkey
French Bread   Sweet Butter
Mustard   Mustard Mayonnaise
Endive   Celery   Radishes   Olives
Cheese Board   Crackers   French Rolls
Fresh Fruit   Fruit Cake

Smoked-Fish Platter

This might include: smoked salmon, sturgeon, whitefish, eel, one or two types of herring (with sour cream and onions or maatjes herring, or both), kippered tuna, and any other smoked or cured fish you can find in your neighborhood.

Serve with thinly sliced pumpernickel, rye bread, sweet butter, thinly sliced onions, capers, olive oil, and a bowl of thinly sliced cucumbers dressed with oil, vinegar and dill weed or fresh dill.

Smithfield Ham

This may be bought ready to eat. Be sure to carve in very thin slices.

Roast Turkey

See p. 314–15.

The fish should be kept coolish, the coffee hot, and the rest of the food can be at room temperature. This will make it easy for you to keep platters replenished through the evening.

A Christmas Breakfast for 12

This is a pleasant custom that takes the place of the more usual Christmas Eve supper. Serve fruit juice or Bloody Marys before eating and white wine throughout the meal.

Fruit Juices
Cheesed Melba Toast
Codfish in Cream with Eggs   Crisp Bacon
Italian Sausages, Hot and Sweet
Raw Mushroom and Bibb Lettuce Salad
Brioche   Stollen   Toasted Muffins
Preserves   Cream Cheese
Fresh Fruit

Fruit Juices

The juices should be freshly squeezed or done to order and should include grapefruit and orange, with perhaps one reconstituted frozen juice, such as pineapple or tangerine. The wine, which is, after all, fermented grape juice, counts as a juice. And those in need will be grateful for tomato juice in the form of a Bloody Mary.

Cheesed Melba Toast

Make your own Melba toast by slicing bread quite thin and drying it out in a 250° oven. When it is crisp, brush with butter and sprinkle with grated Parmesan mixed with a little black pepper and paprika. Add a dash or two of Tabasco, and reheat for a few minutes to blend the cheese. Serve crisp and warm.

Codfish in Cream with Eggs

4 pounds filleted salt codfish
Water
6 tablespoons butter
5 tablespoons flour
2 cups milk
1 teaspoon salt
1/8 teaspoon nutmeg
1/4 teaspoon Tabasco
3/4 cup heavy cream
4 egg yolks
12 hard-boiled eggs, peeled
    and sliced
Chopped parsley
14 pieces fried toast

Soak codfish overnight, changing the water once. Add fresh water, and bring to a boil. Simmer for 6 to 8 minutes or until fish will flake easily. Taste for salt. Break fish up into bite-size sections.

Prepare the cream sauce by melting the butter over low heat, blending in the flour and slowly adding heated milk. When sauce has thickened and is smooth, season with salt, nutmeg and Tabasco. Add the cream and egg yolks. Stir until well blended and thickened over medium heat. Do not let sauce boil. Just before serving add codfish, sliced eggs and parsley. Serve with fried toast.

Crisp Bacon

Arrange 1 1/2 pounds bacon on a broiling pan and bake in 350° oven till desired state of doneness is reached.

Italian Sausages, Hot and Sweet

Poach 2 pounds or more small sausages for 10 minutes in white wine to cover, allowing the wine to cook down a bit. Remove sausages to a broiling pan rack and brown in the oven or under the broiler.

Raw Mushroom and Bibb Lettuce Salad

1 1/2 pounds firm mushrooms,
sliced in rounds
8 to 10 heads Bibb lettuce

Vinaigrette Sauce (see p. 338)
Freshly ground black pepper

Wash Bibb well, and dry it. Nothing is worse than wet salad greens unless it be sandy and gravelly Bibb lettuce. Cut the heads in quarters. Add the sliced raw mushrooms, add a few grinds of fresh pepper, and toss with a basic vinaigrette sauce made with 4 parts good olive oil to 1 part wine vinegar.

Brioche, Stollen, Muffins

To make Brioche, see recipe on page 344.

Unless you are an ambitious baker, buy your stollen from a good bakery that specializes in this holiday delicacy. Slice it very thin.

Toast the muffins to order, or keep a toaster on the buffet table so guests may help themselves.

With these items serve plenty of sweet butter and interesting preserves. Cream cheese is especially pleasant when combined with the preserves.

For a pleasant ending, produce lots of hot coffee and a large, decorative bowl of fruit to which you have added dried raisins and nuts.

My Own Christmas Dinner for 8

This is the Christmas dinner I am apt to serve. My feeling for tradition has changed, and thus the holiday dinner is considerably simplified. It is much more to my taste and it seems to find general approval among my guests, who favor it over yesteryear's feast.

I prefer to begin the festivities with champagne. You may want to serve Scotch, dry martinis, Lillet, or any number of other drinks. With the apéritifs I produce the first course and it is usually a foie gras with toast—not a great deal of it, but enough to be thoroughly savored. If it is a large party, sometimes I make tiny baking-powder biscuits, and sandwich a piece of foie gras in them. They are light and short and make a nice setting for this delicacy. If foie gras is not your dish, you might substitute prosciutto and melon or a bit of smoked sturgeon or some caviar. At any rate, be festive.

Serve a Burgundy of a good year—a Vosne Romanée or a red Chassagne Montrachet—with the meat, vegetable and cheese; after dinner, cognac and eau de vie de Framboise.

Foie Gras   Toast
Roast Sirloin Strip
Browned Potatoes
Braised Brussels Sprouts
Cheese
Apple and Mince Flan

Roast Sirloin Strip

The sirloin roast is a particular favorite of mine. You may buy the loin with the T-bone and a bit of the tenderloin and the sirloin together. Or ask your butcher to give you boneless shells or strips, which roast perfectly, carve easily and look elegant when served.

You will want 10 or 11 pounds at least—or more, if you like cold beef as well as I do.

Rub the roast with salt and freshly ground pepper, place on a rack in a shallow pan, and roast at 325°, allowing about 10 minutes per pound, or until the roast reaches an inner temperature of 120°, for rare. Remove to a hot platter and allow to rest for 12 to 14 minutes. Garnish the platter with watercress and freshly grated horseradish.

For Sauce: When you remove the roast from the rack, spoon off most of the fat from the drippings, add 1½ cups beef broth to the drippings, and bring to a boil. Then add ¼ cup Madeira and salt and pepper to taste. Serve in a sauce boat with the roast.

Browned Potatoes

12 good-sized potatoes *Salt and pepper*
2 cups finely chopped beef suet

Peel the potatoes and cut in half lengthwise. Boil for just 8 minutes in salted water. Drain. An hour before the potatoes go in, place the beef suet in a roasting pan, and melt in the oven. Add the potatoes and roast them for 1 hour or till tender, turning them once or twice to color them nicely.

Braised Brussel Sprouts

3 pints Brussels sprouts *Salt and pepper*
Boiling salted water *Sliced lemon*
¾ cup butter

Trim the sprouts well, and blanch them in boiling salted water for 4 minutes. Drain. Melt butter in a heavy saucepan, and add the sprouts. Cover tightly and cook over low heat till they are just tender when pierced with a fork. Correct the seasoning, and serve at once with thin slices of lemon.

Cheese

Choose several varieties of the finest cheeses, and leave them at room temperature for several hours before serving. Toasted rolls or crisp French bread are best with cheese. Continue with the red wine which you served with the beef.

Apple and Mince Flan or Tart

Rich Pastry (see p. 347)
6 apples
1/4 pound butter
Vanilla

1/4 cup sugar
2 cups mincemeat
   (approximately)
Apricot Glaze (see p. 38)

Make a double recipe of Rich Pastry. Cool for 1 hour. Roll out and fit into 2 9-inch flan rings, a large baking dish, or 2 9-inch pie tins. Chill again.

Peel the apples and cut into eighths. Melt butter in a heavy skillet and add apples and a dash of vanilla. Cover, and steam apples over medium heat till soft but not mushy. Sugar to taste. Cool.

Fill pie shells or flan shells with a layer of apples and a layer of mincemeat. Bake at 450° for 10 minutes. Reduce heat to 350° and continue baking till nicely set and crust is browned. Cool slightly. Glaze with apricot glaze. Serve warm. Some people like to serve mince pie with sweetened whipped cream flavored with additional cognac.

VARIATION: You may make strips of pastry for the top and make a lattice over the mincemeat. In this case brush the pastry with 1 beaten egg blended with 2 tablespoons cream.

Christmas Dinner for 6

This dinner is more difficult but should be delicious whether you serve it in the country or the city. It also would be suitable for a New Year's dinner. Start with your favorite potables, pass some good salted almonds and olives, then move on to the table with a fine Madeira for the soup course. A really great Hermitage should accompany the goose and the cheese. Try to find a rare old one of a fine year. Cognac and coffee are musts after this dinner.

Turtle Soup with Madeira
Buttered Toast
Roast Stuffed Goose with Prunes
and Apples
Watercress
Braised Sauerkraut   Puree of Chestnuts
Cognac and Coffee Ice Cream
Macaroons   Sand Tarts
Raisins, Nuts, Dates, Prunes, Glacé Fruits

Turtle Soup with Madeira

Purchase a fine brand of turtle soup and turtle meat. For 6 persons buy 3 large cans of soup and a can of meat. Cut the meat into small dice, and combine with the soup. Cook for 30 minutes or until the soup has reduced one-fourth. It should be rich and gelatinous. Flavor to taste with Madeira, and correct the seasoning. Serve very hot with buttered toast and a fine Madeira.

Roast Stuffed Goose with Prunes and Apples

1 goose
18 pitted prunes that have
   been soaked in sherry or
   Madeira for 4 days
6 to 8 apples, peeled, cored

and halved
Nutmeg and lemon slices
Salt and pepper
6 potatoes, peeled and
   quartered lengthwise

There is a great deal of fat on a goose. Therefore it should be roasted slowly and on a rack so that the bird will crispen while the fat drips down into the roasting pan. I like to roast potatoes in the goose fat, for they become rather crisp and thoroughly saturated with flavor. Reserve the fat for future cooking. It can be used for many dishes.

Stuff the goose with the prunes and the apples, which have been lightly salted and dusted with a bit of nutmeg. Here and there add a lemon slice. Place the goose on a rack in rather a deep pan, and cover lightly with foil. Roast at 325°. At the end of 2½ hours remove the foil and baste with the drippings. Continue roasting till browned and tender. A large goose should take about 3 or 3½ hours to cook.

If the potatoes are added to the bottom of the pan 1 hour after the goose is placed in the oven, they will be ready with the goose, delicious, crisp, and rich as can be!

I always like to serve a large bowl of watercress with goose. It is so refreshing and seems somehow to offer an appropriate contrast of flavor as well as color.

Braised Sauerkraut

Goose fat
4 pounds sauerkraut, washed
   and drained
1 clove garlic, finely chopped

1 teaspoon freshly ground
   black pepper
White wine
Juniper berries (optional)

Heat 4 tablespoons goose fat in a heavy kettle. Add the sauerkraut, the chopped garlic and the pepper. Cover with a good dry white wine and bring to a boil. Place a lid on the pan and simmer for 2½ hours, adding more white wine if necessary. A few juniper berries may be added.

Puree of Chestnuts

2 cans chestnuts in brine
1/4 pound butter
Salt

Pepper or nutmeg
3 tablespoons cream

Wash the chestnuts and either mash them or put them through a food mill. Melt the butter in a heavy pan, stir in the puree, and heat gently. Season with salt and a few grains of pepper or a dash of nutmeg. Just before serving stir in the cream, and heat again.

Cognac and Coffee Ice Cream

I love real old-fashioned ice cream turned in a freezer. (Although nowadays you can get electric ice cream makers that save a lot of muscle.) This is a favorite.

1 quart heavy cream
1 cup light cream
1 cup sugar
1 teaspoon vanilla

1/2 cup cognac
2 tablespoons instant
coffee, or to taste

Combine ingredients and stir. Add a dash of salt, place in refrigerator, and chill well. Freeze in freezer packed with salt and ice. Follow directions for your particular freezer. If using hand freezer, turn until it will turn no more. Wipe the cover carefully, remove the dasher, and repack with ice and salt until ready to use. Serve with Macaroons (see below) and Sand Tarts (see p. 281).

Macaroons

1 cup almond paste
1 cup confectioners' sugar

3 to 4 egg whites
Granulated sugar

Blend together the almond paste and the confectioners' sugar, being certain that it is well mixed. Add the egg whites, one at a time, until the texture is soft enough to flow through a pastry tube yet firm enough to hold its shape. You may not need all the egg whites.

Force through a pastry bag fitted with a plain tube onto baking paper arranged on a baking sheet, making 1 1/2-inch rounds. Sprinkle with granulated sugar, and bake at 300° for 12 to 16 minutes.

Dinner for a Green Christmas, for 6

Not everyone can experience a white Christmas, so this menu is planned for those who enjoy the winter holidays in sunny climes. I have spent many a Christmas in San Francisco without once eating turkey. One of the dishes I remember having on Christmas Day was roast loin of pork, a favorite of mine and as good a dish for celebration as any.

Drink a California champagne with the first course, and if you like, carry on with it through the meal.

California Caviar
Roast Loin of Pork
Celery Root and Potato Purée
Oven-baked Cabbage
Five-day Plum Pudding

California Caviar

This domestic caviar is excellent and less expensive than Russian but still not plentiful. It should be served like any good caviar from a bowl set in another bowl of crushed ice. All it needs is toast or dark bread and a bit of lemon juice. Two spoonfuls make an ample serving. Instead of caviar you might want to serve a good smoked salmon.

Roast Loin of Pork

5-pound pork loin, trimmed
 and tied
Salt and freshly ground

black pepper
1 teaspoon dried thyme
1 cup chicken or veal stock

Rub the loin well with salt, pepper and thyme. Place fat side up on a rack in a roasting pan and roast at 325° for 25 to 30 minutes a pound, to an internal temperature of 160°. Remove from the oven and let it rest for 10 minutes before carving. Meanwhile skim excess fat from the roasting pan, add the chicken or veal stock, and let the mixture come to a boil. Simmer a few minutes and serve with the pork.

Celery Root and Potato Purée

2 pounds celery root (medium
 size)
2 pounds potatoes
1/2 cup (1 stick) unsalted

butter, softened
1/4 cup heavy cream
Chopped parsley

Wash the celery root and put it, unpeeled, in a saucepan with salted water to cover. Simmer until it is quite tender. Remove and drain. Peel the roots, cut off the root ends, and cut into quarters. Put through a food mill (which will remove any coarse fibers) or purée in a food processor.

Peel the potatoes and put in a saucepan with salted water to cover, and simmer until they are tender, about 20 minutes. Drain, return to the pan, and let them dry over medium heat for a minute or so. Mash or put through a food mill.

Combine the celery root and potato purée, and whip them together with the butter and cream. Spoon into a heated serving dish and top with a dab of butter and chopped parsley.

Oven-baked Cabbage

3-pound head of cabbage
3 tablespoons unsalted butter
Juice of 2 lemons

Salt and freshly ground
   black pepper
1 lemon, thinly sliced

Trim the cabbage, remove the core, and shred. Bring to a boil enough salted water to cover the cabbage. Add the cabbage, and cook until just tender. Pour off the cooking liquid and drain. Place in a gratin dish, dot with the butter, pour the lemon juice over it, and sprinkle with salt and pepper. Garnish with the lemon slices. Bake in a 350° oven for 10 to 15 minutes. Serve at once.

Five-day Plum Pudding

$1/2$ pound beef suet
2 cups all-purpose flour
$3/4$ cup seedless raisins
1 cup sultana raisins
$1/2$ cup dried currants
1 pound dried citrus peel
   (orange, lemon and citron,
   mixed), finely chopped
3 cups fresh bread crumbs
6 or 7 tart apples, cored,
   peeled and chopped
$1/2$ cup ground filberts

1 cup brown sugar
$1/2$ teaspoon ground cloves
2 teaspoons ground cinnamon
1 teaspoon ground ginger
1 teaspoon ground mace
1 teaspoon salt
1 orange
1 lemon
Cognac, rum or brandy
6 eggs, lightly beaten
Cognac Sauce

Chop the suet very fine and sprinkle it with $1/2$ cup of the flour. Place the raisins and currants in a bowl, lightly dust them with flour, and add the suet.

Lightly dust the citrus peel with flour, and add it to the raisin-suet mixture. Stir in 1 cup of the flour, then add the crumbs, apples, filberts, sugar, spices and salt.

Grate the peel of the orange and the lemon, then squeeze the juice from both. Add the peel and juice to the mixture. Then add $1/2$ cup of cognac, rum or brandy, and stir everything well.

Place in a cold spot or in the refrigerator for 5 days, $1/4$ cup more of spirits each day and stirring mixture well. On the last day, stir in the lightly beaten eggs. If the batter is too thick, thin it with a little beer.

Pour the batter in a mold, cover it with a floured, buttered damp cloth or seal with aluminum foil. Place in a large pot, and pour in boiling water to reach halfway up the mold. Cover the pot and cook the pudding over medium low heat for 6 hours, adding water if necessary. Unmold and serve with Cognac Sauce.

BASIC RECIPES

SEASONING

Quatre Épices

¹/₄ cup ground white pepper
1¹/₂ teaspoons ground ginger
1¹/₂ teaspoons ground nutmeg
¹/₂ teaspoon ground cloves

Combine the spices, and blend thoroughly. Store in a sealed jar.

SAUCES

Béchamel Sauce

3 tablespoons butter
3 tablespoons flour
1¹/₄ cups liquid (light cream;
milk; or chicken, fish or
vegetable broth)

Salt
Pepper
Nutmeg
Tabasco (optional)

Combine butter and flour and cook over low heat for 2 or 3 minutes, stirring gently with a spatula, wooden spoon or wire whisk. Gradually pour in heated liquid while stirring, and continue to stir until mixture thickens. Season to taste with salt, freshly ground pepper and a dash of nutmeg. A dash of Tabasco will give this sauce an added lift.

MORNAY SAUCE:

To the above Béchamel sauce, add ¹/₂ cup grated Parmesan cheese and blend thoroughly.

Cheese Sauce:

Add ¹/₂ to ³/₄ cup grated Gruyère, Emmenthal, or cheddar cheese to the Béchamel sauce and stir until melted. Add a good dash of Tabasco.

Sauce Suprême:

To a recipe of Béchamel made with chicken or veal stock, add 1 cup heavy cream mixed with three beaten egg yolks. Stir over low heat until hot through, but do not allow to boil.

Velouté Sauce:

To 1 cup of Béchamel, made with milk or with 1 cup of meat, poultry, fish or vegetable stock, add ¹/₂ cup heavy cream. Stir until well blended and hot.

Basic Brown Sauce (or Sauce Espagnole)

¹/₂ pound butter or clarified butter
2¹/₂ cups flour (approximately)
4 cups strong beef broth or bouillon
2 tablespoons heavy tomato paste

¹/₂ teaspoon thyme
Sprig of parsley
Onion stuck with two cloves
Salt
3 or 4 mushrooms, sliced
2 tablespoons glace de viande or beef extract

Prepare a brown roux, which you may keep in a jar or a tin in the refrigerator for several weeks. Melt butter or clarified butter in a heavy skillet and combine it with an equal amount—in weight—of flour. This would be a little over 2¹/₄ cups. Blend and cook slowly over a very low heat until the roux turns a delicate brown.

For the sauce, 1 cup of the roux is combined with beef broth or bouillon, tomato paste, thyme, parsley, an onion stuck with cloves and salt to taste. Bring to a boil, add mushrooms or some mushroom stems, coarsely chopped, and simmer for 45 minutes. Cool and put through a fine sieve. Add glace de viande or beef extract if you have it.

This is a basic sauce espagnole or brown sauce, which is used as a base for many of the famous brown sauces. It will keep for some time under refrigeration and may be used for the following:

SAUCE BORDELAISE:

6 shallots or 12 small green
  onions, peeled and chopped
1½ cups good red wine
1 tablespoon chopped parsley

1 cup sauce espagnole
Pat of butter
Poached marrow

Combine shallots or onions with wine and chopped parsley. Reduce over a brisk flame to ¾ cup. Strain and combine with sauce espagnole. Bring to a boil and simmer for 1 or 2 minutes. Add a pat of butter and correct the seasoning. Add some poached marrow to the steak or roast with which you are using the sauce.

SAUCE MADÈRE:

6 shallots or 12 small onions,
  peeled and chopped

1 cup sauce espagnole
½ cup Madeira

Sauté shallots or small onions. Combine sauce espagnole with Madeira and bring to a boil. Add shallots, simmer 5 to 6 minutes and correct seasoning.

SAUCE PERIGOURDINE:

To sauce madère above, add 2 tablespoons finely chopped truffles.

SAUCE DUXELLES:

To 1½ cups of the basic sauce madère, add ¾ cup Duxelles (see p. 341) and simmer for 5 minutes. Add a dash of lemon sauce. Correct the seasoning.

SAUCE DIABLE:

1/4 cup tarragon vinegar
3/4 cup white wine
1 shallot, finely chopped
1 teaspoon tarragon
1 1/4 cups sauce espagnole
Dash Tabasco

2 teaspoons dry mustard
Pepper
Parsley, finely chopped
Fresh tarragon, finely
* chopped*

Combine tarragon vinegar and wine with chopped shallot and tarragon. Reduce to one half and add to sauce espagnole with a good dash of Tabasco and dry mustard. Bring to a boil and simmer 3 minutes. Add several grinds from the pepper grinder and strain. Serve with a dusting of parsley and fresh tarragon, both finely chopped.

SAUCE POIVRADE:

Reduce 1 cup port to 1/2 cup and blend with 1 1/2 cups sauce espagnole. Bring to a boil and simmer for 4 minutes. Add 1 1/2 teaspoons freshly ground black pepper and correct the seasoning.

SAUCE PIQUANTE:

2 cloves garlic, finely chopped
4 shallots, finely chopped
1/2 cup wine vinegar
1 cup red wine
1 teaspoon oregano

1 1/2 cups sauce espagnole
3 tablespoons concentrated
* tomato paste*
1 tablespoon Dijon mustard
Dash Tabasco

Combine chopped garlic and shallots with wine vinegar, red wine and oregano. Reduce to 1/2 cup over brisk heat. Strain and add to sauce espagnole along with tomato paste, Dijon mustard and a hearty dash of Tabasco. Blend and simmer for 5 minutes.

Basic Hollandaise Sauce

1/4 pound butter
3 egg yolks
1/2 teaspoon salt

1 tablespoon lemon juice
Dash Tabasco

Cut the butter into three equal parts. Beat egg yolks slightly and add seasonings. Place in an enamel, glass or pottery container over hot water. Using a wire whisk or spatula beat in 1/3 of the butter, then the second piece and then the third. Do not let the water boil.

If the hollandaise should curdle, add a touch of boiling water and continue stirring till it emulsifies again.

FOOD PROCESSOR OR BLENDER HOLLANDAISE:

4 egg yolks
1 tablespoon lemon juice
1/2 teaspoon salt

Dash Tabasco
1/2 cup butter, melted

Place egg yolks, lemon juice, salt and Tabasco in the food processor or blender, and pulse for a few seconds. Heat the butter until it is very hot (but not burning) and bubbly. With the food processor or blender running, steadily dribble in the hot butter until the mixture emulsifies and thickens. This will hold over warm water for several hours.

SAUCE MOUSSELINE:

To 1 cup hollandaise add 1/2 cup heavy cream, whipped.

SAUCE BÉARNAISE:

3 shallots or scallions, finely
  chopped
1 teaspoon tarragon or
1 tablespoon chopped
  fresh tarragon

1/4 cup wine vinegar
1/4 cup white wine
1 teaspoon chopped parsley
Basic hollandaise recipe

Add to shallots or scallions the tarragon, wine vinegar, white wine and chopped parsley. Bring to a boil and reduce to practically a glaze. Add this to basic hollandaise and correct seasoning.

If tarragon is fresh, it is sometimes pleasant to stir in an extra amount.

Anchovy Sauce:

To basic hollandaise, add 4 finely chopped anchovy fillets, a clove of crushed or chopped garlic and a few capers; or if you are making a blender hollandaise, place 4 egg yolks, no salt, the chopped anchovy fillets, a clove of garlic and 1 tablespoon lemon juice in the blender. Turn on and off. Gradually pour in, with the blender at high speed, 2/3 cup bubbling melted butter.

Beurre Blanc

1/4 cup white wine
1/4 cup wine vinegar
1 tablespoon chopped
*   shallots or onions*
1/4 teaspoon salt

1 dash freshly ground black
*   pepper*
12 ounces chilled butter
*   (3 sticks cut into 24 squares)*
Salt and pepper

Boil liquid and onions (in Pyrex or enamel) until they are reduced to 2 tablespoons. Add salt and pepper. Remove the pan from the fire; and with a wire whisk, beat in two pieces of butter. When it begins to cream, beat in another piece; when this begins to cream, beat in another; and continue in this manner, holding the pan over low heat or warm water until all the butter is added. The resulting sauce will be creamy and light amber in color. Do not let it get too hot or it will break.

Basic Mayonnaise

2 egg yolks
1 1/2 cups oil (half olive,
*   half peanut)*
1 tablespoon vinegar or lemon

juice
1 teaspoon salt
1/2 teaspoon dry mustard

Mayonnaise is an emulsion of egg yolk and oil. It may be mixed with a fork, an egg beater, or an electric mixer. Beat yolks well in a soup plate, if you use a fork; a bowl, if you use an egg beater; or in the mixer bowl, if you use an electric mixer. Add oil slowly till the emulsion begins to thicken. Begin with a teaspoon or a thin dribble if you are using the electric mixer. Gradually increase the amount added. When the mixture becomes very thick add vinegar and salt. Finally add dry mustard and continue beating. Taste and add additional vinegar if needed.

BLENDER MAYONNAISE:

1 whole egg
2 teaspoons wine vinegar
¹/₂ teaspoon salt

1 teaspoon dry mustard
1 cup oil (half olive, half peanut)

Place egg, wine vinegar, salt, and dry mustard in the blender container. Turn blender to high and dribble oil through the top till mixture emulsifies and thickens. Takes about 1 minute.

FOOD PROCESSOR MAYONNAISE:

1 whole egg
1 tablespoon vinegar or lemon juice
1 teaspoon salt

¹/₄ teaspoon pepper
1¹/₂ cups oil (half olive, half peanut)

Put the egg, vinegar and salt and pepper in the processor, and pulse 2 or 3 seconds. Slowly—very slowly at first—pour in the oil until the mixture emulsifies.

MUSTARD MAYONNAISE:

Add Dijon mustard to taste and a little dry mustard. About 1 tablespoon Dijon and 1 teaspoon dry mustard makes a good, brisk mustard sauce.

ANCHOVY MAYONNAISE:

Add 2 teaspoons Dijon mustard and 2 tablespoons finely chopped anchovy fillets. Omit salt in this mayonnaise.

Sauces with a Mayonnaise Base

RÉMOULADE:

To 1 cup of mayonnaise add 1 minced clove of garlic, 1 teaspoon of dry or 1 tablespoon fresh chopped tarragon, ¹/₂ teaspoon dry mustard, a finely chopped hard-boiled egg, 1 teaspoon of capers, 1 tablespoon chopped parsley, and a dab of anchovy paste.

GREEN GODDESS:

To 1 cup mayonnaise add ¹/₂ cup mixed, chopped green herbs—parsley, chives, tarragon—and 3 chopped anchovy fillets.

RUSSIAN:

Blend together and allow to stand for 2 hours, 2 cups of mayonnaise, 1 teaspoon dry mustard, 2 tablespoons finely chopped onion, 1 tablespoon Worcestershire sauce, and 2 ounces of caviar.

TARTAR:

Blend 2 cups of mayonnaise, 3 tablespoons finely chopped onion, 2 teaspoons finely chopped parsley, 2 teaspoons lemon juice, and 2 tablespoons finely chopped dill pickle—or fresh dill, if you prefer.

THOUSAND ISLAND DRESSING:

To 1 cup of mayonnaise add 1 tablespoon of finely chopped onion, 3 tablespoons of chili sauce, 1 chopped hard-cooked egg, and a touch of dry mustard.

Sauce Vinaigrette or French Dressing

6 tablespoons olive or vegetable oil	¹/₂ to 1 teaspoon salt
2 tablespoons wine vinegar	¹/₂ teaspoon freshly ground black pepper

Blend the ingredients together thoroughly. You may adjust the vinegar content and salt and pepper to suit the salad or the individual palate.

VARIATIONS

These are endless.

1) Mustard, either dry or Dijon, may be added—a dash of dry and up to a tablespoonful of Dijon for certain salads.

2) Garlic is delicious in many dressings and can be added to your taste. Crush the clove and rub well into the salt before adding oil to the bowl.

3) Add chopped or crushed fresh or dried herbs to the salad. Tar-

ragon is a perfect salad herb. Basil is superb with tomatoes. Dill goes with cucumbers. Rosemary goes with salads that have a little orange or grapefruit in them.

4) Finely sliced onion or chopped green onion or chives make a superb flavoring for salad.

The important thing is to make your dressing fresh each time and adjust it to suit the salad ingredients.

Sauce for Vegetables à la Grecque

²/₃ cup olive oil or peanut oil
1 cup white wine or vermouth
1 teaspoon salt
¹/₂ teaspoon freshly ground

pepper
1 or 2 sprigs parsley
Thyme, rosemary or tarragon

With this base one can experiment and add various flavors—such things as coriander seeds, mustard seed, celery seed, cumin, garlic or Tabasco, allspice or tomato puree.

Poach vegetables in this sauce until crisply tender and then cool and serve in the sauce. Among the vegetables to be serve this way are celery, small artichokes, zucchini, cucumbers, celery root, small onions, fennel and leeks.

Dress with chopped parsley before serving.

Sauce Italienne

1 clove garlic, finely chopped
1 small onion, finely chopped
2 tablespoons olive oil

1¹/₂ cups solid-pack tomatoes
¹/₂ teaspoon basil
1 can (6 ounces) tomato paste

Sauté garlic and onion in olive oil. Add tomatoes and basil. Simmer 30 to 40 minutes. Add tomato paste and allow to simmer 15 minutes.

Strain. If not thick enough, cook over brisk heat several minutes to reduce it, stirring often and being careful that the sauce is not scorched.

Cocktail Sauce

1 cup catsup or chili sauce
2 tablespoons lemon juice
1/2 teaspoon salt

1/4 teaspoon Tabasco
1 tablespoon horseradish

Mix ingredients thoroughly. Chill well before serving. Serve with shrimp, crab or lobster. Makes approximately 1 1/4 cups.

Barbecue Sauce

2 medium onions, quartered
1/4 cup salad oil
1 teaspoon dry mustard
1 tablespoon Worcestershire
  sauce
1/4 cup lemon juice

1/2 cup chili sauce
1 small hot chili pepper
  (peeled green chilies)
1/4 cup brown sugar
1 teaspoon salt
6 peppercorns

Put all ingredients into container of a blender or food processor. Blend for 20 seconds. Pour into saucepan and heat until boiling. Makes 1 1/2 cups sauce.

Oriental Sauce

1 large onion, finely chopped
1 clove garlic, finely chopped
4 tablespoons butter
1 tablespoon curry powder

4 tablespoons flour
1 cup hot chicken broth
1 cup hot water

In a saucepan melt 2 tablespoons of the butter, and sauté the chopped vegetables with the curry powder for 5 minutes. Blend the flour and remaining butter together, then stir in the hot chicken broth. Finally add the hot water and stir until smooth. Add to the vegetables in the saucepan, and cook over low heat about 10 minutes, stirring occasionally, until smooth and thickened. Makes 2 cups sauce.

Mushroom Sauce

1 3-ounce can cooked
   mushrooms or ¹/₂ cup
   Duxelles (see below)
2 tablespoons flour

2 tablespoons soft butter
¹/₂ cup hot chicken broth
¹/₂ cup heavy cream

Into the container of a blender or food processor put mushrooms, flour, butter, and chicken broth. Blend for 15 seconds. With motor still running add the cream. Pour into saucepan and cook over simmering water for 15 minutes, stirring occasionally. Makes 1¹/₂ cups.

Duxelles

Chop 1¹/₂ pounds of mushrooms very finely. Melt 4 ounces of butter in a heavy skillet. Add 1 clove of garlic finely chopped and 2 finely chopped shallots. Add the mushrooms and let them sauté very slightly. Add more butter if necessary until they cook down and turn dark. Sprinkle with 2 tablespoons flour and let them cook down more. Pack in a covered container. Store in refrigerator.

BREADS AND PASTRIES

Basic Homemade Bread

2 cups milk
3 tablespoons butter
1 tablespoon salt
   (approximately)

2 tablespoons sugar
1 cake or package of yeast
6 cups sifted flour
   (approximately)

Scald milk. Combine 1 cup with butter, salt, and sugar. Dissolve 1 cake or package active dry yeast in remaining cup of milk. Combine the 2 cups and work in 3 cups sifted flour. Blend well, gradually beat in remaining 3 cups, or more, flour and knead on a floured board until smooth and springy and tiny blisters form.

Place dough in a buttered bowl and daub top with butter. Cover and place in a warm spot without drafts to rise to double its bulk. Turn out on floured board, punch down and work slightly. Let dough rest for a few minutes, then shape into loaves and place in buttered bread pans. Cover and allow to rise again till almost doubled in bulk. Center of loaf will probably be higher.

Bake at 400° about 45 to 50 minutes.

Sweet Dough

¹/₂ cup scalded milk	*2 cakes or packages of yeast*
¹/₂ cup sugar	*¹/₂ cup warm water*
1 tablespoon salt	*2 eggs, well beaten*
4 tablespoons butter	*5 to 6 cups all-purpose flour*

Combine scalded milk, sugar, salt, and butter and cool to lukewarm. Dissolve yeast in warm water. Combine with the milk and butter mixture and add eggs, and 3 cups all-purpose flour. Work in 2 to 3 more cups flour till you have a soft dough. Knead on a lightly floured board until dough is springy and blisters slightly. Place in a buttered bowl, brush with melted butter and put to rise in a warm, draft-free place. When doubled in bulk, punch down and work slightly.

Use this dough for coffee cakes, kuchen and sweet rolls.

KUCHEN:

Roll out sweet dough ³/₄ inch thick and arrange in an 11- by 14-inch pan that has been buttered. Let rise 5 minutes. Arrange fresh fruit on top, sprinkle with sugar, and, if you wish, dust with cinnamon. Dot with butter and bake at 375° until nicely risen and the fruit is cooked. Apples, plums, peaches, prunes, all lend themselves to kuchen.

CINNAMON ROLLS:

Roll out sweet dough ³/₄ inch thick. Spread or brush well with melted butter. Dust with cinnamon and sprinkle with 1 cup granulated sugar. Brush with butter again and sprinkle with ¹/₂ cup each broken walnut or pecan meats and sultana raisins. Roll and cut into 2-inch sections. Arrange on a buttered baking sheet, brush with melted butter and sprinkle with sugar. Let rise for 15 minutes.

Bake at 375° until the rolls are nicely browned and cooked through—about 20 minutes. Brush with sugar and milk icing if you wish.

Sponge Cake

1¹/₄ cups flour
¹/₄ teaspoon salt
1¹/₄ cups sugar
6 eggs

2 tablespoons lemon juice
1 tablespoon grated lemon rind
2 tablespoons water
¹/₂ teaspoon cream of tartar

Sift together the flour, salt and 1 cup sugar; separate the eggs. Beat the yolks and add the flour mixture, the lemon juice and rind, and the water. Beat well with an electric beater or with a heavy whisk till thick and ribbony. This will require about 4 minutes by hand or 3 or so in the electric beater.

Beat egg whites till they hold soft peaks. Sprinkle cream of tartar over them and add half the remaining sugar and beat until well blended. Add rest of sugar and beat till the mixture holds firm peaks and is glossy.

Fold yolk mixture into whites and pour into a 10-inch tube pan or into a 13- by 9-inch pan or into a loaf pan.

Bake at 350° until cake springs back when tested with finger and is nicely browned, about 30 to 40 minutes

Pizza Dough

1 cake or package of yeast
1 cup lukewarm water
1 teaspoon sugar

2 teaspoons salt
3 tablespoons olive oil
3¹/₂ to 4 cups all-purpose flour

Dissolve yeast in lukewarm water. Stir in sugar, salt and olive oil. Gradually add flour and beat until smooth. Turn out on a floured board and knead until smooth, satiny and springy. Cover and let rise in a buttered bowl for about 1 hour or until double in bulk.

Divide dough into two pieces and knead a few minutes. Roll out into rounds to fit pizza pans. Use any pizza filling you wish. Bake in a hot (400°) oven for about 25 minutes.

Brioche

1/2 cup milk
1/2 cup margarine or butter
1/3 cup sugar
1/2 teaspoon salt
1/4 cup warm water
1 cake or package of yeast

1 egg yolk, beaten
3 whole eggs, beaten
3 1/4 cups sifted enriched flour
1 egg white beaten with
    1 tablespoon sugar

Scald milk. Cool to lukewarm. Cream thoroughly margarine or butter. Add gradually and cream together sugar and salt. Measure into bowl warm (not hot) water (cool to lukewarm for compressed yeast) and sprinkle or crumble in active dry or compressed yeast and stir until dissolved. Stir in lukewarm milk and creamed mixture. Add beaten egg yolk, beaten whole eggs, and flour. Beat for 10 minutes. Cover. Let rise in warm place, free from draft, about 2 hours or until more than doubled in bulk. Stir down and beat thoroughly. Cover tightly with waxed paper or aluminum foil and store in refrigerator overnight. Stir down and turn out soft dough on floured board. Divide into 2 pieces, one about 3/4 and the other about 1/4 of dough. Cut larger piece into 16 equal pieces and form into smooth balls. Place in well-greased muffin pans 2 3/4 inches in diameter by 1 3/4 inches deep. Cut smaller piece into 16 equal pieces. Form into smooth balls. Make a deep indentation in center of each large ball and dampen slightly with cold water. Press a small ball into each indentation. Cover and let rise in warm place, free from draft, about 1 hour, or until more than doubled in bulk. Brush with egg white and sugar mixture. Bake in moderate oven (375°) about 20 minutes.

Croissants

3 ounces fresh yeast
1 tablespoon sugar
2 teaspoons salt

1 cup cold milk
4 cups unsifted all-purpose flour
3/4 pound sweet butter

Cream yeast with sugar and salt. Add cold milk. Then add about three cups of flour, or enough to make a medium firm dough. Work in 1/8 pound (half a stick) of softened butter. Knead dough till it is very smooth and elastic—at least 15 minutes. Let dough rest 20 to 30 minutes covered with bowl.

While dough is resting, cream medium-firm butter with remaining flour. Roll butter-flour mixture between sheets of floured wax paper into a rectangle less than $1/2$ inch thick. If butter becomes very soft and sticky, place in refrigerator till it becomes firm but not hard.

After dough has rested, roll it on a floured cloth into a rectangle three times as long as it is wide. Cut butter rectangle in half and place half in center of dough. Fold one end of dough over butter. Place remaining butter on folded end of dough. Cover butter with remaining dough, sealing ends as well as possible.

Turn dough so that open ends face you. Roll out again into a rectangle. Bring both ends of rectangle to meet in center of dough. Fold in half, making four layers. Wrap in floured cloth or aluminum foil and refrigerate for one hour, or more if desired.

After one hour, place dough on floured cloth, open ends facing you. Roll and fold again, as before. Place in refrigerator for at least six hours, preferably overnight, before shaping into croissants.

To shape, roll dough out, using half at a time, into a sheet less than $1/4$ inch thick. Cut into triangles that are 4 inches wide at the base. Chill triangles briefly. Roll up tightly into croissants. Place on well-greased (or paper-lined) cookie sheets. Chill very well. Brush with beaten egg yolk mixed with a tablespoon of cream. Bake in a 450° oven for 5 minutes, or till croissants are well puffed. Reduce heat to 350° and continue baking till golden brown. Cool slightly before serving. These may be frozen.

Pâte à Choux

$1/4$ cup butter
$1/2$ cup hot water
$1/2$ cup flour

$1/4$ teaspoon salt
$1/4$ teaspoon sugar
2 eggs

Combine the butter and the hot water and place them over the flame. When the butter is melted and the water boiling, add the flour, salt and sugar and stir with a wooden spoon until the mixture leaves the sides of the pan and forms a ball in the middle of the pan. Remove from the pan and continue beating or place in the electric beater. Add the eggs, one at a time, and continue beating until the dough is waxy and smooth. This may be forced through a tube or dropped by spoonfuls into a baking dish or into hot fat. If baked, these should be placed in a 450° oven for 10 minutes and then reduce the temperature to 350°. They should be baked until well browned and crisp.

Baking Powder Biscuit

2 cups sifted flour
2¹/₂ teaspoons double acting
    baking powder
³/₄ teaspoon salt

5 tablespoons butter or
    other shortening
³/₄ cup milk (approximately)
Melted butter

Sift the flour, measure it, add baking powder and salt, and sift again into a mixing bowl. (Some people add sugar to biscuit, but I don't think it necessary. If you prefer it, add 2 teaspoons.) Work in the butter or other shortening with your fingers till it is the consistency of cornmeal. Add milk to make a soft dough. Turn onto a floured board. Knead for a minute, and roll or pat out to ³/₄-inch thickness. Melt butter in a baking pan or a small saucepan. Cut the biscuits according to your taste. Dip each one in melted butter and arrange on a baking sheet or pan. If you want them crisp all around, place them far apart. If you want them crisp on top and fluffy, place them close together.

Bake at 450° for 12 to 15 minutes. Makes 12 to 18 biscuits.

BUTTERMILK BISCUIT:

Add ¹/₄ teaspoon soda to the recipe above, and use buttermilk instead of sweet milk.

Shortcake Dough

Increase butter content of Baking Powder Biscuit recipe to ¹/₄ pound and use heavy cream for mixing. Add 2 tablespoons sugar.

Divide dough into two portions, one twice the size of the other. Use the larger portion for bottom piece. Arrange on a baking sheet and brush with melted butter. Roll out remaining portion. It should, of course, be smaller than the first piece. Dot lower piece with additional butter where the upper piece will rest. Brush top with butter. Bake as for biscuits.

Plain Pastry

2 cups flour
1/2 teaspoon salt
2/3 cup butter or 1/3 cup butter

and 1/3 cup vegetable
shortening
Ice water

Sift the flour and salt onto a pastry board. Make a well in the flour and add the butter and shortening, cut into small pieces. Cut with two knives or blend with finger tips till flour is mealy and the size of small peas. Add just enough ice water to make the flour and shortening form a firm ball. Chill for at least 30 minutes before rolling. Makes 1 2-crust pie or 2 shells.

Rich Pastry

2 cups unsifted flour
3 tablespoons sugar
1/2 cup butter
1/4 cup vegetable shortening
1 1/2 teaspoons grated lemon rind

3 hard-cooked egg yolks or
2 raw egg yolks, or
2 egg whites (see Note)
1/2 teaspoon salt

Make a well in the center of the flour. Add sugar; butter, not too hard, not too soft, cut in small pieces; vegetable shortening cut in small pieces; lemon rind; hard-cooked yolks crushed with a fork; and salt. Work quickly with finger tips to make a firm, smooth pastry. Dough should form a ball and leave table top or bowl fairly clean. Chill pastry for at least 30 minutes before rolling. Makes 1 2-crust pie or 2 shells.

NOTE: If a very rich pastry is desired, use raw yolks of eggs. The whites will make a more brittle and less fragile pastry. If you are making flans or shells you may roll out and fit pastry and freeze till ready to use. Use the pastry frozen. If you are baking a shell, fit the inside of the pastry with foil and fill with dry beans or peas, then bake. Remove the foil and beans and reserve beans for future bakings. If you are baking tart shells you may place the tins one over the other, after having lined them with pastry, and turn them upside down on a baking sheet. Weight lightly and bake.

This pastry may be made in an electric mixer if desired. Use paddle attachment.

Cream Cheese Pastry

1/2 pound butter
1/2 pound cream cheese
1/4 cup heavy cream

2 1/2 cups flour
1/2 teaspoon salt

Cream the cheese and butter together well. Add the cream and whip for 3 minutes. Gradually add the flour and salt, and work into a firm ball. Chill before using.

Puff Pastry

FOR THE DOUGH:

2 tablespoons vegetable oil
*1 1/2 cups unbleached
all-purpose flour*

*1/2 teaspoon salt, mixed
with 6 tablespoons
ice water*

FOR THE BUTTER MIXTURE:

3/4 cup unsalted butter

1 cup flour

For the dough: In a mixing bowl stir the oil into the flour and mix thoroughly. Cut and press with a spatula and a cupped hand until the mixture forms a mass. Add the salted ice water and continue mixing until the dough is pliable but not sticky. Remove from the bowl, sprinkle lightly with flour, and wrap in wax paper. Place in a plastic bag and refrigerate for 1 hour.

For the butter mixture: If using an electric mixer, cut the butter into large pieces, place in the mixer bowl and sprinkle with the flour. With the paddle attachment mix at slow speed until smooth and supple. If working with your hands pound the butter with a rolling pin to make it more pliable, then gather it into a mass. Break into large pieces and smear across the work suface with the heel of your hand. Sprinkle with the flour, gather into a mass and knead until the butter and flour are completely mixed and the mixture is smooth. Work quickly so the mixture stays chilled. Place on wax paper and refrigerate, uncovered, for no more than 20 minutes.

Flour the work surface lightly, unwrap the chilled dough, and flour it lightly. Pat into an 8- by 4-inch rectangle. Cut the chilled butter mixture into small pieces and arrange evenly over 2/3 of the dough, leaving clear the 1/3 nearest you and a 1/2-inch border all around. Fold the unbuttered third over the adjoining third, and the remaining third over that, as if you were folding a letter. Pinch the edges closed.

Rotate the dough a quarter turn clockwise so that the narrow end faces you, and once again roll the dough to make an 8- by 4-inch rectangle. This time fold the top of the dough down and the bottom up so that the edges meet in the center. Fold these two halves together as if you were closing a small book. This process constitutes one quarter "turn" of the dough. Wrap the dough in wax paper, put it in a plastic bag, and refrigerate for 1 hour.

Do two more turns in the same way, placing the dough on the work surface so that the open ends are at the top and bottom: Roll out, fold the ends of the dough inward to meet in the center, then fold in half. Refrigerate the dough for 1 hour after the second turn and for 2 hours after the third, wrapping well until ready to use. Makes about 1 pound of pastry.

Pound Cake

1 pound butter	4 cups sifted flour
2 cups sugar	$1/2$ teaspoon mace
10 eggs, separated	2 tablespoons cognac
$1/4$ teaspoon salt	

Cream butter until light and fluffy. Add sugar and continue creaming until light and very fluffy. Beat egg yolks till light and lemon-colored and add to the butter-sugar mixture. Fold in the stiffly beaten whites to which you have added salt. Add sifted flour, mace, and cognac. Beat well for 5 minutes. Pour into buttered loaf tins or tube pan and bake at 300° for $1 1/4$ to $1 1/2$ hours.

Fruit or nuts may be added to this basic recipe. Mix with $1/4$ cup of the flour and add at the last. You may use about 1 cup fruit or nuts.

Corn Bread for Toasting

This is a simple bread, delicious when baked, split and toasted. It is not light and fluffy but corny, in the best sense of the word.

Combine 1 cup corn meal with 2 cups scalded milk, 2 teaspoons sugar, 1 teaspoon salt and 3 tablespoons melted butter. Spread in a 9-inch-square pan that has been well buttered, or drop by spoonfuls onto a buttered pan. Bake at 350° until brown. You may eat this hot from the oven; or cool, toast, and serve with plenty of butter.

Génoise

1 cup sugar   1 cup sifted cake flour
6 eggs   1 cup clarified butter

Place sugar and eggs in a double-boiler top. Place over hot water and beat for about 12 minutes with a wire whisk, or until the mixture is light and creamy. Place in the bowl of your electric mixer and beat at medium-high speed till it is thick and lemon-colored. If you do not have an electric mixer, a rotary beater is necessary.

Gradually fold in, a little at a time, sifted cake flour, using a wooden or rubber spatula.

Fold in by tablespoons clarified butter—butter that has been melted and siphoned off, leaving behind any water or solid residue. Pour into a 9-inch round or square cake pan that has been buttered and floured, or one that has been lined with silicon baking paper. Bake at 350° about 35 to 40 minutes. The cake will leave the sides of the pan when it is done.

Remove immediately to a rack to cool.

Sable Normande

1 cup (2 sticks) butter
1 cup sugar
1 teaspoon orange-flower water

3 cups all-purpose flour
Pinch salt

Work butter, sugar and orange-flower water together with your hands. Little by little work in a mixture of flour and salt until dough feels sandy in texture. Chill in refrigerator until firm enough to handle. Divide dough in half and roll half at a time, on a lightly floured board, about 1/4 inch thick. Cut with a 2-inch round cookie cutter and place on ungreased cookie sheets. Bake in a preheated 350° oven for about 15 minutes or until edges are rimmed with gold. Makes approximately 50 sables.

Crêpes (Unsweetened)

7/8 cup all-purpose flour
1/8 teaspoon salt
3 eggs

2 tablespoons melted butter
1 1/2 cups milk

Sift flour and salt together and add eggs one at a time, mixing well, until there are no lumps (a mixer at low speed is excellent). Add melted butter. Gradually stir in milk and mix until the batter is the consistency of thin cream. Let batter rest an hour or two before baking.

Bake the crêpes in a 6-inch, well-buttered pan over a medium-high heat. Pour a little of the batter in pan and tip, so it runs over the entire surface. Turn and brown lightly on the other side. Keep hot in the oven.

DESSERT CRÊPES:

Sift 1/4 cup sugar with the dry ingredients; and after mixing in the eggs, add 2 tablespoons cognac or rum and 1 teaspoon vanilla or 1 teaspoon grated lemon rind. Continue as above.

POTATOES

Baked Potatoes

The Idaho is surely the finest baking potato. It is said to be grown in a particular soil that has great lava content and that this greatly resembles soil in Peru, where the same type of potato abounds.

Allow 1 baking potato per person, or, if they are extra large, ½ potato will be ample. Preheat the oven to 375°. Scrub potatoes well and place them on a rack in the oven. Bake for approximately an hour or until the potatoes are soft to the touch.

Split at once and serve with freshly ground black pepper and salt. They are perfect this way, but you may want to add any of the following:

1) Butter
2) Cream, chives, bacon and parsley
3) Butter and paprika

VARIATION:

Preheat oven to 375°. Scrub potatoes well and rub with oil or butter. Make a thin slit in each potato. Bake till just soft—approximately an hour. Split and serve as above.

Stuffed Baked Potatoes

Bake as above. Cut about ¾ inch off the potato with a sharp knife. Scoop contents into a bowl or saucepan. For 6 potatoes add:

¼ pound (1 stick) butter	*1 teaspoon paprika*
1½ teaspoons salt	*¾ cup heavy cream*
1½ teaspoons freshly ground black pepper	*¾ cup grated Swiss Gruyère or cheddar*

Beat in the butter, seasonings and cream. Add ½ cup of the cheese and beat well. Return the potatoes to the shells and top with remaining cheese. Return to the oven to melt cheese and reheat potatoes.

Disgustingly Rich Potatoes

For 6 persons, bake 6 large Idaho potatoes as directed above. When soft, split and scoop out each potato into a mixing bowl. Scrape out the shells.

Add to the potatoes ¾ cup butter, 2 teaspoons salt, 1 cup heavy cream and 1 teaspoon freshly ground black pepper. Mix lightly and transfer to a flat baking dish. Dot heavily with butter and sprinkle with shredded Gruyère or cheddar cheese. Bake at 375° for 15 minutes.

NOTE: Spread the skins with butter and place them on a rack in a 500° oven or under a broiler to crisp. Serve for a cocktail accompaniment—an idea I gleaned from Mildred Knopf.

Sautéed Baked Potatoes

Peel cold baked potatoes and sauté in butter or bacon fat. Add a little cream and let it cook down.

Sweet Potatoes Baked

After baking, peel and slice. Sauté in butter and add a touch of nutmeg and a sprinkling of brown sugar. Then mash and combine with a great deal of butter and a dash of Madeira. Spoon into a baking dish and top with toasted sliced almonds. Dot with butter and brown in a 375° oven.

Sweet potatoes are really best when they are baked and served simply—with butter, salt and pepper.

Browned Potatoes

These are peeled and halved potatoes, preferably Idaho or similar potatoes. Drop them into the fat in a roasting pan when roasting beef or pork or lamb, and allow them an hour. Turn once or twice during the cooking time so that they brown on all sides.

NOTE: You may parboil these potatoes before tossing them into the fat. They will cook more quickly.

Roast Potatoes without a Roast

You may roast potatoes, peeled and halved (or scraped new potatoes or small whole potatoes) in beef drippings, butter, oil or pork drippings. You will want enough dripping to cover the pan to a depth of 1 inch. Peel the potatoes and preheat the oven and the pan to 350°. Add potatoes and roast, turning twice or three times till they are just pierceable and nicely browned. Salt and pepper.

Boiled Potatoes

Estimate ½ pound per person or slightly more for larger appetites. At least 1 potato per person should be the rule. Peel potatoes and boil in salted water till just soft to the fork. Drain and return to the stove for a moment or two to dry. Serve very hot with:
1) butter
2) parsley butter
3) chive butter
4) fines herbes butter
5) plain, with parsley
These are served with fish, stews and ragouts and often with sautéed chicken or other sautés.

Boiled New Potatoes

Small ones are by far the best. Cook them in their jackets, with a "belly band" cut around them, or scrape them if they are freshly dug. Boil quickly in salted water. Drain and dress with butter and salt and pepper.

NOTE: You may use chopped fresh parsley, fresh chervil, fresh chives or fresh mint with these delicious little potatoes.

Mashed Potatoes

Alexander Dumaine was once quoted as saying that "the mashing process should only be an up and down one." Thus he would eliminate that pleasant American term "whipped potatoes." For 6 persons peel and boil 8 medium potatoes. Drain and dry for a second over the heat. Mash the potatoes with a masher. Add ¾ stick butter (6 tablespoons) and salt to taste. Mash again. Add ½ cup heavy cream that has been heated and whip potatoes with a spatula or a whisk. Serve very hot in a hot dish with an extra pat of butter in the center and a dusting of freshly ground black pepper.

If potatoes are exceptionally dry you may add more cream.

VARIATIONS:

1) Whip in a little chopped parsley or chopped chives, or both.

2) Whip together equal quantities of potatoes and yellow turnips that have been mashed with butter.

3) Combine potatoes and mashed celery root.

Duchesse Potatoes

Prepare the same as whipped potatoes, but add 2 or 3 egg yolks before whipping vigorously. Force through a pastry bag fitted with a rosette tube. Form small medallions on a buttered baking sheet or use for a border on made dishes or planked dishes. Brown in a 375° oven.

Sautéed Mashed Potatoes

These may be formed into flat cakes and sautéed quickly in hot butter, beef fat or bacon fat and turned once or twice to give them a lovely golden color. Delicious with almost any dish, hot or cold. Perfect with cold turkey after that holiday dinner.

Home Fried Potatoes

Allow 1 to 1½ potatoes per person. Peel and slice potatoes. Sauté them in a heavy skillet, using butter, olive oil, beef fat or pork fat. Cook slowly, turning them occasionally till they are brown and nicely crisp on both sides. Salt and pepper to taste.

German Fried Potatoes

Peel potatoes (allowing 1 to 1½ potatoes per person) and cut into ⅛-inch slices. Heat 5 tablespoons butter in a skillet (for 4 medium-sized potatoes). Sauté potatoes over fairly intense heat. Turn often with a spatula and salt and pepper to taste. Potatoes should be crisp and brown.

Potato Galette

Peel and slice thinly 4 Idaho potatoes. Melt 6 tablespoons butter in a heavy skillet. Arrange potato slices in rosette fashion in pan. Start with a large slice in center and overlap other slices. Salt and pepper each layer and dot with butter. Cover and cook over fairly low heat for 20 to 25 minutes. Increase the heat and shake the pan lightly. Invert on a hot platter. Serves 4.

NOTE: You may also invert potatoes and return to pan to brown other side.

Hash Brown Potatoes

Allow 1 to 1½ potatoes per person. Peel and slice potatoes and then chop them rather coarsely. Melt butter (1 tablespoon for each potato) or beef fat in a heavy skillet and get the pan quite hot. Add potatoes and press down. Cook till they form a crisp brown crust on the bottom. Invert on a hot plate. If you wish, you may slide the potatoes back in the pan to brown on the other side. Salt and pepper to taste.

Lyonnaise Potatoes

Peel and slice 6 to 8 potatoes. Peel and slice thinly 2 medium onions. Melt 6 tablespoons butter in a skillet. Add the onions and sauté lightly. Add potatoes and turn well till they begin to brown nicely. It may be necessary to add more butter. Just before serving, add salt and pepper to taste and ¼ cup chopped parsley. Turn well and serve very hot. Serves 6 to 8.

O'Brien Potatoes

Peel and cut in ¾-inch dice 6 to 8 precooked potatoes. Peel and slice 1 medium onion. Clean and dice ½ green pepper, and dice 1 pimiento. Melt 6 tablespoons butter or bacon fat in a skillet, add onions and pepper, and cook for 4 minutes. Add diced potatoes and sauté gently, shaking the pan and turning them from time to time. Add salt and pepper to taste and, just before serving, the chopped pimiento and ¼ cup chopped parsley. Serves 6 to 8.

Deep Fried Potatoes

Use any vegetable oil, vegetable fat or even beef fat. Strain through a cheesecloth after frying, for reuse.

Various potatoes require different frying times. Try soaking them in ice water and drying them before frying or frying them without any preparation. Experiment till you find the perfect potato for frying.

For all potatoes of this kind one needs a deep-frying pan with a basket to lower and raise the potatoes. The temperature for deep-frying should be from 350° to 370°. The lower temperature is for blanching potatoes that you will later recook at a higher temperature. Fry a few potatoes at a time. Be sure your temperature control goes back to the original temperature each time. Keep cooked potatoes hot in the oven.

The following are the styles of potatoes most often deep fried:

CHIPS:

These are small new potatoes cut into halves or quarters and cooked in deep fat till crisp and brown.

FRENCH FRIES:

Potatoes cut in 1/4- to 1/2-inch square strips or into dice. These are either fried in fat at 370° or blanched at 350° and refried at 370° later. Salt them well and serve very crisp. Nothing is worse than a soggy French fried potato.

JULIENNE POTATOES:

These are cut into 1/4- or 1/8-inch strips and fried.

SHOESTRINGS:

For these you need an appliance called a "mandoline," which cuts vegetables into various shapes and sizes. Shoestrings are exceedingly narrow cut strings of potatoes that are fried crisp at about 355° to 360°

SARATOGA OR POTATO CHIPS:

These are sliced very thin on the mandoline and deep fried till golden and crisp.

WAFFLE POTATOES:

These are cut on the mandoline in a latticed pattern and cooked crisp at 360°. Delicious hot or cold.

DAUPHINE POTATOES:

Combine 1 cup each Pâte à Choux (*see* p. 345) and mashed potatoes and beat well. Drop by spoonfuls into fat at 370° and fry till golden brown and puffy.

Potatoes Anna

For 6 persons peel and thinly slice 6 medium potatoes. Butter a heavy iron skillet or a baking dish and arrange the potatoes in overlapping layers, dotting each layer lightly with butter and salting. Top with butter and bake in a 400° oven until potatoes are soft in the centers and crisp at the edges and those at the bottom are browned. You may cover the pan for part or all of the cooking time, if you wish. It is impossible to say how long the potatoes will take. I have had them cook in 45 minutes and again have had them take 1¼ hours. Invert the dish on a hot platter.

Boulangère Potatoes

Butter a baking dish and arrange freshly sliced potatoes in layers, dotting each layer with butter. You will need about 1 largish potato per person. Salt and pepper to taste, and, just before putting the potatoes in a 350° oven, add 1 cup or more beef broth or consommé. Cover for 30 minutes. Remove cover and continue baking till potatoes are tender and well soaked with broth. Add additional broth if potatoes cook dry.

Pommes Dauphinoise

Butter a deep baking dish and arrange layers of thinly sliced potatoes. Dot each layer with butter and sprinkle with grated Gruyère cheese or Parmesan cheese. Salt and pepper to taste. Cover and bake at 350° until potatoes are tender.

VARIATION:

Arrange layers of sliced potatoes dotted with butter and sprinkled with salt and pepper. Add 1/2 cup heavy cream, cover and bake at 325° till potatoes are barely tender. Add another 1/2 cup cream and sprinkle top lavishly with grated Gruyère cheese. Return to oven uncovered and cook till cheese has melted and browned.

Cheddar cheese may be used instead of Gruyère; and thin slices of sausage meat may be placed on top before the cheese is added.

Sweet Potatoes Boiled

Sweet potatoes may be boiled and mashed; boiled, sliced and glazed with butter and sugar; or mashed, blended with butter and pecans, rolled in chopped pecans, brushed with butter and baked in the oven for 20 minutes at 350°.

Potato Salad I

Boil 6 to 8 potatoes and as soon as they are cooked run under cold water. Peel and slice while still hot. Transfer to a bowl. Add 1/2 cup olive oil, 2 tablespoons wine vinegar, and salt and pepper to taste. Cool and let stand in refrigerator overnight. When ready to serve add seasonings to taste, such as:

1/2 cup finely chopped onion or scallion	*1/2 cup chopped parsley*
	1/4 cup grated carrot
1/4 cup finely cut celery	*1/4 cup chopped green pepper*
1/4 cup chopped chives	

You may use any of these or all of them if you wish. Correct the seasoning and add more oil and vinegar if necessary. Garnish with hard-cooked eggs and cherry tomatoes.

Potato Salad II

Boil 6 to 8 potatoes and chill. Peel and cut into ³/₄-inch dice. Combine with ³/₄ cup each chopped onion and celery, ¹/₄ cup chopped parsley, ¹/₂ teaspoon freshly ground pepper, and salt to taste. Bind well with mayonnaise or boiled dressing. Spoon into a bed of greens and decorate with sliced hard-boiled eggs and ripe olives.

Hot Potato Salad I

Boil 6 to 8 potatoes in their jackets and peel while still hot. Try out 8 rashers bacon cut in small pieces. Add ¹/₂ cup chopped onion and ¹/₄ cup wine vinegar to the pan. Toss with the potatoes and add ¹/₄ cup chopped green onions and ¹/₄ cup chopped parsley. Correct seasoning.

Hot Potato Salad II

This one should be made with new potatoes. Boil in their jackets and peel while still hot. Cut in halves or quarters. Add ²/₃ cup hot olive oil, 3 tablespoons wine vinegar, and salt and freshly ground pepper to taste. Add finely chopped onion if desired. Serve with sausages, sauerkraut dishes, etc.

A GUIDE TO WINES

WINE	SOURCE	CHARACTERISTICS	SERVE WITH
BEAUJOLAIS (almost always red)	France, from the district of the same name in Burgundy.	Fruity and lively, with a spicy bouquet. Should be full-bodied and is best drunk quite young. Though red wines are normally served at room temperature, this one can (and should) be lightly chilled during the summer months.	Simpler versions of beef, and lamb Pasta Parisienne Terrine Some veal dishes Chicken, roasted or braised A good picnic wine
BEAUNE (both red and white)	France, from the Côte d'Or in Burgundy.	A light, soft wine. Drink young.	Salmon braised in red wine Beef bourguignon Estofat of beef Lamb Game

WINE	SOURCE	CHARACTERISTICS	SERVE WITH
BORDEAUX Regionals (red)	France	*Médoc:* Home of the greatest Bordeaux or clarets. These are slow to mature and shouldn't be drunk in the first flush of youth. *St. Emilion:* Big wines, somewhat similar to Burgundies. Should not be drunk too young.	Turkey Chicken Lamb Duck Steaks Fowl with distinctive flavor Game Spiced braised dishes Leg of lamb
CABERNET SAUVIGNON (red)	A California varietal wine.	This is the grape from which most of the great French Bordeaux are made. Superior California clarets are produced in Napa, Sonoma and Santa Clara counties.	Kidneys Beef Stews Roast fowl Tomato dishes

CHABLIS	France, from Burgundy.	The best are a pale straw color, delicate in bouquet and flinty dry. Drink young.	Apéritif with crème de cassis Delicate fish dishes, such as cold lobster, shad roe, oysters on the half shell Clams
CHAMBERTIN (red)	France, from the vineyards of the same name, near the Côte d'Or in Burgundy.	These are big, fine wines that should have five years or more to develop before they are drunk.	Baby Lamb Coq au Vin de Chambertin Beef Game
CHAMPAGNE (white)	Strictly speaking, these are French wines produced in the Champagne district of France. However, some very fine ones,	Traditionally *the* wine for festive occasions. Serve chilled, of course.	Apéritif with cassis Caviar Smoked salmon Chicken Ham Turkey Seafood Almost any food

WINE	SOURCE	CHARACTERISTICS	SERVE WITH
CHAMPAGNE (cont.)	such as Almaden, Korbel and Beaulieu, are made in California.		
CHASSAGNE-MONTRACHET (red)	France, from the Côte d'Or in Burgundy.	These soft, well-balanced wines are little known in comparison to their white counterparts. They reach perfection in about five years.	Beef roasts Fish cooked with red wine Veal roasts Small game Cheese
CHÂTEAU AUSONE (red)	France; a Bordeaux from St. Emilion.	A big, full wine that matures slowly.	Roast fowl Game Beef Squab Guinea hen Cheese
CHÂTEAU BEYCHEVELLE (red)	France; a Bordeaux from St. Julien.	This is one of the light Médocs that can be drunk young quite successfully.	Fowl Stuffed squab chickens

CHÂTEAU BEYCHEVELLE (cont.)			Lamb Kidneys Cheese
CHÂTEAU CHEVAL BLANC (red)	France; a Bordeaux from St. Emilion.	Another exceptionally full wine that develops slowly.	Roast chicken (formal dinner) Game fowl Beef Great cheese
CHÂTEAU HAUTBRION (red)	France, from Pessac-Graves.	One of the greatest of Bordeaux. Ready to drink as young as five years old.	Holiday turkey Great game dishes Exceptional beef and lamb dishes Cheese
CHÂTEAU DE LASCOMBES (red)	France; a Bordeaux from Margaux.	Shares in the bigness and fullness characteristic of wines from the Médoc. Matures more rapidly than some of its cousins.	Holiday birds Roast beef Game birds Venison

WINE	SOURCE	CHARACTERISTICS	SERVE WITH
CHÂTEAU PRIEURÉ LICHINE (red)	France; a Bordeaux from Margaux.	This is one of the light Bordeaux that can be drunk young.	Fowl Game such as partridge Steaks Squab
CHÂTEAUNEUF-DU-PAPE (red)	France, from the Rhone Valley.	Stout and robust with a full flavor. Should be at least five years old.	Hearty dishes such as cassoulets and stews Game Venison Duck Goose
CHIANTI (most often red)	Italy, though some is produced in California.	Agreeable, though not what one would call distinguished. Should be drunk young.	Classic for Italian dishes Pasta with red sauces Stews and ragouts
FLEURIE (red)	France, from the Beaujolais district of Burgundy	Fruity and lively, and best drunk young. Delicious chilled in summer.	Informal meals Terrines Deviled chicken Chops Roast lamb

GEWURZTRA-MINER (white)	A native of Alsace; quite creditable versions are also produced in California.	A full-flavored, spicy wine with pronounced bouquet. Should be drunk in its youth.	Pig's feet Sauerkraut Poached chicken Fruits Some fish dishes
GREY RIESLING	A California varietal wine.	A delicate, delicious wine. The one produced by Charles Krug is particularly good.	Hors d'oeuvre Sautéed fish White chicken dishes Veal Sweetbreads
MOUNTAIN RED	California	A delightful wine that submits gracefully to light chilling in the warmer months. Louis Martini has an outstanding one, which is also available in bulk.	Beef Turkey Ragouts Perfect picnic wine General use

WINE	SOURCE	CHARACTERISTICS	SERVE WITH
MOUNTAIN WHITE	California	Another case where the Louis Martini vineyards rate special marks.	Shellfish such as lobster Picnics General use
MUSCADET (white)	France, from the Loire.	Very light and dry, this should be drunk quite young. It is a lovely "summer wine" that is excellent when chilled.	Cold trout Grilled shellfish Veal Sweetbreads Brains Any fish dish
HERMITAGE (red; also white)	France, from the Rhone Valley.	A big, full-bodied wine that is long lived.	Lamb Hearty dishes such as roast beef or goose
JULIÉNAS (red)	France, from the Beaujolais district of Burgundy.	Has the fruitiness and freshness characteristic of Beaujolais. It, too, should be drunk young.	Beef Red meats in informal dishes Chops Picnics

MADEIRA	Portugal, from the island of Madeira.	A fortified wine and one of the longest lived. It ranges from the light and dry Rainwater through Sercial and Verdelho, to rich, sweet Bual and heavy Malmsey. Can be put to most of the uses of the corresponding sherries.
Apéritif Turtle soup After a fine dinner		
NEUCHÂTEL (white)	Switzerland	A light, dry wine that is at its best young.
Swiss tarte à l'oignon Fondue Veal dishes Trout		
NUITS ST. GEORGES (red; also white)	France, from the Côte de Nuits.	A full, rich wine that should be at least three or four years old.
Lamb Chicken and fowl Game (White) Veal and fish		

WINE	SOURCE	CHARACTERISTICS	SERVE WITH
PINOT CHARDONNAY	A California varietal wine	A light, delightful wine.	Ham Roast turkey Fish Light chicken dishes For summer drinking
PINOT NOIR (red)	A California varietal wine.	This is quite similar to French Burgundy.	Roast kid Beef Lamb Cheese
PORT	The original and finest come from Portugal, though many other countries make ports.	A fortified wine.	Fruits Cheeses Dessert wine

POULLY-FUISSÉ	France, from Burgundy.	A dry wine with a lovely bouquet. It should be drunk young.	Shrimp Lobster Crab Veal Light dishes
POUILLY-FUMÉ (white)	France, from the Loire.	A light, agreeable wine that is best drunk young.	Smoked fish Perfect luncheon wine Cold dishes
PULIGNY MONTRACHET	France, from the Côte d'Or in Burgundy.	One of the great Burgundies, dry and with deep flavor. Should not be too old.	Sweetbreads Veal White chicken dishes Fish
RIESLING (white)	Produced in Alsace, Germany, California and Chile.	This is a sharp, exceptionally dry wine.	Apéritif Fish dishes Pork

WINE	SOURCE	CHARACTERISTICS	SERVE WITH
ROSÉ	Produced in almost all wine-growing countries. Particularly good are the Tavels from France and the Almaden from California. The latter is available in bulk.	This is a light, refreshing wine that can be drunk with almost anything and, like Beaujolais, should be drunk quite young.	Excellent picnic wine Ham Summer dishes Cold dishes
SANCERRE (white)	France, from the Loire.	Fresh, fruity and dry, it is best when drunk young.	Fish Broiled chicken Veal Summer foods

SAUTERNE (white)	Originally France; now also from New York and California.	A sweet wine.	Desserts Sometimes with hors d'oeuvre
SAUVIGNON BLANC (white)	A California varietal wine.	A charming wine, ranging from dry to sweet.	Hors d'oeuvre Cold dishes Veal Light chicken dishes
SHERRY	Spain; also produced in America.	Sherries, like ports, have a great range of flavor. They go from the pale, very dry Finos to the dark and sweet Creams.	Apéritif (drier ones) Soup Occasionally, hors d'oeuvre
SOAVE	Italy	A dry wine that should be served well chilled. Drink young.	Antipasto Fettucine Veal dishes Chicken

WINE	SOURCE	CHARACTERISTICS	SERVE WITH
TRAMINER (white)	Produced in Alsace, Germany, and California	Especially noted for its marvelous bouquet.	Fish Eggs Light dishes
VALPOLICELLA (red)	Italy	A light wine that should be less than four or five years old. Can be lightly chilled with great success.	Chicken Ragouts Pasta
VERDICCHIO (white)	Italy	Light, dry, and faintly earthy. This should be drunk young.	Antipasto Fettucine Fish Veal
VOLNAY (red)	France, from the Côte d'Or in Burgundy.	A soft and rather delicate wine, pleasing to most palates.	Most meats Fowl

VOSNE-ROMANÉE (red)	France, from the Côte d'Or in Burgundy.	A big, full-bodied wine that is a wine lover's delight. Should be at least five years old.	Beef Cheese Game Duck Goose
ZINFANDEL (red)	A California varietal wine.	A fresh, fruity wine similar to Beaujolais.	Red meats Pasta Ragouts Informal meals

A GUIDE TO APÉRITIFS

WINE APÉRITIFS, OR QUINQUINAS, FROM FRANCE

These are the most common of the quinquinas. They were so called because they formerly contained quinine, which was especially beneficial to those living in the tropics who were exposed to malaria. Some of these are now made in America and sold under the same names, although in a few cases they are slightly altered to please the mythical thing called "the American palate."

Dubonnet:

Probably the most famous of all apéritifs. Comes in dark and blond varieties. Sweet and rather cloying, it may be combined with gin or vodka and ice for a less sweet drink.

Lillet:

A delicate, dryish wine-based drink from Bordeaux. Comes in dark and light varieties. Slightly orange in flavor. Best on the rocks with a strip of orange zest or with a bit of soda.

Raphael or St. Raphael:

A quinquina with a somewhat overpowering bittersweet flavor. Good on the rocks, with soda or with a drop of gin.

Byrrh:

(Pronounced "beer.") Similar to the other bittersweet drinks. It is a lovely color and is best served cold, although Europeans prefer it at room temperature.

La Seine:

A drink that resembles French Dubonnet so closely that it is astonishing. Use like Dubonnet.

AROMATIZED WINES

Dry or French Vermouth:

In addition to being the element that changes straight gin into a martini, dry vermouth is, for many people, the ideal apéritif. It can be served on the rocks, frappéed, or mixed with ice and strained into a cocktail glass. Mixed with a few drops of crème de cassis, with the addition of a strip of lemon zest and a bit of soda, it becomes a Vermouth Cassis.

Sweet White Vermouth:

This is Italian in origin and is usually served straight, either chilled or not.

Sweet Vermouths:

The dark vermouth, familiar to most of us as the additive to whisky in a Manhattan, is perhaps the most popular apéritif in the world. It is especially a favorite in South America, in the Caribbean, and in Europe—served straight, chilled, or on the rocks. Combined with Campari bitters (3 parts vermouth, 1 part Campari) and soda, with a twist of lemon zest, it becomes an Americano. An ounce of sweet vermouth, one of gin and one of Campari, with ice and soda, make a Negroni.

Bitters:

Campari is perhaps the best known and is exceedingly popular throughout the Latin world. It is usually combined with soda or with sweet vermouth. Punt Y Mes is popular in Italy and Spanish-speaking countries, either straight or combined with vermouth.

CHILLED WINES

White Wine:

Chilled white wine without embellishment is a delicious apéritif. It should be on the dry side. Mixed with a few drops of crème de cassis, it makes a most popular apéritif known as *Kir*—approximately 1 teaspoon of cassis to a glass, or to taste.

Champagne:

This, of course, is the greatest of all apéritifs. It may be served with a touch of cassis, but certainly do not use your finest brut.

FORTIFIED WINES

Dry Sherry:

The dry and only the dry ones make good apéritifs. They should be chilled. These include the Montillas, Manzanillas, Finos and Dry Amontillados.

Dry Madeira:

This may also be served as an apéritif and is best when chilled.

A Guide to Liqueurs

LIQUEUR	FLAVOR	AS A DRINK	USES IN COOKING
APRY (French) APRICOT LIQUEUR (French, American, Dutch)	Apricot	Straight. In punches.	To flavor soufflés, apricot glaze for fruit tarts, crêpes, apple tart or charlotte. On pineapple, fruits, ices.
CHERRY HEERING (Danish)	Cherry	Straight or with soda, or with fresh lime and tonic (quinine water). In lemonade, Rum Collins.	In cherry tart, soufflé, duck Montmorency. On fruit, ices.
GRAND MARNIER (French) AURUM (Italian) COINTREAU (American)	Orange, except for Mandarine, which has a tangerine flavor.	Straight, or in long and mixed drinks. Half and half with cognac. Aurum, in coffee.	To flavor orange sauces for duck, crêpes. In soufflés, butter creams, Bavarian cream, mousse, syrup

LIQUEUR	FLAVOR	AS A DRINK	USES IN COOKING
(cont.)			
CURAÇAO (Dutch) TRIPLE SEC (American) MANDARINE (French)			for baba or savarin. On fruit, ice cream. To baste pork roasts.
PEACH LIQUEUR (French, American, Dutch)	Peach	Straight. In punches.	In sauces. On peaches, other fruits, especially raspberries, or ice cream.
FRAMBERRY (French)	Raspberry	Straight. In punches.	To flavor sauces, crêpes, soufflés. On fruit, ices.
CRÈME DE VIOLET (French, Dutch)	Violet	Straight.	In sauces. On parfaits, ice cream.

KUMMEL (French, American, Dutch)	Caraway	Straight. In punches.	In some sauces, soufflés.
TEA LIQUEUR (French)	Tea	Straight, chilled. In hot or iced tea, or lemonade.	On ice cream.
PIMENTO DRAM (Jamaican)	Rum and spice	Straight. In punches.	On pineapple, rum baba.
LIQUEUR D'OR (French)	Aromatic herbs (contains bits of gold leaf)	Straight.	On ice cream. Combine with other liqueurs.
STREGA (Italian)	Herbs and citrus	Straight. In coffee.	In sauces, soufflés.
CHARTREUSE (French)	Herbs	Straight. With cognac, Scotch.	In pudding and ice cream sauces, hard sauce, Bavaroise. On lemon ice, ice cream.

LIQUEUR	FLAVOR	AS A DRINK	USES IN COOKING
BÉNÉDICTINE (French)	Aromatic herbs	Straight, with coffee. In cognac.	In hard sauce, apple pie, mincemeat, soufflés.
B & B or BÉNÉDICTINE AND BRANDY (French)	Aromatic herbs	Straight, with coffee.	
CRÈME DE CASSIS (French)	Black currant	With soda. In Vermouth Cassis, Cognac Cassis, White Wine Cassis.	With raspberry or black currant purée for sauces. In cassis sherbet. On fruit.
CRÈME DE CACAO (French, Dutch, American)	Cocoa	Straight. In Alexander, Grasshopper.	In chocolate soufflé, sauces. On ice cream.
TIA MARIA (Jamaican)	Coffee	Straight. In hot or iced coffee,	In coffee syrups, sauces, or soufflés.

(cont.)

KAHLUA (Mexican) **ESPRESSO** (Italian)		or hot chocolate.	On parfaits, ice cream.
CRÈME DE VANILLE (French, American, Dutch)	Vanilla	Straight. In eggnog, iced chocolate.	In vanilla soufflé, mousse, Bavaroise, ice cream sauce. On ices.
CRÈME DE NOYAUX (French, Dutch)	Almond-hazelnut	Straight. As substitute for orgeat. In Pink Squirrel cocktail.	In sauces, soufflés, fruit coupes. Often combined with fruit liqueur.
CRÈME DE MENTHE, green (French, American, Dutch)	Mint	Straight, or frappé. With water or vodka. In Grasshopper.	With pears. On ices.

LIQUEUR	FLAVOR	AS A DRINK	USES IN COOKING
CRÈME DE MENTHE, white (French, American, Dutch)	Mint	Straight or with water. With cognac in Stinger.	In chocolate or ice cream sauces. With pears.
FIOR DE ALPE (Italian)	Aromatic with rock candy base.	Straight, chilled. In punches.	Same as Chartreuse.
IZARRA (French)	Aromatic herbs	Straight.	On ice cream.
ANISETTE (French, American, Dutch) ANIS (French) OUZO (Greek)	Anise	Straight, on the rocks, or with soda or water.	In certain sauces.
DRAMBUIE (Scottish)	Scotch and honey	Straight. In punches.	In custard sauce for poached fruit, soufflés.
IRISH MIST (Irish)	Irish whisky and honey	Straight.	On sliced oranges.

INDEX

INDEX